DATE DUE

NAPOLEON THE THIRD

from a photograph by W. & D. Downey. 57, Ebury St.

THE LIFE

OF

NAPOLEON THE THIRD

BY

ARCHIBALD FORBES, LL.D.

KENNIKAT PRESS
Port Washington, N. Y./London

THE LIFE OF NAPOLEON THE THIRD

First published in 1898
Reissued in 1970 by Kennikat Press
Library of Congress Catalog Card No: 70-112802
ISBN 0-8046-1068-1

Manufactured by Taylor Publishing Company   Dallas, Texas

CONTENTS

LIFE OF NAPOLEON III

CHAPTER I

PARENTAGE—BIRTH—CHILDHOOD

AMONG the countless victims of the guillotine during the Reign of Terror was Alexandre, Vicomte de Beauharnais, one of the most distinguished generals of the Revolutionary period. Executed in 1794, he left a widow and two children, all of whom were destined to attain to high estate. The forlorn widow of Beauharnais became the first wife of Napoleon the Great. Her son Eugène, who in the evil days had been a carpenter's apprentice, became Napoleon's stepson, shared in most of the campaigns of the Great Captain, and attained the dignity of Viceroy of Italy. Her daughter Hortense, one of the most beautiful and interesting women of her time, rose to the Throne of Holland, and was the mother of a son whose strange and diversified life is the subject of this memoir.

There was an element of romance as well as of chance in the circumstance which is said to have led up to the marriage of Napoleon and Josephine. Soon after the victory of the Paris sections over the Convention in the 13th Vendémiaire (Oct. 5th, 1795)—a day on which he had cleared the streets with grape-shot, pursued the rioters into their hiding-places, disbanded the National Guard, disarmed the populace, and virtually ended the Revolution—Napoleon received a timid visitor in young Eugène Beauharnais, who came to beg for the restoration of his father's sword, of which he had been informed the General had become possessed. The bright countenance and frank manner of the young Eugène pleased Napoleon. When the sword was once again in the lad's hands he kissed it with tears ; and this touching manifestation of affection for his dead father's memory stirred the interest of Napoleon in his young visitor. The sequel, if we are to believe the story, was that Madame Beauharnais considered it her duty to call on the General and thank him for his kindness to her son. Napoleon, it seems, had greatly admired Josephine at first sight ; he returned her visit, they became intimate, and on March 9, 1796, they were married. Napoleon's age was then twenty-seven ; Josephine was considerably older. Napoleon, by no means addicted either to doing or saying pretty things, practised a graceful little artifice having for its motive the diminution of the difference between their ages. In the certificate of their marriage he represented Josephine as six years younger than she really was, while he added more than a twelvemonth to his own age. Napoleon was not born on Feb. 5, 1768, as stated in the marriage certificate, but on Aug. 15, 1769 ; and Josephine's birthday was not on July 23, 1769, but on June 23, 1763.

This is Napoleon's own version in the 'Voice from St. Helena' of the circumstances connected with his marriage with Josephine. Bourrienne's account is pleasant reading enough. 'One day,' he tells in his

Memoirs, 'he (Napoleon) called my attention to a lady who sat opposite at dinner, and the way in which I answered his questions appeared to give him much pleasure.   He then talked a great deal to me about her, her family, and her amiable qualities ; he told me that he should probably marry her as he was convinced that the union would make him happy.   I also gathered from my conversation that his marriage with the widow Beauharnais would probably assist him in gaining the objects of his ambition.   His constantly increasing influence with her had already,' he said, 'brought him into contact with the most influential persons of the day.'   It remains to be said in a sentence that Barras, in an exceptionally abominable passage of his coarse and self-complacent Memoirs, frankly avers that Josephine had been his mistress, and that when tired of her he had, not without some reluctance on her part, cynically arranged the marriage between her and Napoleon.

Eleven days after his wedding Napoleon left Paris to conduct the most brilliant series of campaigns the world had ever seen.   Two years later he was voyaging to Egypt and the conquest of that country followed ; but the stubborn defence of St. Jean d'Acre baulked his most resolute efforts, and in the autumn of 1799 he gave up the command to Kleber and after a hazardous voyage suddenly appeared in Paris.   Mr. Jerrold in his interesting Life of Napoleon III. tells that 'in the autumn of 1798, Josephine, left alone with her daughter Hortense while Napoleon was carrying war through Egypt with her son, young Eugène de Beauharnais, at his side, busied herself with the pleasant duty of finding a retreat for the hero when he should return. . . . Josephine fixed on Malmaison, near Rueil, and she paid for the modest château and domain chiefly with her dowry.' Josephine's 'dowry' was rather of the character of a negligible quantity, nor did Napoleon bring back from Egypt great store of wealth. Bourrienne asserts, however, that Napoleon returned from his Italian campaigns in possession of more than three million francs ; and that money it probably was with which Josephine made of Malmaison a rare and delightful retreat, of which Napoleon 'never tired until the purple drew him to the statelier splendours of St. Cloud and Fontainebleau.' Mr. Jerrold continues in a charming strain : ' Malmaison was the nursery of the Empire : its cradle and its grave. Within its peaceful bounds the scattered elements of polite society were first drawn together after the storms and excesses of the Revolution. At Malmaison the first great salon was thrown open ; and here, amid the laughing school-girls of Madame Campan and her "*vieux généraux de vingt ans*," were formed the manners that prevailed during the Empire.'

But before the pleasant life of Malmaison began, scenes had occurred which had taught the ingenuous Hortense that life was not a long frivolity—a knowledge which was to come home to her with a deeper personal bitterness in no long time. There can be no question that Josephine had behaved, to use a mild term, with great indiscretion during the absence of her husband in Egypt ; and that when Napoleon's arrival in France was announced she was, in the words of Madame Junot, 'a prey to great and well-founded uneasiness.' The recollections of the past, the ill-natured reports of his brothers, the hints of Junot in Egypt and the exaggeration of facts, had irritated Napoleon to a very high pitch and he received Josephine with studied displeasure. On Josephine's return to Paris after having missed her husband Napoleon refused to see her, and actually did not do so for three days. Eugène and Hortense strove long in vain to overcome his resistance. 'Napoleon,' says Madame Junot, 'could not with any degree of propriety explain to Eugène or Hortense the particulars of their mother's conduct. He was therefore constrained to silence and had no arguments wherewith to combat the tears of two innocent creatures at his feet, exclaiming, "Do not abandon our mother, she will break her heart!" . . . The scene, as Napoleon confessed, was long and painful; and the two, brother and sister, at length introduced their mother and placed her in his arms. The unhappy woman had awaited his decision at the door of a small back staircase, extended almost at full length upon the stairs, and suffering the acutest pangs of mental torture. . . . Whatever might have been his wife's errors Napoleon appeared entirely to forget them and the reconciliation was complete.' Madame Junot adds: 'It was to the earnest entreaties of her children that she owed the recovery, not of her husband's love—for that had long ceased, but of the tenderness acquired by habit and that intimate intercourse in virtue of which she still retained the rank of consort to the greatest man of his age.'

In a public sense the arrival in Paris of Napoleon from Egypt on Oct. 16, 1799, was for him singularly opportune. The Government of the Directory was promptly overthrown without a word of regret; a new Constitution was sanctioned by an overwhelming majority of votes; and Napoleon became First Consul, appointed

for ten years with the whole administration in his
hands. From this time thenceforth he was the
unquestioned ruler of France. The Tuileries were his
official residence and there Josephine presided over the
Court.

But the picturesque Château of Malmaison a few
miles west of Paris in a charming country, the modest
home which Josephine and Hortense had made for
husband and stepfather while Napoleon and Eugène
were abroad, was a delightful alterative to the Tuileries,
of which Napoleon said in a scornful mood that they were
triste comme la grandeur. Thither Josephine brought
the graces and the politeness of the social world to which
she had belonged and which she was now gradually
restoring. The old and the new order of things, to
Napoleon's great satisfaction, mingled in his wife's salons ;
under the shady trees and in the *bosquets* of Malmaison
the young heroes of the Republic made love to the girl
graduates of Madame Campan's famous seminary whom
that wise and accomplished lady sent forth into the world.
And on the close-shaven lawn there were games of active
play in which middle-aged generals and young subalterns
of family engaged with vivacity. A participator in the
Malmaison romps has described for us ' Napoleon
throwing himself heart and soul into the fun, and rolling
on the ground in a fit of laughter before surrendering
himself to the enemy, while Hortense, full of audacity
and cunning in feints, continued to baffle her pursuers.'

But there were shadows of deep gloom behind this
fascinating scene of mirth and sun-glow ; and there were
jealousies and plotting among the seemingly light-hearted
company. Josephine had ever before her the painful

presentiment of an unhappy future ; for she knew herself hopeless of progeny and the object of dislike and jealousy on the part of her husband's family. But there was an exception in Louis, the fourth of the Bonaparte brothers, and him she desired to make her son-in-law by his marriage with her daughter Hortense, with the hoped-for result that he might support her against the adverse spirit on the part of the other members of the Bonaparte family. Josephine's policy so far succeeded that she brought about the marriage on which she had set her heart, but the further results which she hoped for were not very apparent.

It is not easy to diagnose the character of this Louis Bonaparte whom Josephine desired for husband to her daughter. He was nine years younger than Napoleon, who had taken Louis under his especial care, treating him as a son rather than a brother. Between teacher and pupil were natural antagonisms which the friction of opposite characters constantly exacerbated. Napoleon esteemed Louis a good but unambitious soldier. ' In the attack on Saorgio,' wrote Napoleon from St. Helena, ' I stationed him for the first time under cannon-fire. He persisted in placing himself in front of me to protect me from hostile bullets. His courage,' continued the Emperor, ' was brilliant, but by fits ; and he remained indifferent to the praises which his valour stimulated. At the passage of the Po he placed himself at the head of the attacking columns ; at Pizzighettone he was the first in the breach ; at the assault of Pavia he was on horse-back at the head of the sappers charged to destroy the gate. The destruction of the famous university of this city made a deep impression on him, and he became still more taciturn.' Louis preferred to converse with savants rather than with soldiers; and Jerrold suggests that he probably regretted the events which had drawn his family from their birthplace. Queen Hortense, it is said, always held that he had a dislike for women; but he retaliated that it was not women, but their love of show, that displeased him. Madame Rémusat, on the other hand, gives Louis no quarter. Writing of him as she noted his character in 1806, she says that he made his wife's life miserable. ' Her husband's tyranny was exercised in every particular; his character, quite as despotic as his' brother's, made itself felt by his whole household. Until now his wife had courageously hidden the excess to which he carried his tyranny '; but it had become the more intolerable because since his return from Egypt he had suffered from a malady which so affected his limbs that he walked with difficulty and was stiff in every joint. The ailment was described as infectious, but further details cannot be given.

Louis was well aware of Josephine's desire to have him for a son-in-law; and all authorities appear to agree in fixing the responsibility of his unhappy marriage on Napoleon's wife. Hortense certainly had no *tendresse* for the morose and taciturn Louis. Constant in his Memoirs writes: ' Previous to her marriage with Louis Hortense cherished an attachment for Duroc, who was at that time (1802) a handsome man of about thirty and a great favourite of Napoleon. But the indifference with which Duroc regarded the marriage of Louis Bonaparte sufficiently proves that the regard with which he had inspired Hortense was not very ardently returned. It is certain that Duroc might have become the husband of Mdlle. de Beauharnais had he been willing to accede to the conditions on which Napoleon offered him his stepdaughter's hand. But Duroc looked for something better ; he declined the proposed marriage ; and the union of Hortense and Louis which Madame Bonaparte, to conciliate the favour of her brothers-in-law, had endeavoured to bring about, was immediately determined on.'

Josephine had her way, sacrificing her daughter for the furtherance of her own purposes. The dutiful daughter submitted ; and on Jan. 4, 1802, Louis and Hortense were married. Louis endured to have forced upon him as a wife a woman who had always avoided him as much as possible. She nevertheless seems to have honestly tried her utmost to like the man whom her mother and Napoleon presented to her as a husband. The union was bitterly unfortunate, yet Napoleon has stated that when Louis and Hortense first came together they loved each other. But Hortense had been disappointed in regard to Duroc, while Louis wrote of his marriage day, 'Never was there a ceremony so sad ; never did two espoused persons feel more vividly a presentiment of all the horrors of a forced and ill-assorted marriage.' Jerrold remarks that 'the aversion, with all its bitterness, came afterwards.' That view is destroyed by Louis' shuddering testimony. The pair took up their residence in the beautiful Château of St. Leu. The crypt of the handsome church of the village of that name built by Napoleon III. is the burial-place of the Bonapartes. In its vault there lie Napoleon Louis Charles the eldest son of Louis and Hortense, Napoleon Louis their second son, ex-King Louis himself, and old Charles Marie Napoleon of Corsica, the father of all the stock.

Although her nuptials had been sombre Hortense made the best of the situation in her married life. She essayed to make of the old château another Malmaison. The parterres blazed with the flowers she loved, and quaint surprises of light and shade met courtiers and senators in their stroll through the umbrage. She gave birth to her first child, Napoleon Louis Charles, on Oct. 10, 1802. Upon this child, the adopted son and heir-presumptive of Napoleon, rested for a time the hopes of the Emperor, who had often been seen playing with the beautiful and interesting boy on the terrace of St. Cloud. But the hopes were dispelled when, on May 5, 1807, the child died of croup at The Hague. Hortense was broken-hearted; when the sad tidings reached the Emperor he wept; and the unfortunate Josephine exclaimed in her agony, 'I am lost! My fate is decided—he will forsake me!'

A second child, Napoleon Louis, had been born to Louis and Hortense in 1804 who was to live until 1831. It was on the afternoon of April 20, 1808, in her *hôtel* in the Rue Cérutti, now the banking-house of the Rothschilds in the Rue Lafitte, that Queen Hortense gave birth to her third son, the future Napoleon III. The Empress was then at Bordeaux and the Emperor at Bayonne. Talleyrand, with other high officers, had been commanded by Napoleon to be present at the impending accouchement of Queen Hortense. She thus notes regarding him : 'The visit of M. de Talleyrand aggravated my nervous state. He constantly wore powder the scent of which was so strong that when he approached me I was nearly suffocated.' Talleyrand looked down solemnly on the new-born infant; some thirty years later in Lady Tankerville's drawing-room in London, he did not choose to recognise the son of Hortense by whose birth he had stood. The heir of the Empire was then an exile; and Talleyrand was serving a new master. The high authorities of the Empire stood around the bed of Hortense while the certificate of birth was being prepared by the Archchancellor Cambacérès; and there were also present Madame Mère, Cardinal Fesch, and Admiral Verhuel the Ambassador from Holland. It was not until June 2 that in accordance with the Emperor's instructions the infant received the christian names of Charles Louis Napoleon. He was baptized in 1810 at Fontainebleau by Cardinal Fesch his grand-uncle; his godfather the Emperor Napoleon and his godmother the Empress Maria Louisa. His birth was celebrated with great rejoicings throughout France as that of a presumptive heir to the Imperial throne; for by the law of succession (dated 28th Floréal, year 12, and 5th Frimaire, year 13) the Crown, in default of direct descendants of the Emperor himself—and he at that time had none—could be inherited only by the children of two of his brothers, Joseph and Louis. But Joseph had no male offspring, and the sons of Louis in consequence became for the time heirs-presumptive, until the birth of the King of Rome.

The Emperor himself stood sponsor at little Louis' baptism. When the child was still in his cradle, the prospects of his elder brother and himself were imperilled by the Emperor's marriage with Maria Louisa;

and were apparently blighted when in 1811 a son was
born to Napoleon himself. Louis, however, was in
great measure brought up in the Tuileries and was a
great favourite with the Emperor. A curious story was
extant of the last words which passed between those
two. It was at the moment when Napoleon was setting
out on the campaign which proved to be his last. The
little boy on hearing that his uncle was to leave within
an hour became strangely agitated. He sought out the
Emperor in his cabinet, and taking hold of his arm
burst into tears. The Emperor asked what ailed
him. 'You will not go!' cried the child. 'The enemy
will get you. I shall never see you any more.' Napoleon was deeply agitated, took the child to his mother,
and said, 'Look well to him. Perhaps, after all, this
little fellow is the hope of my race.' Those were the
last words that his little nephew heard him utter.
Louis never saw the Emperor again. But the words
sank deep into his mind, to awaken afterwards as the
voice of destiny.

The King of Holland was present neither at the
birth nor at the ceremony of June 2; nor do the documents show that he was represented. It is possible, it
is true, to accept the hypothesis that he was represented
by Admiral Verhuel, to whom has been attributed the
paternity of the Prince. Did the repeated absences of
King Louis infer his disavowal of the paternity? Some
colour is no doubt given from the circumstance that
their Majesties were notoriously estranged, and that
about nine months before the Prince's birth the Queen
and Admiral Verhuel were together in the Pyrenees.
But, as it happened, King Louis was there also; and it

may be said that if he was with his wife neither before, during, nor after her confinement, it was because he was excessively annoyed, it seemed, because she refused to lie in at The Hague. There need be no reticence in regard to the errors of Hortense. It is unquestioned that in October, 1811 she gave birth to a son the father of whom was the Comte de Flahault—a son who was consequently a half-brother of Napoleon III. and who was the well-known Duc de Morny of the Second Empire. But the evidence seems fairly conclusive that Louis Napoleon was the veritable offspring of the unfortunate King of Holland; although it is true that neither in features, in physique, nor in mental characteristics did he bear any resemblance to any member of the Bonaparte family. It is certain that during the summer and early autumn of 1807 Hortense and her husband were living at Cauterets ; and that when they parted, the husband to return to Holland the wife to proceed to St. Cloud, Louis was aware that Hortense was *enceinte*. In the early spring of 1808 he wrote to her expressing the hope that 'you will reach your time without accident,' and desiring her to choose a doctor in view of the impending event. Louis' letter was cold but not unfriendly, and in it he mentioned that he had formally communicated to his Ministers at The Hague the news of the Queen's condition. As soon as he learned of Hortense's accouchement the King announced the event to the people of his capital collected under his balcony, and received the customary felicitations. He wrote again to Hortense : 'I should like the little one to be solemnly baptized here in Holland ; but I subordinate my wishes to yours and to those of the Emperor.'

It seems evident, then, that King Louis was in the full belief that he was the father of the infant to whom his wife gave birth on the afternoon of April 20, 1808, in her house in the Rue Cérutti. He proved that conviction on his part by leaving all his property to his son Louis Napoleon, whom he described in his will as 'my only surviving son.'

King Louis' four years' tenure of the throne of Holland had been constantly troubled by the highhandedness of the Emperor Napoleon. At the Emperor's instigation a deputation from Holland had come to Paris in June, 1806, to desire that Prince Louis should accept the Batavian throne. In vain did he attempt to shun the proffered honour. When he pleaded his ill-health Napoleon sternly replied, ' It is better to die a king than live a prince ' ; and Louis was proclaimed King of Holland at St. Cloud. He went to Holland accompanied by Hortense, who quitted St. Leu with bitter tears and who took an early opportunity of returning to France. But for the vexations to which he was continually exposed on the part of the Emperor Louis might have had a useful reign in Holland. But the bitter insults heaped on him by Napoleon in letter after letter stung him beyond endurance. Reduced to the harsh alternative of crushing Holland with his own hands or of leaving that task to his autocratic brother, Louis determined to lay down his sceptre. He abdicated in favour of his elder son Napoleon Louis, and in his default, of Charles Louis Napoleon his younger son, afterwards Napoleon III. In July, 1810, taking the title of Comte de St. Leu, he quitted Holland and repaired to the waters of Toeplitz, where he was living in retirement when he learned that Napoleon had united Holland to the French Empire. His protest, in which he declared 'the pretended union of Holland with France mentioned in the decree of the Emperor to be null, void, illegal, unjust, and arbitrary in the sight of God and man,' was in effect a dead letter, its circulation strictly prohibited by the police. Some time before the abdication of Louis he and Hortense had become entirely estranged, and years elapsed before they had any friendly intercourse in their common solicitude regarding their sons.

That Napoleon III. intended to write his autobiography is proved by a fragment which Mr. Jerrold has printed, and which is now in the possession of the Empress Eugénie. He did not pursue his design, and the 'Souvenirs de ma Vie' written in after-life are but the casual beginnings of an abandoned project. 'I can still see,' so wrote Napoleon III., 'the Empress Josephine at Malmaison covering me with her caresses, and even then flattering my vanity by the zest with which she retailed my childish *bons mots*. "Louis," said the Empress once, "ask for anything that will give you the greatest pleasure," and I requested to be allowed to go and walk in the gutters with the little street boys. . . . One day I entered into conversation with the old soldier on sentry duty. I called to him, " I, too, know my drill —I have a little musket." Then the grenadier asked me to command him, and there I was, shouting "*Présentez armes ! Portez armes ! Armes bas !*"—the old grenadier obeying, to please me. . . . My brother and I often went to breakfast with the Emperor. He used to take us by the head between his hands and in this attitude stand us on the table. This way of carrying us frightened my mother very much, Corvisart having told her it was extremely dangerous to children. . . . When the first news of the Emperor's return from Elba came there was great irritation among the Royalists against my mother and her children—the rumour ran that we were all to be assassinated. One night our governess came with a servant and took us across the garden of my mother's house in the Rue Cérutti, to a little room on the boulevards where we were to remain hidden. We were flying from the parental roof for the first time, but our young years prevented us from understanding the meaning of events, and we were delighted with the change.' This fragment vividly suggests how interesting would have been Louis Napoleon's full autobiography from those early days down the long varied years to the quiet residence at Chislehurst.

Louis Napoleon had scarcely attained the age of six years when the fortunes of the French Empire were overcast by terrible reverses. In the early summer of 1813, broken and mutilated soldiers, the survivors of the ill-fated Russian campaign, were seen in the streets of Paris. The Emperor's star, indeed, had begun to pale ever since his divorce from Josephine. He bade Hortense reopen the doors of her salons, and *fêtes* and balls were to be resorted to as expedients to exorcise the gloom now lowering over the Imperial fortunes. A woman of a staunch and loyal heart, Hortense did her best to meet his wishes ; but the gaiety she strove to simulate was forced and hollow. Yet she played her part gallantly ; and she retired to the grateful repose of St. Leu only after Napoleon had quitted Paris in April, 1813, to conquer still occasionally, but ultimately to be defeated in the long bloody struggle around Leipsic. In the seclusion of St. Leu Hortense had her children, of whom she was proud, and in the rudiments of whose education she maintained a constant interest. The brothers were bright, high-spirited, affectionate children; but the younger, Louis, was in his childhood very feeble.

Hortense would not be absent from the Emperor's farewell to the National Guard previous to his departure to join his sorely depleted army on Jan. 23, 1814. Spite of his extraordinary activity his corpulence had increased and in his pale face was an expression of melancholy and irritability. The sombre silence was profound until, in a firm and sonorous voice but with a certain lack of confidence, Napoleon spoke to the assembled officers. His opening words were very solemn: 'I set out this night to take the command of the army. In quitting the capital I confidently leave behind me my wife, and my son in whom so many hopes are centred.' After a short brilliant campaign during which, always against superior numbers, he fought and won battle after battle, he gave his enemies the opportunity of which they availed themselves with an unwonted celerity; and when the Allied artillery was bombarding Montmartre Napoleon was far away at Troyes. He speeded back, but when he approached Fontainebleau Paris had already capitulated.

When in the disastrous *finale* of the campaign of 1814 the enemy were at the gates of Paris and when every hour brought tidings of some new defection and some new disaster, Hortense maintained her courage and protected her children sedulously. She had hastened to the Tuileries to advise the Empress Marie Louise not to

leave Paris, but courageously to remain at the post where
her husband had placed her. The Empress would not
listen to Hortense's high-minded advice. Hortense
determined to stay with the Parisians and share their
fortunes. But Paris was officially declared untenable,
the Cossacks were at hand, and maternal love asserted
its natural sway. A friend furnished the refuge of a
country house at Glatigny ; but there on the following
morning was heard the roar of the cannon with which the
Allies had begun to batter the feeble defences of Paris.
It was resolved to make for Rambouillet, which was
reached very late, and where the fugitive Bonapartes and
the Ministers were found at supper. They were all
bound for Blois ; but the intention of Hortense was to
join her mother at the Château of Navarre in the Eure.
A crust of bread was requisitioned, not without difficulty,
by Hortense for her children. The whole vicinity of
Rambouillet was being scoured by Cossacks ; but at
Maintenon the resolute Hortense found a French cavalry
regiment from the commander of which she obtained an
escort, and thus protected she proceeded in much greater
safety towards the Château of Louis, whose owner had
begged her to spend the night there. Cossacks were
still occasionally visible ; but they seemed not to advance
beyond Louis. It happened, therefore, that all that part
of the country traversed by the refugees was in a condition of delightful tranquillity, and they journeyed with
elevated spirits through shady lanes and along the
windings of beautiful valleys which presented exquisite
pictures of pastoral life. The escort was dismissed with
gracious thanks. Queen Hortense regarded herself, her
children, and her entourage as now in safety. Next

morning by daylight the cortège set out towards the Château of Navarre where her mother was residing, and where Josephine and Hortense with her two sons remained throughout the period of negotiations which was ended by the departure of Napoleon for his new domain of Elba.

CHAPTER II

EXILE—BOYHOOD—ADOLESCENCE—INSURRECTIONIST—
CONSPIRATOR

IT was not until April 20, 1814, that Napoleon quitted
Fontainebleau for Elba; and meanwhile Josephine and
Hortense, with the children of the latter, remained at
Navarre in mournful retirement.   Josephine would fain
have joined Napoleon in his exile; Hortense trembled
for the future of her boys.   In a letter to Mdlle. Cochelet
of April 9 she exclaims: 'Ah! I hope they will not
demand my children, for then my courage would fail me.'
The mother and daughter returned to Paris as soon as
affairs had calmed down.   Hortense went to her town
house in the Rue Cérutti, to find it empty ; her servants
had deserted.   The Emperor Alexander—chivalrous
gentleman that he was—made haste to pay her a visit
and expressed his anxiety to be of service.   He advised
her to rejoin her mother at Malmaison, whither he
presently followed her and continued to protect her with
delicacy and true kindness during the time he remained
in Paris.   Malmaison became a sort of rendezvous of
the Sovereigns then assembled in Paris.   All the Kings,
Princes, and chief men of the Allies united to evince their
respect for the fallen Empress and her beautiful daughter.   One day the King of Prussia brought to Malmaison

his two sons, the Princes Frederick William and William, stalwart striplings who were amused in their Teuton manner by the *naïf* innocent remarks of the boys of Hortense.   More than half a century later King William of Germany and Louis Napoleon still then Emperor of the French, who had seen each other for the first time in Queen Hortense's salon at Malmaison, met for the last time in the Château Bellevue on the morrow of Sedan, surrounded by the dead and wounded of the great battle the issue of which lost Napoleon his Throne and sent him into exile.

Grief had done its work on Josephine.   She died at Malmaison on May 29, 1814, after a short illness; her last utterances were, ' Bonaparte—Elba—Marie Louise.' After the funeral of her mother Hortense retired with her children to St. Leu until the return of Napoleon from Elba.   It was then that her husband King Louis, living in retirement in Rome, demanded that his two sons should be given up to him by their mother.   They and she had been exempted from the general proscription of the Bonapartes, and as the children were in France he had to sue in the French Courts.   Hortense resolutely fought the claim ; and while she was still in mourning for Josephine the cause came to trial.   The result brought anguish to the mother, who would have made every sacrifice to keep her sons in France.   But the finding of the Court was that the elder boy should be given to the father, and share his exile.   The verdict, however, was not acted on until a later period.

Simultaneously with this wrench to her tenderest feelings, Hortense was informed that Napoleon had landed at Cannes and was marching on Paris.   She was

warned to take precautions—the Bourbons were quite
capable of seizing her children as hostages.   She herself
might be in danger.   But she found safety for her children
and herself under the hospitable roof of her brother's old
nurse.   From that humble shelter she wrote to her
brother Eugène : ' I have just seen him (Napoleon).   He
received me very coldly.   I think he disapproves of my
having remained here.   My God! if only there is no
more war! . . . Ah! speak to him for peace—use your
influence with him ; humanity demands it.   I have been
obliged to hide myself for the last twelve days because
all sorts of reports were circulated about me.'

During the ' Hundred Days ' Hortense and her sons
were present at the lukewarm ceremony of the Champ-
de-Mai ; during which the mother saw the Emperor, in
the absence of his own son the little King of Rome,
present her two boys to the troops in the Place du
Carrousel.   When Waterloo had been fought and lost
and when Napoleon's extraordinary career had come
near to its ending, Hortense accompanied her stepfather
to Malmaison, leaving him for a time at the door of the
bed-chamber in which the dying Josephine had uttered
his name with her last breath ; and she and her two sons
were the last to take a sad farewell of the fallen man
when he set forth to his captivity on the rock of St.
Helena.   The figure of an eagle cut in the sward of the
Malmaison lawn long marked the spot of French ground
last pressed by the foot of Napoleon ; but Josephine's
beautiful château has undergone many vicissitudes ; and
the shell fire of the last sortie from Paris in January,
1871, utterly wrecked Malmaison and the charming
amenities which once surrounded it.

It has been said that Hortense and her sons had been exempted from the general proscription of the Bonapartes. But after the Restoration rumours, absurd but venomous, of conspiracies directed against the safety of the Allied Sovereigns, had come into circulation, in which the name of Queen Hortense was malignantly and falsely involved. Hortense was not a conspirator, but she was an impulsive woman ; and she was probably over-eager to be of service to unfortunate Bonapartists lurking in Paris because unable to make their escape. Some ill-feeling had been engendered against her by the Royalists, who grudged her the exceptional exemption from proscription and who were chagrined because Louis XVIII., as the result of repeated solicitation on the part of the Emperor Alexander, nominated Hortense to the title of Duchesse de St. Leu, giving her at the same time the estate of that name as an independent duchy.

Early on July 17, 1815, an aide-de-camp of the Prussian General Müffling, who was then the Military Governor of Paris, called at the *hôtel* of the Duchesse de St. Leu and informed her major-domo by his superior's instructions that within two hours the Duchesse must leave Paris with her children. The reason alleged for an order so sudden and so peremptory was that she was held to be concerned in a plot for assassinating all the foreign Princes then in the capital—a ridiculous pretext, considering Hortense's cordial relations with many of the high personages alluded to. Ultimately she obtained a few hours' delay ; but the order was explicit that she must be outside the walls before nightfall and withdraw from French territory without delay. She had to be beholden to the courtesy of alien soldiers for safe conduct to the

frontier for her children and herself. Prince Schwarzen-
berg had the chivalry to appoint his own adjutant the
Count von Voyna to act as escort to the refugees, a
mission which that brave officer performed with delicacy
and courage.

The journey was full of incident and peril. At Dijon
a rabble surrounded Hortense's carriage with shouts of
'Down with the Bonapartiste!' During von Voyna's
temporary absence several Royalist officers broke into the
apartment of the Queen, averring that they were ordered
to arrest her in the King's name. The Austrian troops
quartered in the city came to the rescue at the instance of
von Voyna. All night the heroic Frenchmen drank, swore,
and strutted, brandishing their swords and clattering with
the scabbards. But the Austrian soldiers maintained a
steadfast front; and Hortense was protected and passed
out of the city under cover of a general review of
French troops, mustered to prevent the risk of a collision
between the French and Austrian soldiers. After much
anxiety and danger the fugitives reached Geneva only
to be ordered away at a day's notice, and von Voyna
had difficulty in obtaining permission for the party to
remain for a few days pending further instructions from
Paris. Aix, in Savoy, proved more hospitable, and
there Hortense temporarily established herself and family
in a small house. When the Abbé Bertrand arrived his
pupils' lessons were resumed, and Hortense had the help
and sympathy of Mdlle. Cochelet. But she soon found
herself surrounded by Royalist spies from France and
precautions had to be taken for the safety of her children.
A crowning trouble occurred to the harassed woman in
the practical success of her husband's lawsuit for the

possession of his elder son. The day arrived for the departure of Napoleon Louis, escorted to Rome by his father's emissary the Baron de Zuite; and his mother was in despair. 'I cannot describe,' wrote Mdlle. Cochelet, 'the grief I felt at seeing Prince Napoleon tear himself from the arms of his mother and his young brother. I could not calm the grief of my dear Prince Louis, nor amuse him when he was left alone—the deeper his woe because he had never before left his brother for an instant.' Louis is described as having been at this time a gentle, timid child, speaking little but thinking and feeling a great deal. He had now in effect become the only child of his mother, who thenceforth concentrated on him the greater proportion of her maternal tenderness.

Quitting Aix in the early winter of 1815 and journeying towards Constance, Hortense was met by a letter from her relative the Grand Duchess of Baden —the Stéphanie de Beauharnais of Madame Campan's Academy, one of the bevy of laughing girls who had once made Malmaison gay—intimating very courteously that no member of the Bonaparte family was permitted to reside in the Grand Duchy. Hortense pleaded illness and she had passports authorising her sojourn at Constance, in the vicinity of which she found a house which although out of repair was habitable. Its position was charming, on the tongue of land near Constance where the narrowing channel of the waters barely affords a passage for the Rhine, which connects the upper and the lower lake. Settled here, at least for a time, Hortense concentrated herself on the education of her son. Louis in his childhood was a slow and reluctant student, although he used his natural gifts as well as his feeble health permitted. The Abbé Bertrand in course of time gave place to M. Lebas, who became the boy's private tutor when in 1816 Louis entered the College of Augsburg where, with intervals of home life, he remained for eight years. It was in 1817 that his mother bought and established herself in the Château of Arenenberg, a residence which Hortense greatly beautified, in which she died, and which now belongs to the Empress Eugénie. To this delightful spot she had been attracted not only on account of the hospitable invitation of the good people of the Canton of Thurgau, but also because of the vicinity of relatives. The Château of Arenenberg stands on a magnificently wooded hill, about 1,400 feet above the level of the sea. It overhangs, not the Lake of Constance itself, but what is known as the 'lower lake,' between Constance and Schaffhausen, an expansion of the Rhine where the river leaves the lake; and it is charmingly situated opposite to the isle of Reichenau.

Prince Louis is described as having been a singularly amiable and attractive child, and in youthtime and in after-years he exercised an equal charm. He was possessed of many accomplishments, both physical and mental. He was a remarkable swimmer—he is said to have once swum across the Lake of Constance. He excelled in all bodily exercises—as a gymnast few equalled him in excellence ; and he was an admirable horseman. To accomplish all this he had to struggle against the defects of a constitution naturally effeminate ; yet he came to develop an uncommon energy and power of will.

On the completion of his civilian education the Prince adopted the military career, and naturally followed his great uncle's example in choosing the artillery arm of the

service. Presently he joined the camp of Thun as a vo...
teer under the orders of Colonel Dufour, one of Napoleon's old officers. Although never quite robust in health
he took his part stoutly in the roughest duties. The young
officers, it seems, fared in many respects like common
soldiers, marching out for the day's work with tools and
instruments in their knapsacks and camping for the night
in the open. 'The exercise,' Prince Louis wrote to
his mother, 'does me much good. I have double my
ordinary appetite. We muster at six o'clock in the
morning and march, drums beating, to the Polygon,
where we remain until near noon. At twelve we dine,
and at three we are on the Polygon again until seven.
We sup at eight and then go to bed, for we are quite
prepared for sleep. During the entire day we have
barely two hours free, in which time there are notes to
copy and drawings to make.'

The third Lord Malmesbury, who for the first time
made the acquaintance of Prince Louis in 1829 in the
drawing-room of Queen Hortense at Rome and who
remained his close friend throughout Napoleon's eventful
life, furnishes in his Memoirs a description of the Prince
at this period of his life. 'Here,' wrote Lord Malmesbury, 'I met for the first time Hortense's son Louis
Napoleon, then just of age. Nobody at that time could
have predicted his great and romantic career. He was
a wild, harum-scarum youth, or what the French call *un
crâne*, riding at full gallop through the streets to the
peril of the public, fencing and pistol-shooting, and
apparently without serious thoughts of any kind, although
even then he was possessed with the conviction that he
would one day rule over France. We became friends,'

bury, then Lord FitzHarris, was just one
in Prince Louis,—'but at that time he
markable talent nor any fixed idea but the
mention. It grew upon him with his
increased daily until it ripened into a certainty. He was a very good horseman and a proficient
in athletic games ; although short he was very active
and muscular. His face was grave and dark, but re-
deemed by a singularly bright smile. Such was the
personal appearance of Louis Napoleon in 1829, at the
age of twenty-one years.'

In 1830 the Prince was full of intense interest in the
Revolution of July of that year, which exiled Charles X.
and his family, gave the throne of France to Louis
Philippe, and supplanted the *drapeau blanc* of the
Bourbons by the tricolour of the Orleanists and
subsequently of the Second Empire. But that interest,
fervent though it was, did not distract the Prince from
his military duties at the camp of Thun. He quietly
worked and watched ; corresponding occasionally with
his elder brother, who had married a daughter of King
Joseph and was then living in Florence in attendance
on the invalided father of the brothers.

It was a serious discouragement for Prince Louis and
his elder brother to learn that one of the conditions on
which the Great Powers were prepared to recognise Louis
Philippe was, that he should continue to maintain in force
the sentence of exile which the Bourbons had passed on
the family of Napoleon, and which of course included
the sons of Hortense. She was informed on the part of
Louis Philippe that she herself was free to return to
France, but only without her children. The scorn with

which she repelled such a condition may be imagined. Under disabilities so stringent it would have been utter folly on the part of the brothers, even if a secret possibility had existed, to take any measures in the direction of attempting to form a Napoleonist Party in France. But both were full of energy and were eager to make a career. The elder brother had conceived the project of joining the Greek cause, but was dissuaded by the urgent representations of his mother. The warmest ambition of Prince Louis was to win his rank in the French army, but that opportunity was denied him by the proscription under which he writhed. When the Liberal Party in France was striving to force the Government to hinder Russia from sending her troops into Poland to quell the insurrection in that territory, the Italian patriots became encouraged ; and the young Princes rejoiced in the fleeting assurance that the Citizen-King would support the principle of non-intervention. Such was the influence of the name of Napoleon that the chiefs of the Polish insurrection offered the young Louis, in 1831, the command of their legions 'as the nephew of the greatest captain of all ages,' and also the Crown of Poland ; but the capture of Warsaw by the Russians put a stop to this proposal. Prince Louis at Thun and Prince Napoleon at Florence caught echoes of the shouts of the exulting Liberals of the boulevards. They saluted the tricolour as the emblem of the Revolution and of French glory ; and, to use the stirring words of Jerrold, 'they imagined that all the romantic dreams of liberty which the excited band of young journalists then in the ascendant described in glowing language were speedily to come to pass.' It was long a moot question whether Louis Napoleon, afterwards Napoleon III., ever actually took the oaths as a Carbonaro. Cavour was convinced that he had done so, and used his knowledge of the fact to a notable purpose. Count F. Arese, till the death of Napoleon III. his close and true friend, has not spoken positively on the point. ' It cannot,' he has written, ' be said that at this first period '—presumably in 1829-31—' Louis Napoleon was a Carbonaro ; for the Prince always appeared strongly opposed to sects of all descriptions. But it may be said that he was one in his young days—for in effect all were Carbonari who laboured to drive the Austrians and their representatives out of Italy.' The question, however, has been decided beyond a doubt by the authoritative statements made by Count Orsi in his ' Recollections of the Last Half-Century.' [1] Count Orsi writes as follows : ' The organisation of secret societies which began in 1821 had in 1829 developed itself in every part of Italy to such an extent as to form a nucleus in the remotest and poorest villages of the country. As those societies were the only means of communication left to the people, every possible device that could be invented to avoid detection was resorted to by their leaders. . . . The most powerful of those societies was that called the " Carbonari," of which Prince Napoleon Louis and his brother Prince Louis Napoleon had become members.' [2]

Count Orsi, in later pages of his book, proceeds to afford further proof of Louis Napoleon's membership of the ' Carbonari.' He thus writes : ' I attended the meeting convened by Prince Napoleon at my house on the night of Feb. 26, 1831, at which were present his brother

[1] Longmans, Green & Co., London, 1881.
[2] Count Orsi's *Recollections*, p. 5.

Louis Napoleon, Ciro Menotti's brother, three delegates from various provinces, and myself. . . . One of the most remarkable features of this meeting was the complete silence of Prince Louis Napoleon. He had just arrived from Rome, and the information he was expected to give us concerning the real position and plan of the insurrectionary forces already in the field was the very thing I had been anxiously awaiting. Not a word was uttered by him. . . . Speaking for the first time, Prince Louis Napoleon remarked :

' " You lose sight of the engagements we have entered into, and which we swore to perform."

' " Engagements ! With whom ? " said I.

' " With the secret society of Carbonari, of which we are members," answered the Prince.

' " I was not aware of it," said I ; " and such being the case I cannot help feeling even more anxious than I did before." '

In October, 1830 Queen Hortense accompanied by her younger son Prince Louis set out from Arenenberg to pass the winter in Rome in accordance with their wonted custom. On their way they spent a fortnight at Florence with Prince Napoleon, the elder of the brothers. Hortense and Louis arrived in Rome about the middle of November. What actually were the designs of the Bonaparte family at this time it is impossible to determine with certainty ; but there are strong evidences that most of the members of it were deeply concerned in fomenting the anarchy prevailing throughout the Peninsula. A mother not devoid of personal ambition and yet more ardent in ambition for the advancement of her sons, it is probable that Hortense was neither surprised nor dis-

appointed to find in the Papal city an assemblage of
the leading members of the Bonaparte family keenly
watching impending events. In December a sort of
family conclave was held in the palace of ' Madame
Mère,' at which among others were present Cardinal
Fesch, Jerome Bonaparte, Queen Hortense, and Prince
Louis. From the wreck of the Empire the older
members of the family had salvaged large amounts of
money, and they were prepared, it was believed, to
utilise their opulence in the furtherance of the schemes
which they were secretly promoting. The opportunity
was tempting. The misgovernment and anarchy which
unquestionably existed in the Papal States, in the Lom-
bardo-Venetian kingdom, in Piedmont, Bologna, Parma,
and even in Tuscany, went to encourage the aspiration
that the House of Bonaparte, exiled from France though
it was, might still erect for itself an empire beyond the
Alps. From the family council-board at Rome agents
and emissaries were being despatched in various directions to stimulate the co-operation of the well-wishers of
the family and to hurry on affairs to a crisis. The heads
of the house had their own ends to serve ; and it by no
means followed that the objects for which they were
engaged in conspiring were intrinsically deserving of
censure. Had they succeeded in their enterprises, it
was impossible that they should have proved worse
rulers than the potentates whom they would have supplanted, and it is extremely likely that they would have
proved much better. The whole country from the Alps
to the Faro of Messina was in a state of great excitement, and all those secret societies which for years had
been labouring to bring about a revolution were now

sanguine that the time was at length at hand when the accomplishment of the longed-for purpose was to be achieved. The effervescence of the public mind was perhaps most active in the Romagna, where the desire for political emancipation penetrated through every rank of society. Unfortunately the people contented themselves in a great measure with applauding the approaching advent of the Revolution, instead of passionately and purposefully espousing its cause. Immersed in a supineness the shame of which they were not capable of recognising, the masses were more disposed to hail the march of the liberators than to take an active and resolute part in the patriotic ranks. Leaders, moreover, were lacking; there was no unity, no guiding hand. In Bologna, Modena, Parma, and Reggio there had sprung up as many extemporary Provisional Governments—not rivals one to the other, but distinct—and even deprived of the idea of combining their efforts by a foolish holding to the principle of non-intervention.

Day by day the state of Italy became more anarchical. In the streets of Rome the enthusiastic patriots shouted for ' Louis Philippe, the giver of independence to the nations ' ; they believed in their simplicity that he was preparing for a crusade against the oppressed—that he would deliver Poland out of bondage and drive the Austrians from Italian soil. It is needless to add that Louis Philippe had not the slightest intention of doing anything of the kind. What he did do, however, was to ' assure the Holy Father by an express message, of his protection and intervention for the maintenance of the Papal States under the government of the Holy See.' But meantime men from the Sabine mountains, from

the quarries, the marshes, and the mines began to show
their fierce and rugged figures in the purlieus of Rome.
Knots of conspirators gathered muttering in the public
places. Among the lower classes of the multitude an
inexplicable movement was discernible. The Papal
Government was obviously disquieted and the death of
Pius VIII. increased the effervescence among the Italian
youth, in whose minds the Revolution of July and the
installation of a Constitutional King in France had engendered the idea that the time had come to strike.

The spirit of disorderly agitation was greatly
intensified when one day, with an obvious and inten-
tional significance, Prince Louis rode along the Corso
with the tricolour ostentatiously displayed on his head-
gear and saddle-housings. The boldness of his attitude,
while it stirred the patriots, gave umbrage to the authorities, both of which results the Prince probably desired.
The chief of the Papal police went to Cardinal Fesch
and demanded that Prince Louis should depart from
Rome, adding that a person less powerfully protected
would have been arrested and sent to prison. The
Cardinal, himself concerned in revolutionary intrigues,
maintained that the Prince had committed no offence
and insisted that he should not be made to leave the
city. His mother was in great anxiety; she was aware
that there was an extensive revolutionary conspiracy in
Rome and that the conspirators looked to her son to
support and lead them.

One afternoon the chief of the Pope's guard was
announced; the palace of Hortense was surrounded
and her son was seized and carried off across the frontier
of the Papal territory. In spite of her ambition on

behalf of her son, she dreaded a repetition in the Eternal City of those bloody tragedies which near the close of the previous century had made of Paris a human shambles ; and she was not sorry that Prince Louis should be removed from the impending outbreak. Maternal solicitude outweighed with Hortense all other considerations, and her mind was at rest when she learned that her sons were with their father in Florence. She wrote cautioning them to enter into no rash undertakings, and warning them that the Romagna alone was preparing to raise the standard of revolt. She was not aware till later that on Feb. 5, 1831, an insurrection had broken out in Bologna and had spread rapidly through all the Romagna. The tricolour had been hoisted in Perugia, Spoleto, Foligno, and Terni ; the insurrection raged in the provinces of Umbria and Trasimene ; Cardinal Benvenuto was a prisoner at Cosimo ; Ancona surrendered to Colonels Sercognani and Armandi ; and Maria Louisa fled from her States, to which the conflagration had spread. The standard of Young Italy soon floated over the heights of Ottricoli, and terror reigned in the Vatican. The sons of Hortense, without her cognisance, had been fighting during most of this turbulent period. The character of the answer of the Princes to the wise and discreet letter of their mother had tranquillised the mind of Hortense, and she remained quietly in Rome until at length in the beginning of March insurrection broke out in that capital. Her sons immediately wrote to their mother imploring her to leave Rome, and after a hazardous journey she reached Florence.

The expectation that she would find her sons there was not fulfilled. A servant of Prince Louis handed her the following letter : ' Your affection will understand us. We have accepted engagements, and we cannot depart from them. The name we bear obliges us to help a suffering people who call upon us.' The brothers had displayed conduct and valour. Menotti, one of the most fervent leaders of the insurrectionary movement, had gone to Florence and addressed himself to the Princes. He had appealed to the name they bore, and the young men had become devoted to the cause. A practical soldier who had studied the art of war, Prince Louis had been of especially valuable service, and he it was who had planned the preliminary operations for a *coup de main* on Civita Castellana. Napoleon, the elder brother, with 200 men had repulsed a considerable body of Papal troops who had attempted to capture the towns of Terni and Spoleto ; and Louis with another detachment was now preparing for the assault on Civita Castellana. Solicitude for her sons had temporarily brought together the long-estranged King Louis and Queen Hortense, and courier after courier was sent with messages of recall to the young men. But their answer to their parents was that they were recognised by all the youth of the country as their leaders ; and that they were on the eve of seizing Civita Castellana and of delivering the prisoners who had been immured for years in the dungeons of that place.

But jealousies and the youth of the brothers rendered it inexpedient that they should retain commands in the revolutionary army, which were placed in the more experienced hands of Generals Sercognani and Armandi. They were informed that their position threatened to become a hindrance to the national cause and might even occasion a fresh danger to the patriots in the event of failure. Content to resign command, Napoleon and Louis remained in the field, insisting on continuing to fight in the capacity of simple volunteers. But even this service was not permitted to them; and then their troubles began. It seemed that their mere presence with the revolutionists involved the brothers in danger at the hands of the neighbouring Governments. The Provisional Government of Bologna looked askance on them. They were banned from Tuscany and the approaching Austrians would probably accord them a short shrift, for they were excepted from the amnesty proclaimed by the army of the Emperor on entering the Papal territory. In fine, the brothers were in a dangerous dilemma, for Austrian troops were approaching Ancona.

It was then that the intrepid mother resolved to carry her sons into safety by an unsuspected route to an unsuspected destination. An English gentleman furnished Queen Hortense with a British passport in the name of an English lady travelling from Italy through France to England; and on March 10 she quitted Florence in search of her sons. After delays at Foligno and Perugia she at length was informed that they had recently been seen at Forli. On the way thither the disastrous news was brought to her that her elder son was dangerously ill and desired ardently to see her. She hurried forward in a state almost of delirium; but at Pesaro she was informed that Napoleon was dead. Then, sunk in unconsciousness, she was laid on a bed in her nephew's palace only to be roused by the arrival of Prince Louis, who threw himself on her bosom and told her that his brother had died of measles and fever in his arms. He himself was very ill. Accompanied by the whole population of Forli he had followed his brother to the grave, on the eve of the occupation of the town by the Austrians.

CHAPTER III

TRAVELLING IN DISGUISE—FRANCE—ENGLAND—
RETURN TO ARENENBERG

WHILE Hortense lay in Pesaro prostrated by her
bereavement she was informed that the Austrian troops
on land were almost in sight and that their ships were
visible in the offing. She realised that she had still one
son left, whom she must endeavour to save at all hazards.
She and Louis reached Ancona after a hurried drive,
only to find that there was greater danger in Ancona
than there had been in Pesaro. The imminence of the
danger stimulated the resourceful ingenuity of Hortense.
Her English passport was for a lady travelling with two
sons; and in order to avoid suspicion on the contemplated journey it was necessary that she should
find a substitute for the son in his grave at Forli. At
this time there was temporarily in Ancona the Marquis
Zappi, a young nobleman whose position was seriously
compromised, since he was the bearer of secret despatches to Paris from the Revolutionary Government
of Bologna. Hortense offered him the place of her lost
son during the journey she was about to make to Paris;
Zappi consented, and preparations were at once made
for departure. But meanwhile Louis fell ill of the
disease which had carried off his brother. In this

dilemma she caused a berth to be taken for her son in a vessel about to sail for Corfu and procured for him a passport for that port duly signed by the authorities of Ancona. She spread the report that it was she herself who was ill, and had a bed made up for her son in a cabinet close to her own room. Her servants were ostentatiously carrying baggage from the palace of Hortense to a vessel which was to sail the same evening; it duly departed at nightfall and no one doubted that Louis Napoleon had left Italy in the little craft.

It happened that the general commanding the Austrian vanguard which had entered Ancona was the officer who had escorted Hortense and her sons from Paris to the frontier in 1815. When after eight days of anxiety and danger Prince Louis was pronounced in a condition to travel, Hortense apprised the Austrian commander of her approaching departure. The General courteously furnished her with a pass through the Austrian lines; and she informed him that she would leave Ancona early on the morning of Easter Sunday. One of her servants feigned sudden illness and Prince Louis dressed himself in the livery of the lackey; the Marquis Zappi, who had lain concealed in the house of a friend, joined the cortège in the livery of another domestic. Before daylight Hortense, and her son disguised as a footman, descended the great staircase at the foot of which the guard permitted her to pass without interference. Louis Napoleon stood in livery on the footboard of his mother's carriage and Zappi on that of the second vehicle. At the gate of the town the passports were duly examined without occasioning any suspicion. By-and-by Hortense halted to pray in the church of Loretto and then continued the journey. At Tolentino a wretched Italian who recognised the Prince notwithstanding his disguise, pointed him out to the commander of the Austrian detachment stationed there ; the officer replied that the lady's passports were in perfect order and that he was not there to arrest people.

Hortense made no pause until she had passed the last Austrian outpost. Worn with fatigue and anxiety she nevertheless pushed on through Foligno and Perugia, whose inhabitants awaited with apprehension the approach of the Austrian masses. On nearing the Tuscan frontier her anxieties and apprehensions were increased ; for all over Tuscany Louis and his brother had been familiar figures. The frontier was passed in the dead of night. The Commissioner of Police was absent and had left orders that nobody should pass the barrier until his return. Ultimately Hortense's courier found the Commissioner, who *visé'd* the passport on the courier's assurance that Prince Louis was not of the party. At Camoscia the travellers were to leave the high road and go by short stages to Siena. But no relays of horses were procurable at Camoscia. Hortense waited in her carriage in the street, for the inn was full. Prince Louis, the future Emperor of the French, in the dress of a flunkey slept on a stone bench out in the open until at length horses were procured.

After driving through the charming valley of Chiana during the whole day, the travellers reached a quiet little town where they ventured to take a night's rest.

' Without that night's sleep,' wrote Hortense, ' I should have died.' On this little-frequented road the travellers were in comparative safety. But the incognito could not

be long maintained. Queen Hortense had to go through
Siena, where she was well known, since she had been
in the habit of passing through the place every year on
her way to Rome. She now took the bold course of
passing through the city openly in full day ; but this
would have been imprudent for Prince Louis. While
the Queen's passports were being examined at the gate
Louis jumped from behind the carriage, and dodging along
the bye-lanes made quickly towards the street leading
to the Florence gate. Owing to the number of travel-
ing English swarming in the town a stay in Siena
was impossible ; so the party repaired to a roadside inn
outside the town, the Prince having been taken up after
a search for him on the way.

Early on the following morning the travelling party
was safe in Pisa. By this time Prince Louis and
Zappi had changed their clothes, and as Fritz, Queen
Hortense's old domestic, expressed himself, 'the servants
had ceased to be masters.' From this time Queen
Hortense was an English lady travelling with her two
sons, although Prince Louis was the only member of the
party who could speak English, and he then only with a
marked French accent. Their incognito went for very
little. At Lucca the landlord of the inn recognised the
courier of the travellers, and the jeweller of the Court
of Florence did not need to look at them twice. It was
in the valley of Sevarezza near Pietra Santa where the
elder son of Hortense had formerly lived with his wife,
that Hortense for the first time could breathe freely.
Perhaps no spot in Italy is more lovely. 'It unites,' so
wrote St. John, 'the magnificence of Switzerland with
the softness of the south—delicious valleys, marble

mountains, lofty spreading trees, glimpses of the distant sea, and a sky of deep azure tinged towards the horizon with the soft glow of evening.' The thoughts of the mother, like those of her son, were with the dead. Here Hortense persuaded herself that it would be delightful to pass what remained to her of life, plunged in soft melancholy and communing quietly with her own ideas. The mother and son proceeded until they came within sight of the foundations of the house which the young Napoleon had begun to build for himself. The grass was now springing up among the stones, as he lay at rest in the church of Forli.

The party hurried through a dependency of the Duchy of Modena, where there was reason to fear the vigilant police of the Duke. Finally Genoa was reached, where the British Consul affixed his *visé* to their passports without any difficulty. At length, after having been recognised times out of number but never betrayed, the fugitives found themselves once more on French soil. They had entered territory from setting foot on which they had been proscribed ; but after sixteen years of exile they were in their native land once again, and they slept happily that night at Cannes.

The members of the Bonaparte family were by law exiled from France and forbidden to return on pain of death. But Hortense and her son had little apprehension that in their case the law would be sternly enforced, although they took the precaution of travelling under names different from their own. When Hortense had been sent into exile in 1815, she had carried with her letters from Louis Philippe's mother and from his aunt the Duchess of Bourbon, in which they had thanked her warmly for having obtained pensions for them and for permission to remain in France—letters which were long extant. Louis Philippe had commissioned the Grand Duchess of Baden to inform Queen Hortense that she might always rely on his good offices. The resolution of Hortense and her son was to travel direct to Paris, to make known to him their presence, and to place themselves in his hands.

Hortense in her Memoirs recounts with what happiness she noted that as they journeyed forward towards Paris, her son threw off the weight of melancholy which had oppressed him since the death of his brother. 'When we stopped anywhere,' she wrote, 'he would go for a walk in the streets, enter the *cafés*, gossip with the people whom he met, and then return and relate to me all that he had seen and heard. In some places, finding that he had come recently from Italy he was asked about the death of young Napoleon, the questioners little imagining to whom they were addressing themselves. But it was when we passed through a garrison town that he hastened to examine the soldiers and their equipments with the greatest minuteness. . . . My son, electrified by the atmosphere of the country he loved so much, had only one desire—to remain in it, to serve in it as a simple soldier.' This was the object of the following letter which Louis Napoleon addressed to King Louis Philippe, from which some passages were excised by the advice of M. Casimir Périer:

' " Sire,—I venture to address myself to your Majesty, as the representative of the Great Nation, to ask you a favour which is the sole object of my ambition. I pray you, Sire, to open the gates of France to me, and

to allow me to serve as a simple soldier.   I could console
myself for absence from my country when, in an unfortunate land, liberty called me under her standards ; but
now that courage has been compelled to yield to numbers,
I have found myself obliged to fly from Italy.   Nearly
all the States of Europe are closed against me.   France
is the only one where it would not be reproached to me
as a crime that I had embraced the sacred cause of a
people's independence; but a cruel law banishes me.
Separated from my family, inconsolable for the loss of
my brother who died in Romagna after having given so
many proofs of his love of liberty, life would be insup-
portable to me if I did not continue to hope that your
Majesty will permit me to return as simple citizen to the
French ranks—happy if one day I may die fighting for
my country.   France and your Majesty might rely on
my oaths and on my gratitude.'

M. Périer expressed his approval of this appeal, which
he undertook to present to the King ; but so far as is
known no notice was ever taken of it.   Louis Philippe
desired in the French army no ambitious and ardent
young scions of the House of Bonaparte.   He was wise
in his generation.

M. Guizot thus describes in his Memoirs the arrival
in Paris, in April, 1831, of Queen Hortense and her son :
'On her arrival, Queen Hortense addressed herself to
Count d'Houdetot the King's aide-de-camp, begging
him to inform the King of her position.   The King
received her secretly at the Palais Royal ; whither the
Queen and Madame Adelaïde came also to see her.
The Queen and Queen Hortense were seated on the
bed, the King and Madame Adelaïde upon the only two

chairs. The King and Queen showed the kindest interest in the condition of Queen Hortense. She wished to be permitted to return to France, or at any rate to go to the waters of Vichy.

' " Vichy, yes," said the King, " for your health ; it will be considered quite natural. And then you can prolong your stay, or you can return."

' She desired also to press some pecuniary claims on the Government. The King promised all the help in his power ; but referred M. Casimir Périer to her, whom she did not receive without misgivings. " I know, sir," she said, as the Minister entered her room in the Hôtel de Hollande, " that I have violated a law ; you have the right to arrest me."

' " Legally, yes ; justly, no," answered the Minister, and presently he departed, having offered Hortense any help she required, which she refused.'

Queen Hortense has contradicted in many particulars the account of M. Guizot. Her version was that Louis Philippe when informed of the arrival in Paris of Hortense, was exceedingly incensed and sent M. d'Houdetot to intimate his refusal to see her. That emissary told her that the King had said that ' he deplored the audacity of the Duchesse de St. Leu in returning to France, and that he could not consent to an interview with her.' But later his Majesty sanctioned a visit to Hortense on the part of M. Casimir Périer the President of the Council, the result of which was that the King consented to see her in the Palais Royal. The ladies of Louis Philippe's family were present at the interview. Nothing could exceed their politeness and their insincerity. His Majesty received Queen Hortense with all the

graciousness and courtesy which were the distinguishing
characteristics of the 'Citizen-King.' After a short pre-
lude he began to speak of the subject which he knew lay
nearest to the heart of Hortense, the abrogation of the
sentence of exile. 'I know,' said he, 'all the bitterness
of exile, and it is not my fault that yours is not yet ended.
But,' he added, 'the day is at hand when there shall be
no more exiles! I shall have none during my reign.'
Hortense informed his Majesty that her son had accompanied her to Paris; and that he desired to beg of the
King that his Majesty would allow him to enter the
French army. It seemed that the King had suspected
the coming of the Prince; and he was very desirous that
the presence in Paris of the mother and son should be
kept quite secret—he had divulged the fact to none of his
Ministers except M. Casimir Périer. He added that if
circumstances permitted he should be happy to fulfil the
aspiration of Prince Louis. 'I wish you to understand,'
said Louis Philippe to Hortense, 'that in every respect
I shall consider it a pleasure to serve you. I am aware
that you have a claim for considerable sums, and that
the State has hitherto neglected to do you justice. Write
down everything which France owes you, and send the
account to me. I know something about this sort of
business and I will be your *chargé d'affaires.*'

Hortense believed in the King's honesty and friendship, and was greatly touched by his affability. Queen
Marie Amélie, as well as Madame Adelaïde, showed her
great sympathy. But it was significant that the latter
asked Hortense how long she meant to remain in Paris;
and that when Hortense replied that she would probably
prolong her stay for three days, Madame Adelaïde

exclaimed, in obvious alarm, 'So long? Three whole days? Are you aware that there are a great many English families here who have seen your son in Italy and may recognise him?'

When Hortense returned to her hotel from her visit to the Palais Royal, she found, so she tells, her unfortunate son in bed suffering from a recrudescence of the fever from which he had suffered in Italy. The physician called in declared that he had, besides, a dangerous inflammation of the throat. This is the account of Hortense. It must, however, be stated that another version is extant for which M. Thirria, the author of 'Napoleon III. avant l'Empire,' is responsible. His story is that on the morning after Hortense's visit to the Palais Royal M. Casimir Périer said to Louis Philippe at the Cabinet Council,—'Did not the Duchess of St. Leu present to you the excuse on behalf of her son that he was confined to his room by illness? Well, believe me, his plea of indisposition was feigned. At the time your Majesty was receiving the mother the son was in conference with the chief leaders of the Republican Party, and was devising with them the means whereby your throne might be overthrown.' Thirria adds that there could be no question as to the Prince's relations with the Republicans, and that they existed more or less actively until December, 1848.

This anecdote must be taken for what it may be worth. Louis Philippe and his Minister could afford to disregard the efforts of the Republican Party to subvert the throne. The Bonapartists were not more formidable. In the Revolution of 1830 scarcely any voices were heard uttering the name of the great Emperor in a

city which had so long echoed to that sound.   Ladvocat
and Dumvulin, two men without influence, military
reputation, or celebrity of any kind, had conceived for a
moment the idea of proclaiming the Empire : both were
jeered at as visionaries.   Old General Gourgaud, who
had returned from St. Helena, alone made a feeble
effort to stir the dulling pulses of his brother-veterans ;
and he went so far before he flickered out as to protest
against the nomination of the Duke of Orleans.   But in
effect, at this time there existed no Bonapartist Party.
The nominal head of the House of Napoleon was the
Duke of Reichstadt, an Austrian prince living in Vienna
under surveillance.   Joseph's protest from America was
at once futile and belated.   Most of the members of the
Bonapartist family were living in Italy possessed for the
greater part by local ambitions, in aid of which they had
a sufficiency of means.   The Chamber of Deputies gave
the crown of France to Louis Philippe in virtue of the
fact that he was the only possible compromise of a
dangerous position ; the only safeguard, in the words of
Thiers, ' against a republic and its inevitable tempests.'
As for Prince Louis Napoleon, he was a mere negligible
quantity now and for five years later ; a grown man he
nevertheless dangled on his mother's apron-strings.

Sick or shamming, Prince Louis remained in bed in
the Hôtel de Hollande ; and his mother never left him
except to receive M. Périer's daily visit to inquire in the
King's name as to the Prince's health.   The Minister
and Queen Hortense became very friendly.   ' As regards
you personally, a ready consent,' said Périer, ' would be
given to your return to France ; but your son's name
would be an obstacle in his case.   If later he should

aspire to enter the French army he would have to relinquish his name.' Louis overheard the remark and broke out into a passion. 'What!' he exclaimed, 'sacrifice my name? Who dares to make to me such a proposition? Let us return into obscurity. You were right, mother; the hour of the Napoleons has passed— or has not yet arrived!'

For the time Louis Philippe needed to feel no concern regarding the young man whose letter, if he had received it, he had not deigned to answer. It was really by a *façon de parler* that Louis Napoleon could call himself a Frenchman. He was now in his twenty-third year, and since the age of seven he had seen scarcely anything of his native land. He needed to assume no incognito; his old nurse of the Rue Cérutti would not have recognised him. There was in Paris a varied wealth of intense interest for this curiously belated quasi-Frenchman; but he had the misfortune to be debarred from making any pilgrimages or any explorations. Hortense and her son had been eleven days in Paris, and Louis was reported to be still in a very serious condition. On the afternoon of May 4, M. d'Houdetot, the aide-de-camp of the King, came in great haste to insist that the departure from Paris of Hortense and her son could no longer be postponed. This imperative urgency was occasioned by the circumstance that the following day chanced to be the anniversary of the death of Napoleon the Great. The celebration was an annual remembrance of the name which France will never allow to fall into oblivion; but in 1831 the occasion was honoured with exceptional warmth, because the Premier had carried in the Chamber the proposal to reinstate the

statue of Napoleon on the Vendôme Column, and the
work was actually in progress. Already great excitement
prevailed throughout the capital ; and it was with feelings
of apprehension that Louis Philippe's Government, not
yet a year old, regarded an anniversary so charged with
momentous memories. From the earliest dawn throughout the long day dense crowds gathered around the
Vendôme Column, loading the eagles and the railings
surrounding it with garlands and crowns of flowers.
Hortense had been watching the interesting spectacle
from the window of her apartment looking into the
Place, and possibly she was recognised. What occurred
was in effect that a hasty knock was heard at her door,
and that M. d'Houdetot, pale and confused, entered the
room. ' Madame!' he said hurriedly, ' you must depart
at once. I am ordered to tell you that not another
hour will be allowed unless the doctor is prepared
to state that Prince Louis' life will be absolutely en-
dangered by a journey so sudden.' Ultimately the
travellers started for England on the early morning of
the 6th.

A few days later they arrived in London, where the
unfortunate Louis was promptly attacked by jaundice.
The best people called on the exiles, who thoroughly
enjoyed themselves in the free atmosphere of England,
dined at Holland House and other notable mansions, and
paid a lengthened visit to Woburn Abbey. Talleyrand,
then the French Ambassador to England, lost no time
in inquiring the object of the visit of Queen Hortense
and her son. The reply was that they were on their
way to Switzerland by way of Belgium, an answer which
threw the diplomatic world into a temporary commotion,

since that little monarchy had been very recently constituted. Prince Leopold, indeed, had not yet been elected
to its throne ; and the voice of rumour had it that Prince
Louis intended to try his fortune in that direction.
Leopold, an old friend of Hortense, rallying Prince Louis
as to the *canard*, said jocosely, ' You'll not pocket my
little kingdom as you go home, I hope.' On the surface
the stay in England of Louis and his mother had no
political character or significance. Apparently mother
and son were wholly absorbed in the courtesies and
pleasures of society. They visited, they dined at great
houses, they to all appearance had no concealments and
no concerns ; but in reality they lived in an atmosphere
of plot, intrigue, and jealousy. The Duchesse de Berri,
who was then living at Bath, had at once hurried to
London to watch Hortense. This bold and enterprising
lady was already engaged in preparations for an expedition
to France, in the forlorn hope of fomenting an insurrection having for its object a revolution which should
restore the Legitimist dynasty and place on the throne
of France her son, the Comte de Chambord, a boy of
eleven. She suspected, and probably with reason, a
counterplot on the part of Hortense having a similar
character and object.

Joseph Bonaparte had quitted his retirement at Bor-
dentown—a spot in the American State of New Jersey,
where he had bought a property on which he had built
himself a mansion, in which he had resided under the name
of Comte de Survilliers—on the errand of ascertaining
whether it would be worth while to take a hand in a plot
against Louis Philippe. But the discovery was made
that the Bonapartists of character and devotedness were

at this period not strong in France; and the idea was suggested that an advantage might be gained by a coalition with the Republicans. A well-known politician has written: 'Lafitte and Lafayette were won over, and several other Republicans of distinction repaired to London in the hopes of being able to ripen that notable scheme of fusion. Several generals of Louis Philippe's army displayed considerable eagerness to transfer their allegiance; but not being able to invent any reasonable pretext for visiting the British capital, they instead went clandestinely to Ostend, where Prince Louis Napoleon met them. What was to have formed the basis of the new revolution had it occurred, was never divulged. In all likelihood it would have been Republican in name, but certainly Bonapartist in reality. About the mode of carrying it out Louis Napoleon and Joseph differed essentially, the former being desirous of pushing things at once to extremities, while the latter, with the characteristic timidity of age, sought all manner of pretexts for procrastination. Meanwhile the actual conductors of the journal 'La Tribune,' having discovered the design of the conspirators denounced it with great severity. They went back over the bloody history of the Revolution; they enumerated the victims of Napoleon I.'s perfidy and despotism, and they earnestly and vigorously cautioned the French nation against being deluded a second time by any member of the Bonaparte family, against which they inveighed as a tyrannical cabal utterly irreconcilable with liberty. This outspoken philippic was attributed to the suggestion of Louis Philippe, with some colour of reason; but with whomsoever it originated, it had its effect in thwarting the designs of the Bonapartes and in postponing for nearly twenty years their advent to power.'

It ultimately became evident to Prince Louis that any attempt in the direction of action would at this time be premature. The French Ambassador furnished him and his mother with passports, and they returned to Arenenberg through France, travelling incognito. During the journey they discovered that there had not been time for the French people to grow tired of King Louis Philippe, who, indeed, was then still quite popular with the bulk of his subjects. Since no wider field of action lay open to Prince Louis, he cheerfully concerned himself with his neighbours and his local surroundings. Having become a Swiss citizen—he had bought his citizenship in the village of Ermatingen, just below the Château of Arenenberg—he was duly called upon to undergo his statutory term of military service ; and, along with Mocquard (later his Minister), he served as an officer of artillery in the Swiss army at the camp of Thun. He became greatly interested in his special arm, regarding which he had already made some important scientific studies ; and he elaborated a number of novel combinations regarding explosive cannon balls which at that period were still chiefly of a spherical form. He employed a manufacturer of scientific instruments in Schaffhausen to construct for him finely worked brass models or patterns of those inventions. Having acquired the Swiss-German language, he lived on friendly terms with the worthy inhabitants of the vicinity of Arenenberg, especially with his nearest neighbours the villagers of Ermatingen, where he was quite a familiar visitor and was at one time a member of the *Gemeinde Rath* or Communal

Council. He had many friends throughout the Canton
of Thurgau in which Arenenberg is situated, among
whom was Dr. Kern, later, under the Empire, Minister
Plenipotentiary of the Swiss Confederation in Paris.

The Prince was a very good marksman with the then
very heavy arm of precision used by the Swiss Sharpshooters, and he frequently took part in the regular
rifle meetings held in the neighbouring Swiss towns.
On one of those occasions, a yearly festival of the Society
of Sharpshooters at Schaffhausen, he experienced some
unpleasantness by being forcibly ejected from the shooting stand in consequence of his refusing to conform to
the standing rules ; and this ejection, by a curious coincidence, was executed by the descendant of a French
Protestant family which had long previously been expelled from France.

But the chief employment of Louis Napoleon at
this comparatively uneventful period of his life was with
his pen. He was a copious writer. His first work was
entitled ' Political Reflections,' including a project for a
new French Constitution. The manuscript had the
advantage of being revised and altered on several points
by the illustrious Chateaubriand, who happened at that
time to be on a visit at the Château of Arenenberg.
The ' Political Reflections' may be accepted as the
political programme with which Prince Louis was by-
and-by to appeal to France. It was, in effect, the
carefully elaborated result of his study of his great
uncle's life and works, adapted according to his own
personal views, to the wants and desires of the French
people. It was the outline, in short, of the *régime* which
he was prepared to establish ; and it embodied in effect

the form of Constitution with which in his hand the
Prince was later to make his attempt on Strasburg.

The ' Reflections' were presently followed by a pamphlet in a yellow paper cover, on the title-page of which
were the words ' Political and Military Considerations in
regard to Switzerland.' The author's brief and modest
preface is as follows : ' I commend to the indulgence of
my readers these reflections, which I submit to their
judgment. If, in speaking of Switzerland, I have been
unable to prevent the frequent recurrence of my thoughts
to France, I trust that my digressions may be pardoned,
for the interest wherewith a free nation inspires me
naturally augments my love for my own country. I
counsel the Swiss to be always the allies of France,
because their local interest invites, because their interest
as a civilised nation impels them to that result.' This
brochure published in 1833, was mainly the outcome of
the studies which the Prince had been pursuing at Thun.
It was the result of some thought, reading, and experience. The views he advocated were naturally those
of a Frenchman of the Napoleonic School. He was at
this early period of his career a Republican, although he
found a crucial difficulty in reconciling his political ideas
with the traditions of his family—above all, with his
reverence for Napoleon. Among his chief mental idio-
syncrasies derived from that homage were his hatred of
England and the aspiration, then cherished more or less
deeply by nearly all Frenchmen, of avenging the defeat of
Waterloo. What of philosophy he then possessed had
not yet taught him to regard with calmness the events
of history, and to reflect that it is the destiny of great
nations to have to experience alternations of victories

and reverses. It had not yet come to him to realise that the animus of revenge is incompatible with civilisation in its best sense ; and Mr. Jerrold has shrewdly pointed out that the young author would not or could not recognise that Frenchmen might as well chafe at the remembrance of Cressy, Poictiers, and Agincourt, as at the fresher memory of Waterloo. The 'Considerations' nevertheless are not destitute of interest and suggestion. Their author wrote with strong convictions in favour of freedom although he seldom permitted himself to be impassioned or enthusiastic.

In evidence of their appreciation of this careful and friendly study of Switzerland the Cantons of Thurgau and Berne conferred on the Prince the rank of Captain of Artillery. In acknowledgment of this honour he wrote : 'I am proud to be placed among the defenders of a nation where the sovereignty of the people is the foundation of the Constitution, and where every citizen is ready at any time to sacrifice himself for the liberty and independence of his country.'

In the intervals of his literary work the Prince from time to time found change in his duties at the camp of Thun, where 12,000 men were assembled on a war footing and where he first appeared in the character of a captain of the Swiss Confederation. He drew up a 'Manual of Artillery' for the Swiss army, which was accepted and taken into use. It was not without a certain modesty that he now regarded himself as the practical head of the House of Bonaparte ; for the Duke of Reichstadt had died in 1832, King Joseph had become heir to the Imperial Crown, King Louis being next in succession, and his son Prince Louis being third. But

Joseph was now old and never had been adventurous; King Louis was a permanent invalid; and the hopes of such Bonapartist Party as there still existed were vested in the son of Queen Hortense. From this time forward the whole life of Louis Napoleon, speculative and practical, was devoted to his realisation of what now became his 'fixed idea'—the conviction that he was destined to occupy the throne of France.

CHAPTER IV

THE ATTEMPT ON STRASBURG

PRINCE LOUIS NAPOLEON in 1836 had been quietly
watching public opinion in France for a considerable
time, and had been in constant communication with some
of the leading men of the country. He was aware that
discontent in France with the government of Louis
Philippe was gradually becoming profound and general.
In writing to his mother after his failure he declared that
in undertaking the Strasburg expedition he acted on
calmly settled convictions, and that it was after mature
reflection and after very careful calculations that he
resolved once again to raise the Imperial eagle within
the borders of France. ' What,' he continued, ' care I
for the shouts of the vulgar, who now call me fool because
I did not succeed, and who would have exaggerated my
merit had I been triumphant ? I take all the responsibility of the attempt upon myself, for I acted from
conviction and not by impulse.'

Laity, the chronicler of the enterprise, avers too
sanguinely yet not wholly without warrant, that a revolution consummated at Strasburg by the nephew of
the Great Emperor in the name of liberty and the
sovereignty of the people, would have stirred France to
its depths. ' Had this city been secured,' in Laity's

ardent words, 'the National Guard would have manned the ramparts and protected it from assault without. The youth of the city, formed into corps of volunteers, would have been added to the garrison. The march on Paris would have been begun with 12,000 men, 100 guns, a full military chest, and spare arms for the enthusiasts rallying to the cause. Every garrison in Alsace would have fallen into line. The route of march on Paris would have been through the Vosges into Lorraine, and Prince Louis might have entered Champagne at the head of 50,000 men.' Instead of which hypothetically swift and amazing successes, the Prince was fast in prison a few hours after he had entered the fortress which he had come to conquer. Yet he was not so very far from winning the *coup* which he had projected; he had friends in many of the cities of Eastern France and he had the ardent good wishes of a great many influential inhabitants of Alsace and Lorraine.

Nephew of the Great Emperor yet condemned to the vexations of an obscure youth, his kindred proscribed, while he himself was exiled by an unjust law from the country which he loved and in which the memory of Napoleon was still alive, Louis Bonaparte probably did believe himself destined to uphold the honour of the great name he bore, to punish the persecutors of his family, and to reopen for his country a path to fame and glory. The attempt was hazardous; and Prince Louis, although capable of having conceived it, was not strong enough to carry it through. Louis Blanc with rare perspicuity has thus described the character of the Prince at the opening of his active career: 'To be insensible and patient; to care

for nothing but the end in view ; to dissemble ; not to
expend one's daring on mere projects, but to reserve it for
action ; to urge men to devotedness without putting implicit
faith in them ; to seem strong, in order to be so ; such, in
the egotistical and vulgar meaning of the phrase, is the
genius of the ambitious. Now, Prince Louis possessed
scarcely any of the constituent elements of that genius,
whether good or evil. His easily-moved sensibility
exposed him unarmed to the spurious officiousness of
subalterns. Through haste or good nature he often erred
in his judgment of men. The impetuosity of his aspirations deceived him or hurried him away. Endowed with
a natural straightforwardness injurious to his designs, he
exhibited in curious combination the elevation of soul
that loves the truth and the weakness of which flatterers
take advantage. He was prodigal of himself to augment
the number of his partisans. In a word, he possessed
neither the art of husbanding his resources nor that of
dexterously exaggerating their importance. But on the
other hand he was generous, enterprising, prompt in
military exercises, and the uniform sat upon him with a
manly grace. There was no braver officer, no more
gallant cavalier. Though the expression of his countenance was gentle rather than energetic and impe-
rious, though there was an habitual languor in his looks
often dashed with thought, no doubt the soldiers
would have loved him for his frank bearing, his honest
and hearty speech, his small figure resembling his uncle's,
and the lightning which the passion of the moment
kindled in his blue eyes.'

In July 1836 Prince Louis left Arenenberg for a
temporary residence at Baden-Baden, a place which he

found suitable to his purpose from its vicinity to Alsace, and from the opportunities it afforded him of covering his designs under the mask of pleasure. It was there that the preliminary arrangements for the project were made, and whither gathered around him some of his most trustworthy adherents. Colonel Parquin, an old soldier of the Empire, had been long an intimate of Arenenberg, having married in 1822 Mdlle. Cochelet, Queen Hortense's reader and school-time friend. The Colonel's regard for the Prince and his estimation of the latter's qualities, had helped to draw to the vicinity of Arenenberg many soldiers of the Empire. Colonel Vaudrey was a scar-worn officer who had commanded a battery at Waterloo and who was now in command of the artillery force in Strasburg. Fialin (afterwards Comte, and later Duc de Persigny), a *ci-devant* cavalry officer who had been cashiered, had attached himself devotedly to the fortunes of the Prince and in his later career proved a man of remarkable ability and character. The plan of the project was bold and had a specious aspect of feasibility, mingled, however, with fantasy. The Alsatian democrats were to be gained over, the garrison of Strasburg was to be captivated by the cry of ' *Vive l'Empereur !* ' ; the citizens were to be summoned to liberty, the young men of the schools to arms; the ramparts were to be entrusted to the holding of the National Guard. And then the pictures which presented themselves in the glowing mind of Prince Louis were of towns surprised on the march to Paris, of garrisons swept onward with the movement, of young men eagerly enlisting under the tricolour, and of old soldiers quitting the plough to salute the eagle in its advance, amid acclamations caught up by echo after echo along the valleys and over the hills.

The decisive blow was to be struck in Strasburg. Two months before the actual attempt Prince Louis was brought into that city under cover of night, and introduced into a room in which a friend of the cause had assembled twenty-five officers of the garrison representing the different arms of the service. He was received with unanimous enthusiasm. ' The nephew of the Emperor was welcome,' was the cry ; ' he has nothing to fear. We would defend him with our lives!' He made the officers a short speech which appeared to stir them greatly; and according to Laity, one and all declared that the Prince should no longer live in exile and assured him that they would exert themselves to restore him to his country.

The preliminary arrangements had the pretence of secrecy, but it is certain that many persons must have been aware that a conspiracy was in the air. So frank, indeed, was the Prince, that he himself made overtures to General Voirol, in chief command at Strasburg and military governor of the Department of Bas Rhin. Voirol was an old soldier of the Empire, but he was true to his salt. He repelled the advances of the Prince and warned him off French territory. He further considered it his duty to acquaint the Prefect of Strasburg with the projects in progress on the frontier. The Prefect wrote on the subject to the authorities in Paris, adding that he had a secret agent about the person of the Prince. Louis Philippe's Government apparently regarded the matter as trivial ; at all events no obstacles were offered to the designs of the conspirators.

During the stay in Baden a strange element was

imported into the enterprise in the person of a certain
enthusiastic Madame Gordon, said to be the daughter of
a captain in the Imperial Guard and to have been brought
up in the worship of Napoleon. While giving concerts in
the Kursaal in the character of a professional singer she
became fully initiated into the secrets of the plotters, and
she threw herself ardently into their designs, devoting
herself to gathering in partisans for the Prince. He had
returned from Baden to Arenenberg on a short visit to
his mother, and when on Oct. 25 he took farewell of
her ostensibly to join a hunting party in the Principality
of Heckingen, Hortense showed more emotion than a
temporary separation seemed to warrant. It is probable that she was aware of the danger which her son
was about to encounter ; for pressing him to her heart,
she slipped on his finger the marriage-ring of Napoleon
and Josephine, which she regarded as a talisman. A
rendezvous in the Grand Duchy of Baden with some
important persons on whom the Prince had counted
somehow miscarried ; he found no one at the place
appointed ; and at length on the morning of the 28th
he quitted Friburg along with Parquin, Vaudrey,
and Fialin, and reached Strasburg late the same
night. Next day was spent in consultations and arrangements with Parquin, Vaudrey, Laity, an officer of
pontonniers in the Strasburg garrison, and the rest of
the fifteen faithful participators in the adventure of the
morrow. The Prince presented a report on inquiries
which he had directed to be made in Neu-Brisach,
Colmar, and other frontier towns ; and the result seemed
to afford the conviction that their garrisons and civilian
inhabitants were prepared to rise so soon as an imposing

military force should be known to have raised the Imperial eagle in Strasburg.

The first condition towards success, then, was to secure the adhesion of a regiment. The garrison of Strasburg consisted at the time of the 3rd and 4th regiments of artillery, a pontonnier battalion, and the 14th, 16th, and 46th regiments of line infantry. The 16th, quartered in the citadel, was isolated by a fortified neck from the ramparts surrounding the town. The 14th regiment, quartered in the Margarethen barracks, in the western section of the city beyond the Ill, was quite outside of the prospective line of operations. The nearest military quarters to the house in which the conspirators were in consultation were the Austerlitz barracks occupied by the 4th artillery; of which, as well as of the 3rd artillery, Colonel Vaudrey had the command. Diagonally across the town from the Austerlitz barracks was the open space of the Place d'Armes, otherwise known as the Broglie-Platz, the further extremity of which abutted on the north-eastern section of the ramparts. Bordering the Place d'Armes were the Hôtel de Ville, the General's quarters, the Préfecture, the military establishments, and the quarters of the 3rd artillery regiment. Some distance away, close under the northern extremity of the ramparts, were the Finkmatt barracks, separated from the ramparts only by a narrow enclosed court and occupied by the 46th infantry regiment. There were two accesses to the Finkmatt—one by the broad thoroughfare of the ramparts, and the other by a narrow lane from the Faubourg Pierre.

It was finally determined that the first regiment to be attempted was the 4th artillery. Its rank and file were strongly Bonapartist—it had been Napoleon's own regiment, and it had opened the gates of Grenoble to him on his return from Elba. The attachment of the soldiers to their chief, Colonel Vaudrey, a brave soldier devotedly attached to Prince Louis, seemed to give assurance that his regiment would be most easily carried. The fulfilment of the plan consisted in repairing as soon as possible from the Austerlitz quarters to the Finkmatt, where, as has been said, were the barracks of the 46th. According to the plan, the leaders would have arrived there before the movement should become known and therefore before any opposition should be encountered. On the way along the Place d'Armes they would pass the residences of the Chief Authorities, who would either be won over or secured. The 46th once brought into acquiescence with the design of the Prince the military difficulties would have been surmounted; since while the 46th was being dealt with the officers of the 3rd artillery and of the pontonnier battalion who were in the confidence of the Prince, would form their respective corps and bring them on without delay to the general rendezvous on the Place d'Armes.

The morning of Oct. 30, 1836, was dark and cold. As day dimly broke and the cathedral bells chimed the hour of six, Prince Louis and his handful of some twenty adherents set forth on what the less sanguine hearts of the party must have felt to be a forlorn hope. But all wore a good front and tramped sturdily towards the Austerlitz barracks, whither Colonel Vaudrey had gone in advance. Parquin, now dressed as a general officer, walked alongside the Prince, as holding the rank of second in command. De Querelles, a retired cavalry officer, carried the shrouded eagle which he was to display before the soldiers whom Vaudrey was preparing to muster.   Lombard, a military surgeon of Strasburg, was on his way to the printing-office to have the proclamations printed and distributed.   Louis, like most Frenchmen, was addicted to proclamations ; and, unlike his great uncle, he preferred that they should be long.   His first proclamation was addressed to the French people, and its opening sentence was certainly to the point. ' You are betrayed,' it said ; ' your political interests, your commercial interests, your honour, your glory, are all sold to the foreigner.'   The second proclamation was to the army, and had a certain reminiscence of the ' little corporal's ' bulletins : ' Soldiers ! the time has come to regain your ancient renown.   The Government, which betrays our civil interests, would also tarnish our military honour.   The simpletons ! do they think that the race of the heroes of Arcola, of Austerlitz, of Wagram is extinct ? '   The third instalment of bunkum was addressed to the citizens of Strasburg, and began in this wise : ' Alsatians ! my name is a flag that should recall great memories to you ; and this flag—you know that it is inflexible before factions and the foreigner—will droop only before the Majesty of the People.'   Alas that Lombard should have destroyed efforts so striking, if also so full of platitudes !   Persigny and Madame Gordon were more purposeful when they committed to the flames all the compromising documents left by the Prince.

The trumpet-sound calling Vaudrey's soldiers to fall in was the signal in the barrack-yard for the appearance of the Prince and his sparse following.   Laity, an eyewitness, has recorded the scene : ' The officers pressed

closely round him as the Prince entered the yard.
" Forward, Prince!" they shouted ; " France is following
you!" The Colonel was in the centre of the square ;
as the Prince advanced the regiment presented arms.'
At the close of the inevitable harangue the Colonel
cried, ' Shout with me, " Long live Napoleon! Long live
the Emperor!"' The soldiers replied 'with indescribable
enthusiasm.' Then the Prince signified that he desired
to speak ; and when silence had been restored he spoke in
a strong deep voice : ' Soldiers! I present myself in the
first instance to you, because between you and me grand
memories exist. It was in your noble regiment that the
Emperor Napoleon, my uncle, served as a captain ; it
was with you that he made himself illustrious at the
siege of Toulon ; and, again, it was your brave regiment
that opened the gates of Grenoble to him on his return
from Elba.

' Soldiers! the glory of beginning a great enterprise be yours! Yours be the glory of having first
saluted the eagle of Austerlitz and of Wagram!' Here
the Prince seized the eagle which one of his officers
carried, and presenting it to the regiment, he continued :
' Soldiers, there is the symbol of French glory,
destined henceforth to be also the emblem of liberty!
During fifteen years it led our fathers to victory. It
has shone over every battlefield. I confide it to your
honour, to your courage. Let us march together against
the oppressors of their country, to the cries of " Long
live France! Long live liberty!"'

The Prince's address was scarcely finished when
every sword was drawn. The men held their shakoes
aloft, cheering with prolonged vehemence, their cries

mingling with the sounds of martial music.   But now, the regiment gained to a man, no time was to be wasted. The regiment, with the Prince and Colonel Vaudrey at its head, Parquin and the other conspirators following, began its march, its band in the advance.   Lombard hurried faster to the printing-office to hasten the publication of the proclamations.   A detachment took possession of the railway station.   The officers of the 3rd artillery hurried to bring their men on to the parade ground and an officer was sent off to notify in advance the distant 46th at the Finkmatt.   The Prince with his staff led the 4th artillery through the city to the headquarters on the Place d'Armes.

Though still early, crowds thronged the streets and considerable enthusiasm was visible.   The Prince doubtless felt assured at that moment that he had not mistaken the sentiments either of the army or of the people. General Voirol, however, to whom the Prince appealed with great fervour, remained staunch to his duty notwithstanding the pleadings and expostulations of the Prince ; the latter could not shake the allegiance of the loyal old soldier and he was held a prisoner in his quarters.   But in the general glow of enthusiasm Voirol's obduracy reckoned as but a momentary check.   The advance of the 4th artillery, still headed by the Prince, was resumed.   But whereas the proper route to the Finkmatt barracks was along the broad ramparts on which a body of men could march on a wide front, he led the column into the Pierre Faubourg, which was connected with the main entrance to the Finkmatt quarters by an extremely narrow lane.   The barracks themselves were separated from the ramparts only by a

long narrow yard at one end of which was an iron gate
locked. Leaving the mass of his force in the Faubourg
the Prince followed the lane, and he presently found
himself with a weak escort in a narrow and overhung
yard which, if fortune had failed him might easily have
become his prison or his grave.

It was a serious misfortune that the officer sent in
advance to apprise the 46th of the Prince's coming
should not have arrived. The infantrymen of that regiment were thus taken by surprise, but they crowded to
the windows and the doors when they heard the name of
Napoleon. The cheers of the gunners were caught up by
the foot-soldiers ; and, in short, the reception of the
Prince was at first as hearty and unanimous as it had
been at the Austerlitz barracks. Success now seemed
assured on all sides. General Voirol and the Prefect
were under arrest, as were the General of brigade and
the Colonel of the 3rd artillery ; and that regiment
was hurrying to the general rendezvous on the Place
d'Armes. Several companies of the 46th had already
been formed by the Prince and his officers. An old
sergeant exclaimed that he had served in the Imperial
Guard, stooped down to kiss the hands of the Prince,
and embraced him with tears. Emotion seized the
soldiers at this spectacle ; already the Prince was surrounded with marks of devotion ; already the cry was
heard of ' Vive l'Empereur ! ' ; when suddenly a strange
clamour astonished the bystanders, and Colonel Tallandier,
the officer commanding the 46th, came storming forward
with drawn sword, shouting loudly to his men, ' Soldiers,
you are being deceived—this man is an impostor ! ' A
staff officer called out, ' He is not the nephew of the

Emperor! I know him—he is the nephew of Colonel Vaudrey!' An infantry lieutenant named Pleignier rushed forward to seize the Prince. Himself arrested by the artillerymen the wildest confusion ensued. Linesmen and gunners became mingled in a general struggle; muskets were loaded, bayonets were fixed, and swords were drawn. The Prince was parrying with his sword the bayonets pointed against him by the infantrymen when a rush of artillerymen rescued him; but both he and they were driven back up against the barrack wall. The court-yard resounded with menaces; swords were out and flashing in all directions. The artillerymen who had been left in the Faubourg hearing of the Prince's imminent danger, moved forward; suddenly they were seen rushing in great crowds into the barrack-yard; and with them entered pell-mell sixty mounted cannoneers. The infantry thus driven back to both ends of the yard, formed again with shouts of fury and returned fiercely on the Prince's partisans, who were pushed and knocked down by the horses against the base of the ramparts. Here stood the foot-soldiers with bayonets charged; there the gunners with levelled carbines; on the ramparts the populace cheering for the Prince and throwing volleys of stones down on the infantry, amidst wild clamours, roll of drums, clash of arms, and neighing of horses.

But the end soon came. The people on the ramparts were scared by a few shots fired in the air by order of Colonel Tallandier. Gricourt and Querelles would have cut a passage sword in hand for the Prince, but he rejected the offer and was made a prisoner. Colonel Vaudrey wisely dismissed his men and surrendered

himself. Parquin and Laity followed his example ; and
later all the members of the Prince's following with the
exception of Persigny who adroitly escaped, found themselves in prison. The daring attempt, almost at the
moment of seeming success, had suddenly and utterly
collapsed.

The late Mr. Kinglake, the virulent enemy of Louis
Napoleon, remarks on this Strasburg fiasco as follows :
' In some of its features this attempt was a graver
business than was generally supposed. At that time
Louis Napoleon was twenty-eight years old. He had
gained over Vaudrey, the officer commanding a regiment
of artillery which formed part of the garrison. Early in the
morning of Oct. 30 the movement began. By declaring
that a revolution had broken out in Paris and that the
King had been deposed, Vaudrey persuaded his gunners
to recognise the Prince as Napoleon II. Vaudrey then
caused detachments to march to the houses of the Prefect
and of General Voirol, the General commanding the
garrison, and made them both prisoners, placing sentries
at their doors. All this he achieved without alarming any
of the other regiments. . . . Louis Napoleon was brought
into the presence of the captive General, and tried to
gain him over but was repulsed. Afterwards the Prince
surrounded by men personating an imperial staff, was
conducted to the barrack of the 46th regiment ; and the
men, taken entirely by surprise, were told that the person
now introduced to them was their Emperor. What they
saw was a young man with the bearing and countenance
of a weaver—a weaver oppressed by long hours of
monotonous indoor work, which makes the body stoop
and keeps the eyes downcast ; but all the while—and yet

it was broad daylight—this young man, from hat to boot, was standing dressed up in the historic costume of the man of Marengo and Austerlitz. It seems that this painful exhibition began to undo the success which Vaudrey had achieved ; but strange things had happened in Paris before, and the soldiery could not with certainty know that the young man might not be what they were told he was—Napoleon II., the new-made Emperor of the French. Their perplexity gave the Prince an opportunity of trying whether the sentiment for the Bonapartes were really existing or not ; and if it were, whether he was the man to kindle it. But by-and-by Tallandier, the Colonel of the regiment, having been at length apprised of what was going on, came into the yard. He instantly ordered the gates to be closed ; and then—fierce, angry, and scornful—went straight up to the spot where the proposed Emperor and his " imperial staff " were standing. Of course, this apparition—the apparition of the indignant Colonel whose barrack had been invaded—was exactly what was to be expected, exactly what was to be combated ; but yet, as though it were something monstrous and undreamt of, it came upon the Prince with a crushing power. . . . In a moment the Prince succumbed to the Colonel. Some thought that after what had been done that morning, the Prince owed it to the unfortunate Vaudrey to take care not to let the enterprise collapse without testing his fortune to the utmost by a strenuous, not to say desperate, resistance ; but this view did not prevail. One of the ornaments which the Prince wore was a sword ; yet without striking a blow he suffered himself to be publicly stripped of his grand cordon of the Legion of Honour and of all his other decorations. According to one account the angry Colonel inflicted this dishonour with his own hands, and not only dragged the grand cordon from the Prince's breast but trampled both epaulettes and cordon underfoot. When he was thus stripped, the Prince was locked up. The decorated followers who had been personating the imperial staff, underwent the same fate as their chief. . . . Louis Napoleon could not alter his nature, and his nature was to be venturesome beforehand, but to be so violently awakened and shocked by the actual contact of danger as to be left without the spirit and seemingly without the wish or motives for going on any further with the part of a desperado. The truth was, that the sources of his boldness were his vanity and his theatric bent ; and those passions, though they had power to bring him to the verge of danger, were not robust enough to hold good against man's natural shrinking from the risk of being killed. Conscious that in point of hat and coat and boots, he was the same as the Emperor Napoleon, he imagined that the great revoir of 1815 between the men and the Man of a Hundred Fights could be acted over again between modern French troops and himself. But it was plain that this belief had resulted from the undue mastery which he had allowed for a time to his ruling propensity and not from any actual overthrow of the reason ; for when checked, he did not, like a madman or a dare-devil, try to carry his vengeance through ; nor did he even, indeed, hold on long enough to try fairly whether the Bonapartist sentiments to which he wished to appeal were really existent or not. On the contrary, the moment he encountered the shock of the real world, he stopped dead ; and becoming suddenly quiet, harmless, and obedient, surrendered himself to the first firm man who touched him. The change was like that seeming miracle which is wrought when a hysteric girl who seems to be carried headlong by strange hallucinations is suddenly cured and silenced by a rebuke and a sharp angry threat.' The diagnosis is actually vitriolic in its bitterness, but it loses much of its venom because of its obvious and indeed undisguised animus.

The Prince remained a prisoner in Strasburg until Nov. 9. In charge of two officers he was then brought to Paris, where he arrived in the early morning of the 11th, and was confined in the Prefecture of Police. His mother had already hastened to Paris and had addressed to the King and his Ministers petitions in favour of her son. His Majesty and the Council had already resolved not to try Prince Louis at the bar of justice, but to despatch him in a frigate to the United States. After a detention of but two hours in Paris he was hurried to the fortress of Port Louis near Lorient, where he remained until the 21st, when he sailed for America in the *Andromède* frigate. He had written a manly letter to the King entreating his mercy and generosity on behalf of his companions in misfortune, who, he said, had been led away by him and 'seduced by the charm of glorious recollections.' It may be said here that after a trial which lasted for twelve days, the associates of Prince Louis in the attempt on Strasburg were acquitted by the unanimous verdict of a jury, to the great disgust of Louis Philippe and his Ministers. When the *Andromède* was on the point of sailing the sub-prefect of Lorient asked the Prince whether he had any means wherewith to meet his immediate wants on arrival in America. ' None,' replied the Prince. ' Well, then,' said the sub-prefect, ' His Majesty the King has desired me to hand you this case, which contains 15,000 francs in gold.' The Prince accepted the case, the sub-prefect landed, and the *Andromède* set sail.

Prince Louis had assumed, with considerable right, that the frigate was bound direct to the United States. But as soon as the captain opened his sealed letters when some days out from port, it appeared that in his orders from Paris he was directed in the first instance to make a détour by way of Rio de Janeiro, to take in fresh water and provisions there, to keep the Prince on board during the *Andromède's* stay in the roadstead, and finally to convey him thus circuitously to the United States. Ultimately he was put ashore at Norfolk in Virginia, in March, 1837, and was there greeted by the cheering tidings of the acquittal of his Strasburg associates. Joseph Bonaparte, who had been in England since the death of the Duke of Reichstadt, Prince Louis had known would risk nothing to assist the fortunes of the family, and his nephew was well assured that he had disapproved of the Strasburg attempt. Nevertheless, before his departure from France Prince Louis had written to his uncle, begging for a few letters of introduction for Philadelphia and New York and requesting Joseph to inform him through his American agent what land he would sell him. Louis, so he wrote, had determined to turn farmer ; and perhaps, he added, he would never return to Europe. On his arrival in New York Prince Louis found that his uncle was more incensed against him than he had apprehended, and that Joseph had not written him a line. This was discouraging, but he allowed himself to be

disheartened neither by the indifference of his family nor
by his distance from France. It was seldom that Louis
Napoleon was pathetic, but in one of his letters of this
time to his mother he reveals a sorrow. Among his
cousins was one, Mathilde, a daughter of King Jerome,
to whom he was attached, who was believed to return
his affection, and who is still alive, the last survivor
of her generation. The little passage is as follows :
' When, a few months ago, I was returning through the
park of Arenenberg, after having accompanied Mathilde
home, I came on a tree riven by the storm. I said to
myself, " Our marriage will be broken by fate." This
vague, passing thought has become the truth. Have I
exhausted, then, all the stock of happiness life had in
store for me ? '

Prince Louis' stay in America was shorter than he
had anticipated ; but in two months and a half he
assimilated a vast quantity of information in travelling,
visiting, and conversing. There is no doubt that in a
marvellously short time he made himself fully acquainted
with the laws and form of government of the United
States. He is said to have lived much with such people
as FitzGreene Halleck, Generals Scott and Watson
Webb, the Schuylers, the Hamiltons, the Clintons, the
Livingstones, the Bayards. His friends, of the best
houses in the States, found him silent and reserved, but
conceived a sincere and lasting regard for him ; and they
contrasted his conduct and manners with those of his
dissipated and rowdy cousin Prince Pierre Bonaparte,
who was in America at the same time. One prominent
gentleman of New York wrote of Prince Louis : ' His
bearing was always quiet, gentlemanly, and reticent ; he

seldom laid aside his grave demeanour. He associated almost exclusively with our best and oldest families, and he always evinced a fondness for ladies' society. He mixed occasionally in a small but refined French circle. I never heard of his having committed any imprudence ; he always sought the company of persons older than himself and preferred grave topics of conversation.' Another friend wrote : ' He was winning in the invariableness of his amiability, sometimes playful in spirits and manner, and warm in his affections. He was a fondly attached son and seemed to idolise his mother. When speaking of her, the intonations of his voice and his whole manner were as gentle and feminine as those of a woman. It was said that he was without means and lived on loans which he never repaid ; but this was wholly untrue. Funds were awaiting his arrival in New York and money was always at his command.'

This, certainly, seems explicit enough. Yet there is not lacking evidence of quite a different character. Some strange circumstances concerning Louis Napoleon's short residence in America are still claimed to be authentic. He is stated to have lived in a dingy street of Hoboken, a squalid suburb of Jersey City over against New York. ' His room,' says this informant, 'was in the attic of a large frame building, the basement and upper floor of which were occupied by stores and the intervening storeys in rooms let out to mechanics. Louis Napoleon's room looked to the east. There were no decorations on the walls but such as the plain boards afforded, and no furniture except a small iron bedstead and three chairs— two small ones and a kind of armchair in which he sat when he wrote. His wardrobe was of the scantiest description,

and sometimes he presented as sorry a specimen of seedy
gentility as one need look at, in worn-out and threadbare
coat. How he succeeded in appeasing the wants of the
inner man was a mystery which soon attained solution in
the neighbourhood when he was seen under cover of
night to steal out and buy bread at an adjoining baker's.
He always managed, however—how, few could tell—to
have a good bottle of wine in his room and never to be
out of tobacco. He was the steadfast customer of a
little Alsatian Frenchman named Sangler who kept a
tobacco store across the road from his tenement, and
many a discussion was held between the two.'

Apparently Louis had no intention of persevering in
the farming project—at all events until he should receive
from Europe some definite advice. With General
Watson Webb's assistance he was planning a year's
tour through the States of the Union, with intent to
study their institutions and observe the practical operation
of their political systems. But a letter from his mother,
delayed in transmission, reached him, intimating her
intention to undergo an operation which she had assured
herself would prolong her life. The doctors knew
differently, and therefore it was that the faithful and
skilled Conneau wrote on the envelope the. fateful words
'*Venez! Venez!*' Sailing by the first packet the Prince
reached London on July 10, only to be refused passports
for Switzerland by the representatives of the Great
Powers. And now it was charged against him that when
deported to America by the French authorities instead
of being tried for high treason, he had given an undertaking not to return to Europe within a period of
ten years. Nevertheless the Prince, having suddenly

returned from America, persistently denied that he had
entered into any such undertaking ; and that so far from
agreeing to any conditions, it had been his ardent desire
to remain in France and present himself for trial at the
head of his adherents ; not only that he might accept the
whole responsibility of the Strasburg expedition, but also
prove to the world how much more serious and more
nearly approximating to success was that enterprise than
the journalists in the hire of Louis Philippe were instructed
to represent it. His contention was upheld later when,
referring to the Strasburg affair a servant of the Government of July, M. Franck-Carré, *Procureur-Général* to
the Court of Peers, exclaimed at the Prince's subsequent
trial in 1840 : 'Conquered without a fight, pardoned
unconditionally, ought he not to have remembered that
his machinations were not feared ? '

Prince Louis was at length fortunate enough to obtain
the use of a friend's passport ; and after a rapid journey he
reached the Château of Arenenberg in the dead of night.
Conneau told him that his mother was asleep and that
it would be unwise to disturb her. In the early morning
the quick ear of the sick mother was on the alert, and
a few minutes later her son knelt by her bedside. The
first glance told him that Hortense was stricken for
death ; and relay on relay of medical men whom he
requisitioned as forlorn hopes told him that no human
hand could save her. Day after day Louis spent by her
bedside until the end came. She lingered until Oct. 5,
1837. Her last physical effort was to clasp her son in her
worn arms. And as the early sun rose over the Swiss
mountains, Hortense de Beauharnais, Queen of Holland,
Duchesse de St. Leu, passed from a world in which she

had paid for a brief period of splendour and joy with more than twenty years of exile, harassment, and suffering. Her son closed her eyes, in the light of which he had lived so long, and fell weeping on the bed. Her dying entreaty that her remains might lie by the side of her mother in the church of Rueil, near Malmaison, was granted by the French Government.

In July that Government, to which the return of Prince Louis to Switzerland occasioned great uneasiness, wrote to the Swiss Federal Directory requesting his expulsion from the republic. For the moment the matter rested, M. Molé being content to wait until Queen Hortense should have passed away. After her death the Duc de Montebello presented himself at Lucerne to communicate the demand of the Cabinet of the Tuileries that Prince Louis Napoleon should be compelled to quit Swiss territory without delay. The demand was answered by a firm refusal. The French emissary was peremptory for immediate expulsion and there ensued a close combat of words, gradually threatening actual hostilities between France and Switzerland. The situation was abundantly satisfactory to Louis Napoleon. He became for the nonce an European celebrity ; the newspapers were full of him, and he acquired for the first time real importance in the eyes of the Napoleonic Party throughout France. He was no longer a mere adventurer, but was elevated into the position of a serious political opponent of the French King. Switzerland actually armed to resist the French demand for his expulsion ; and a French army was in course of concentration to coerce the Switzers and enforce the extradition of Prince Louis Napoleon. Had the situation become further exacerbated, there was a possibility that the Prince might be crushed between the upper and the lower mill-stone. For the present Louis Napoleon had made himself sufficiently conspicuous in the eye of the world ; and he prudently put an end to the trouble by voluntarily withdrawing himself from Swiss territory. He sold his carriages and horses by auction at Arenenberg, paid his farewell respects to the Diet, and travelling through Germany and Holland, returned to London in the end of October, 1838.

CHAPTER V

THE FIASCO OF BOULOGNE

PRINCE LOUIS NAPOLEON had many staunch and influential friends in England, and as a consequence of the futile folly of Louis Philippe and his Ministers he brought with him to London, in October 1838, an European prestige. The days of obscurity were passed in the case of a man to remove whom a great State had put an army in motion. In all respects London was a more convenient place of residence for Prince Louis than had been his mother's château in an obscure Swiss canton. No molestation could reach him in the bosom of the great and free British nation. In London he was in every sense nearer Paris than he had been in Switzerland; he found in England his uncle Joseph and he was in the midst of a number of well-affected fellow-countrymen. He at once made good his footing in the best circles of the British capital, and he became immediately a personage of high social interest and importance. He seems to have been on terms of intimacy with the leading members of the aristocracy; he was welcomed in the best country houses, and notwithstanding his silent and reserved manners he was a favourite in ladies' society. He frequented the literary and intellectual society of Gore House and soon after his arrival in England he went on a tour of the manufacturing districts, afterwards making a round of visits which extended to some of the most notable houses of Scotland. In the famous Eglinton tournament which was held in August 1839 the Prince took an active part. Armed cap-à-pie as a knight of the days of chivalry he broke a lance with an antagonist. Their spears riven, the combatants drew their swords and their armour rang under the heavy blows. The Prince had been always addicted to exercises requiring spirit and skill. His training at Thun had given him skill in the use of arms and he excelled in the management of the lance, a circumstance which no doubt gave the Eglinton tourney a special attraction in his eyes.

During the London seasons of 1839 and 1840 Prince Louis, so far as the outside world was concerned, led the life of a man of fashion. He has been accused of having been dissipated and a spendthrift. No doubt he had his share in the fashionable vices of a lax and dissipated period. But a man who thought, worked, and schemed so assiduously as did Louis Napoleon, could not have been altogether absorbed in pleasure ; for he lived in daily preparation for the destiny of which he had assured himself. That he had a mission to perform, as those who knew him most closely recognised, was throughout a fixed idea in Louis Napoleon's mind. The man who wrote the ' Idées Napoléoniennes,' which were published in 1839 and speedily ran through four editions in France, was assuredly a thoughtful, serious, and earnest-minded person. ' The " Idées," wrote Mr. Jerrold, ' are the brightest and fullest expression of the mind of Prince Louis Napoleon. His political life was this work in action. By its lights his conduct as President and as Emperor must be judged. It is the text-book of his policy, the code of his personal law, the last result of his unwearied study of the man under whose inspiration he lived and died. Yet the " Idées " are not a mere summary of the intellectual manifestations of Napoleon I.; they are rather new developments of those manifestations, applications of them to the changed aspects of the political world, the Napoleonic ideas amplified and carried forward for the government of society by a later Napoleon.'

The Prince had brought with him to London a suite of seven devoted adherents, among whom were General Montholon (who had shared the St. Helena exile with Napoleon I. until the death of the latter in 1821), Persigny, Colonels Vaudrey and Bouffet de Montauban, and the faithful Dr. Conneau. His confidential servant was Charles Thélin, who later became a person of some importance. On leaving Fenton's Hotel the Prince established himself at first in Lord Cardigan's house in Carlton Terrace, whence in the winter of 1839 he removed to the house of Lord Ripon in Carlton Gardens. His domestic habits during this period are thus described in the ' Lettres de Londres ' :—' The Prince is an active working man, severe towards himself, indulgent towards others. At six A.M. he is in his study, where he works till noon—his hour of *déjeuner*. After this repast, which never lasts longer than ten minutes, he reads the newspapers and has taken notes of the more important events and opinions of the day. At two he receives visits ; at four he goes out on his private business ; he rides at five and dines at seven ; then, generally, he finds time to work again for some hours in the course of the evening.' It has been said of him by unfriendly writers that the Prince, once established in London, gave himself up to the dissipations of the town and degenerated into the mere spendthrift votary of pleasure. One hostile author has permitted himself to aver that, instead of learning how to command armies and govern nations, his time was almost wholly spent on the turf, in the betting-room, or in clubs 'where high play and desperate stakes roused the jaded energy of the *blasé* gambler.' But Mr. Jerrold maintains this description to be untrue. 'Prince Louis,' according to that writer, 'was no saint either before, during, or after his residence in London. He had his full share of the fashionable vices. He kept a mistress. He was fond of sports ; he delighted in racing ; he was expert in all manly exercises. Both in the hunting-field and the park his horsemanship was remarkable.' In a word, he lived among the most fashionable men of the day ; and if he were in a measure dissipated, he was dissipated among gentlemen. His earnest belief in his star even when fate seemed most unpropitious, struck his English friends with mingled astonishment and amusement. To most of them it was a sort of fetish betokening weakness of mind and strength of vanity. But no badinage or discouragement impaired his faith in the ultimate fulfil-ment of his destiny. That he had a mission to fulfil was a fixed conviction in Louis Napoleon's mind. His manner for the most part was grave and taciturn ; he was wrapt in the future and seemed indifferent to the present.

In the spring of 1840 the Prince of Joinville was voyaging to St. Helena in the *Belle Poule*, on the

errand of restoring to France the ashes of Napoleon the
Great; and the statue of the 'Little Corporal' now
surmounted the Vendôme Column. Prince Louis in-
discreetly and prematurely deemed the time favourable
for making a second effort towards the restoration of the
Napoleonic power in France. The chiefs of the party
certainly did not respond with ardour; nor did the
emissaries despatched to test the feeling of the French
Army of the North bring back favourable reports.
Among the Prince's adherents detailed for this service
were Parquin, Lombard, and a new recruit, de Mésonan,
to whom was confided the forlorn-hope attempt of
bringing over to the Prince General Magnan, then in
command of the Army of the North with his quarters at
Lille. Mésonan sapped up towards his purpose with
but little address; and after several visits to the General
he seized a moment which he deemed propitious, and
produced for Magnan's perusal a letter to himself from
the Prince, the terms of which were as follows: 'It is
important that you should promptly sound the General
in question, whom I have marked to be one day a
Marshal of France. You will offer him 100,000 francs
down, and deposit 300,000 more with his banker to
meet the contingency of the loss of command.'

The General, stupefied by a communication made so
bluntly and so abruptly, shouted in passion: 'This to
me—to me—such a letter! I had thought better of you.
I will never betray my oaths—never be a traitor. But
you are mad! My attachment to the memory of the
Emperor will never lead me to betray my oaths to
the King. Were I so base as to accept this offer, I
should be a thief whom the meanest corporal would have

the right to take by the collar! I ought to have you arrested, were it not that I cannot denounce a man whom I have received at my table. For God's sake, in regard for me, for your own honour, renounce your projects! I shall not expose you.' The General opened the door of his room, and as he thrust Mésonan out he exclaimed, ' Go and get yourself hanged somewhere else!'

This was not an encouraging episode. The Prince, having failed in regard to General Magnan and not having succeeded in corrupting any officers of the Lille garrison through the machinations of Parquin and Lombard, abandoned his original idea of causing a rising in a large town ; and having decided to act without any more delay, he fixed his choice on the seaport of Boulogne. To that coast-town the access was comparatively easy ; its garrison was very weak, and there had already been suborned a member of it in the person of Lieutenant Aladenize, an officer who belonged to the infantry detachment of two companies of the 42nd regiment then in garrison in Boulogne. Muskets were purchased in Birmingham ; a number of old French soldiers were hired for whom French uniforms were provided ; and Dr. Conneau himself sewed on them buttons stamped with the figure 40, the number of the regiment quartered in Calais and Dunkirk. A printing-press was purchased for printing the several proclamations which were to be issued in France—to the soldiers, to the inhabitants of Boulogne and the Pas-de-Calais, and to the French nation. The specific *rôles* of the principal adventurers as well as the details of the execution of the enterprise were prepared in advance.

Including the Prince, the expeditionary body con-

sisted of fifty-six persons, more than half of whom were
servants. Among the superiors a few indeed were
cognisant that some such enterprise as the attempt on
Strasburg was impending; but apart from Persigny and
Conneau, and the two officers ordered to Boulogne to
warn Aladenize, every person implicated denied more or
less directly at the subsequent trial having been aware
of the time of sailing, or even when once aboard, what
was to be the object or the destination. The steamship
Edinburgh Castle had been chartered for a month from
Aug. 1, ostensibly for a party of pleasure-seekers, with
freedom to go whithersoever the charterer might desire.
On the night of Aug. 3–4 the vessel came alongside
the Custom House Wharf near London Bridge, and
early on the morning of the 4th there were put on
board ship under the superintendence of Count Orsi,
two heavy vehicles, nine horses, a number of packages
of uniforms, and a quantity of wine and spirits. It was
charged against the followers of Prince Louis that on
arriving at Boulogne they were nearly all drunk. Captain Crow, the skipper of the *Edinburgh Castle*, testified
before the Boulogne authorities that the drinking on
board was enormous, and that sixteen dozen of wine,
besides a quantity of spirits and liqueurs, were consumed
during the stay at sea, or at the rate of about four bottles
of wine per man. Probably among the miscellaneous
throng of underlings there was a considerable consump-
tion of wine, but it is certain that not one of the conspirators was found when arrested to show any token
of inebriety. The 'wild orgie' was of a piece with the
story of the 'live eagle' which, it was said, was carried
on the shoulder of the Prince on entering Boulogne.

The story of this historic fowl was very simple. Colonel Parquin during a delay while the *Edinburgh Castle* was anchored off Gravesend, was obstinately determined to go ashore for the purpose of purchasing some decent cigars, those on the ship being detestable. He had his way in spite of all remonstrance ; and on the way to the cigar-shop accompanied by Orsi and Thélin, he noticed a boy on the wayside feeding an eagle with shreds of raw meat. The eagle had a chain fastened to one of its claws, with which it was secured. Returning towards the landing-place Parquin, whose obstinacy was sustained, approached the boy and looking at the eagle asked, ' *Est-il à vendre ?* ' The boy turned to Orsi and said, ' I do not understand the gentleman.' Orsi entreated, ' My dear Colonel, I do hope you don't intend to buy that eagle ? For my sake don't think of such a thing ! ' The stubborn Parquin insisted, ' Why not ? I will have it. *Combien veux-tu ?* ' The boy shrugged his shoulders ; and at last Parquin asked him in broken English, ' How mooch ? '

' One pound,' answered the boy. The eagle was put into the boat, Parquin insisting vehemently. On arrival aboard the eagle was fastened to the main-mast by the boy, and from that moment was taken no further notice of until it was discovered and seized by the Boulogne authorities. It remained on shipboard, and to use the sententious words of the sub-prefect of Boulogne, ' filled no *rôle* in the affair.' The ' eagle,' indeed, seems to have been a common vulture, and it subsequently found a temporary residence in the slaughter-house of the town, whence it escaped ; but, altering its mind, it returned for a time, and ultimately belonged to a charcoal merchant of Arras.

From the outset the Boulogne enterprise was an utter fiasco. Between London Bridge and Gravesend Orsi in the *Edinburgh Castle* picked up at various wharves detachment after detachment of adventurers. In giving Orsi his instructions for the arrangements regarding the steamer the Prince had particularly insisted on the former being at Gravesend on the 4th at three P.M. precisely; 'because,' said he, 'we shall have to proceed to sea without delay, since we must land at Wimereux near Boulogne at four A.M. of the 5th.' But the hours passed at Gravesend; it was nearly six P.M. and the Prince had not yet made his appearance. His house in London was actually *gardée à vue*; wherever he went he was followed and closely watched. The French police were much more suspicious and active than usual. A council was held, as the result of which Orsi took a post-chaise and hurried to Ramsgate, whither General Montholon, Colonel Voisin, and Colonel Laborde had been sent by the Prince to wait for him. Orsi reached Ramsgate at a very late hour and with no news of Prince or steamer. Voisin, who was one of the three officers whom Orsi found at Ramsgate, waited until the other two went to bed and then expressed to Orsi his utter despair at the non-arrival of the Prince with the *Edinburgh Castle*. 'Do you not know,' said he, 'that the success of our undertaking depends entirely on our reaching the Boulogne barracks at four o'clock to-morrow morning—the 5th? The only man we dread is Captain Col-Puygelier, commanding the detachment at Boulogne; besides being a man who will do his duty unflinchingly, he is a Republican, and nothing could induce him to join an Imperial Pretender.'

'Well,' observed Orsi, 'we shall have to deal with this Hector; whether it be to-morrow or next day does not seem to matter.'

'You are mistaken,' replied Colonel Voisin; 'Captain Col-Puygelier will be absent from Boulogne all day to-morrow. The Prince had purposely fixed the 5th for the enterprise, because he is aware that Col-Puygelier has been invited to a shooting party on that day some distance from Boulogne, and probably he will not return until late. If we miss our landing to-morrow morning we are doomed to utter failure.'

Between one and two A.M. of the 5th the steamer stopped off Ramsgate. Thélin came to announce that the Prince had arrived and that he desired everyone to come aboard. It had been expected that the debarkation at Wimereux should be accomplished by three o'clock in the morning of the 5th. It was now two A.M.; the adventurers were still at Ramsgate and the programme of the enterprise was dislocated if not destroyed. The undertaking now, if attempted at all, had clearly become a most hazardous and difficult adventure. Out of the twelve men of superior standing whom the Prince had called in to deliberate with him as to the future, three advised the Prince to return to London. Nine were urgent for the landing taking place; for a desperate dash being made towards the barracks in order to secure the adhesion of the companies of the 42nd at any price and by all available means; and leaving the town promptly, reach by a quick march St. Omer where other important elements of success might be anticipated. Forestier, Count Persigny's cousin, was promptly sent across the Channel in a row-boat, with instructions to make all speed to Boulogne and inform Aladenize and Bataille of what had occurred, enjoining them to get everything in readiness so far as was possible, for the following day, the 6th.

After deliberating for some time as to the advisability or the reverse of remaining at Ramsgate during the whole of the 5th, it was unanimously resolved, that in order to avoid the risk of suspicion it was the safest policy to go tacking about at sea until nightfall of the 5th. Once out in the Channel the steamer cruised about frequently changing its direction so as not to anticipate the time of landing arranged with Aladenize. On the 5th the Prince collected his adherents on deck and made them a short address. 'Companions of my destiny,' said he, 'it is for France that we are bound. The only obstacle is Boulogne ; that point once gained, our success is certain. Support me bravely and in a few days we shall be in Paris ; and history will relate that it was with a mere handful of gallant fellows such as you are that I shall have accomplished this great and glorious enterprise!' It has been stated that the Prince had with him a sum of 16,000*l.*, left to him by his mother ; and that shortly before the debarkation Bure, his paymaster and foster-brother, distributed by order of the Prince 100 francs to each person of the band. Count Orsi, however, who at this period was one of the henchmen of the Prince, states in his 'Recollections' that it was he who financed Louis Napoleon at this juncture. The Prince, says Orsi, required 20,000*l.*, of which 10,000*l.* was to be paid at once, and another 10,000*l.* on the day previous to the departure for the projected enterprise. Orsi testifies: 'A fortnight of difficult negotiations enabled me to comply with the Prince's wishes. On June 21 I handed him 10,000*l.* in gold and notes. The second payment of 10,000*l.* took place on Aug. 3, the day before the start.'

On the early morning of the 6th the *Edinburgh Castle* anchored about a mile off shore opposite Wimereux, a petty port about two and a half miles north of Boulogne. In four successive trips between two and three o'clock the whole force of the expedition had been landed; and Forestier, Bataille, and Aladenize had been found waiting on the beach. A Customs officer had observed the coming and going of the ship's boat, and had hailed it. A voice had replied out of the gloom, 'We are soldiers of the 40th regiment on voyage from Dunkirk to Cherbourg; but one of the paddles of our steamer is broken and that is why we are debarking.'

A superior officer of Customs asked for some further information. He was told that there was no time for talking and that by will or by force he would have to act as guide to the body which had just landed. Montauban asked Brigadier Guilbert of the Customs, 'Do you know whom you are to escort? It is Prince Napoleon!' The unhappy *douanier* replied that he would lose his place by acting as a guide. 'Men don't lose their places,' was the answer, 'who are constrained by force. Have no fear. The family of the Prince is rich; it will not forget you.' General Montholon offered the man money, but he would not accept it; and the

Prince, noticing that he was troubled, permitted him to go
free on condition that he would keep silence. The lieutenant of Customs pleaded fatigue when ordered to lead
the way to Boulogne. 'Fatigue or no fatigue,' cried de
Mésonan, 'you must tramp'; and Parquin threatened
the poor fellow with his hand on his sword, shouting
'Come, march!' But the Prince again interposed and
permitted the officer to remain. The man was staunch
in refusing Montholon's offer of money, nor would he
accept the Prince's promise to pension him should he
lose his place. At length the expedition started on the
march for Boulogne.

The plan of action was very simple, if not altogether
practical. It consisted, above everything, in seizing the
barracks occupied by the two companies of the 42nd
regiment, in bringing over the soldiers, in seizing and
holding the castle which served as arsenal, in taking
possession of the principal public buildings, in guarding
all the exits, and then in rapidly organising a military
force which should march on Paris, gathering up on the
way an irresistible army borne onward by a popular
impulse.

About five o'clock on the morning of the 6th the
expeditionary column entered the town. It reached first
the Place d'Alton, where there was on duty a post of four
men and a sergeant. The sentry recognised Aladenize
who was heading the advance; then came Lombard
carrying the flag, and behind him was visible a brilliant
staff followed by a few soldiers. The sentry shouted,
'Guard, turn out!' and the men of the post presented
arms. Aladenize exclaimed, 'Behold the Prince!
sergeant, come with us'; but the loyal sergeant would

not quit the post he commanded in spite of Aladenize's alluring representations. The sergeant shrewdly noticed that the Imperial eagle was above the flag which Lombard carried and that no member of the strange band knew the watchword; so he ordered his men to stand to their arms and reiterated his refusal to quit his post, giving no heed to Parquin's threat that he would be punished for his recusancy.

The stout sergeant's staunch attitude was ominous, and as the band of conspirators were marching along the Grande Rue there occurred a second rebuff. An officer of the garrison, Sub-Lieutenant Maussion, was met, and one of the Prince's principal adherents accosted him, asking, 'Do you not know the Prince? Come, I will present you!' Maussion declined, but a sort of forced presentation was nevertheless made; and the Prince begged the young officer to join his enterprise. Maussion, however, stammered out a negative, made a pretext for quitting the Prince, and hurried away to give warning to his superior officer Captain Col-Puygelier, of the extraordinary and alarming event which was in course of progress. The Captain hastened to get into uniform, all the more quickly because tidings had also reached him that a detachment, seemingly of the 40th regiment, had strangely appeared at the barracks of the 42nd. The news was true; the expeditionary column had reached the barrack gate. 'To arms! don't you see the Prince?' shouted Aladenize to the sentry on the gate. The soldier obeyed without hesitation the command of his officer; the guard promptly turned out and presented arms; and the Prince, followed by his suite, entered the barracks of the 42nd without the slightest hindrance.

Two sentries were at once posted on the gate with orders to prevent any officer from entering and to permit nobody to leave the barracks. Already a crowd had gathered outside, into which one of the Prince's officers was throwing money and calling for shouts of ' *Vive l'Empereur !* ' It need not be added that the crowd shouted accordingly with a hearty unanimity so long as the distribution of franc-pieces held out. A couple of sergeants, just as they entered the barrack-yard, were taken hold by Aladenize each by an arm and brought up to the Prince. ' This man,' said he, ' is an old soldier who fully deserves a pair of epaulettes ' ; and the Prince replied, ' I make you at once captain of grenadiers!' Shaking the other sergeant's hand he said, 'And you, *mon brave*, I make you an officer also ! ' Then the assiduous Aladenize presented a sergeant-major, whom the Prince made a captain and desired to bestow on him the cross taken from his own breast. But in attempting in vain to detach it he tore his uniform, whereupon he consoled the sergeant-major by assuring him heartily that he was none the less a Chevalier of the Legion of Honour. Sub-Lieutenant Maussion having come on duty, Aladenize begged him earnestly to cry ' *Vive l'Empereur !* ' but in vain. Maussion shouted ' *Non ! jamais ! Vive le Roi toujours !* '

Now appeared Captain Col-Puygelier in great excitement. At the gate of the 42nd barracks a retainer of the Prince promptly accosted him. ' Captain ! ' he entreated, ' do join us ; here is the Prince ; your fortune is made.' Col-Puygelier's prompt answer was to draw his sword and shout ' Clear the way—let me get to my soldiers ! ' He was surrounded, but he fiercely resisted. 'Fine men of honour,' he roared, 'to commit such a treason as this!' The Prince addressed him: 'Captain, I am Prince Louis; join us, and there is nothing which you may not expect to have.' 'Prince or no Prince,' replied the staunch soldier, 'I don't know you —get out of my barracks!' Then, turning to his men he cried: 'Soldiers! You are being artfully deceived! *Vive le Roi!* Rally round me!' The rest of the loyal officers had now arrived with their swords drawn, and Col-Puygelier formed up his troops preparatory to marching out for action. It was then that Prince Louis in his rash excitement fired a pistol, and the bullet wounded a grenadier in the mouth. Col-Puygelier promptly distributed ball-cartridges to his men, and rapidly gave orders to certain of his officers to strengthen the barrack-guard, seize the port, and send a detachment to the upper town to prevent the seizure of the castle and the pillage of the arsenal.

By this time it was six o'clock, and the civil authorities were now on the alert. Informed that strange men were traversing the streets with treasonable shouts, they mustered the gendarmes and warned their subordinates to turn out for duty. Meanwhile the band of conspirators, driven out of the barracks by superior strength, headed for the castle, spreading proclamations and scattering money. As they passed the sub-prefecture, the sub-prefect stepped out into the street and summoned them in the King's name to disperse and at once lay down their flag. The Prince gave the order to push him aside and pass on. As the sub-prefect showed an intention to bar the way, he was struck full in the chest by a blow of the eagle surmounting the flag, and in defending himself his hands were wounded so that he was obliged to give way to the Prince and his followers ; but he hastened to collect the National Guard, some two hundred of whom rendezvoused in the Place d'Alton under the command of Colonel Sausot.

The adventurers failed to seize the castle, nor did their axes make any serious impression on the closed Calais gate in the ramparts of the upper town. Without any apparent object they hurried to the Column of the Grand Army half a mile from Boulogne, ascended it, and planted on its summit the Imperial flag. A pursuit by horse and foot was promptly organised, whereupon the adventurers scattered and fled in all directions. The Prince in despair would fain, it has been alleged, have committed suicide on the spot but that his adherents prevented him. Aladenize and six others were captured when hiding in the adjacent fields. Desjardins was apprehended in the act of mounting a peasant's horse ; Ornano was routed out of a hut in which he had hidden. General Montholon and Colonel Parquin were captured near the port. The main body of adventurers closely pursued by soldiers and National Guard hurried down to the water's edge shouting, but in vain, to the captain of the *Edinburgh Castle* to take them aboard. Most of the fugitives surrendered on the beach ; some few, among whom were the Prince, Persigny, Conneau, and Mésonan, plunged into the water and attempted to seize a boat which by chance lay at anchor near the shore. Then the Royalist soldiers opened fire at close range on the defenceless unfortunates and the boat capsized while they were attempting to scramble aboard. Colonel Voisin was hit on the

loins and breast, the Prince was struck by a spent ball,
Viengiki was severely wounded in the shoulder and
d'Hunin was drowned.   Faure was killed.   The lieutenant of the port manned a boat, and in the face of
the hot fire rowed to the people in the water and
rescued the Prince along with four of his officers.   The
sub-prefect and the mayor bundled the Prince, numbed
and shivering, into a carriage and had him driven to
the castle.   Persigny, Voisin, Conneau, and Mésonan,
streaming with water, followed in another carriage
escorted by gendarmes.   The Prince obtained permission to divest himself of his wet clothes and to go to
bed at once.   By eight A.M. the affair was at an end—
the outbreak, from beginning to end, having lasted just
three hours.   The band of filibusters were incarcerated
en masse.

Lord Malmesbury has given in his Memoirs a version
of the affair, which differs in some particulars from
the account detailed above.   The Prince and some of
his followers, it is stated, had taken possession of a
lifeboat which was swamped; and the Prince was picked
up by a steamer while clinging to a buoy a short distance from the shore.   He would have been drowned,
it is added, but that the Custom House officers brought
the *Edinburgh Castle* close enough to permit of his
being conveyed aboard.   Some of the party were said
to have made their escape by taking forcible possession of horses belonging to some English gentlemen,
but were pursued and most of them taken ; some of
the adventurers, however, were killed by the French
soldiers after they had surrendered.

Early on the morning of the 7th two carriages

entered the castle-yard. The sub-prefect and some of
the other authorities presented themselves and desired
the Prince to follow. As he came out into the yard his
adherents thronged the windows of their cells with
shouts of ' *Vive l'Empereur !* ' Halting for a moment
the Prince turned to them and said in a loud voice,
' Adieu, my friends ! I protest against this forcible
removal ! ' His farewell, uttered with emotion, was
answered by a loud voice from the officers' prison,
' Adieu, Prince ! the great shade of the Emperor will
protect you ! ' He was escorted to the fortress of Ham
by a detachment of lancers and a body of municipal
guards. At midnight of the 8th the Prince arrived at
the fortress, with the grim walls of which he was soon to
be familiar during a long and weary captivity. But for
the present Ham was merely a temporary resting-place.
He was brought to Paris on the 12th, and in the cell in
the Conciergerie which Fieschi had occupied he was
imprisoned under the close surveillance of three warders,
without permission even to have the services of his
valet.

Kinglake's comments on the Boulogne fiasco are
very biting. ' If,' he remarks, ' Louis Napoleon was
wanting in the quality which enables a man to go well
through with a venture, his ruling propensity had
strength enough to make him try the same thing over
and over again. His want of the personal qualifications
of this sort being now known in the French army and
ridicule having fastened upon his name, he could not
afterwards seduce into his schemes any officers of higher
rank than a lieutenant. Yet he did not desist. Before
long he was planning another "return from Elba" ; but

this time with new dresses and decorations. So long as he was preparing counterfeit flags and counterfeit generals and counterfeit soldiers, and teaching a forlorn London bird to play the part of an omen and guide the destiny of France, he was perfectly at home in that kind of statesmanship; and the framing of the plebiscites and proclamations which formed a large part of his cargo was a business of which he was a master. But if his arrangements should take effect, then what he had to look for was, not only that at an early hour on a summer morning he would find himself in a barrack-yard in Boulogne surrounded by a band of armed followers and supported by one of the garrison whom he had previously gained over; but also having to do with a number of soldiery of whom some would be for him and some inclined against him and others confused and perplexed. Now, this was exactly what happened to him; his arrangements had been so skilful, and fortune had so far lured him on, that whither he meant to go there he was at last, standing in the very circumstances which he had brought about with long design afore-thought. But then his nature failed him. Becoming agitated and losing his presence of mind, he could not govern the result of the struggle by the resources of his intellect; and being also without the fire and joyfulness which come to warlike men in moments of crisis and of danger, he was ill-qualified to bridle the hearts of the bewildered soldiery. So, when a firm, angry officer forced his way into the barrack-yard, he conquered the Prince almost instantly by the strength of a more resolute nature, and turned him out into the street with all his fifty armed followers, with his flag and his eagle and his counterfeit headquarter staff, as though he were dealing with a mere troop of strolling players. Yet only a few weeks afterwards this same Prince Louis Napoleon was able to show by his demeanour before the Chamber of Peers, that when the occasion gave him leisure for thought and for the exercise of mental control, he knew how to comport himself with dignity and with a generous care for the safety and welfare of his followers.'

Louis Philippe's Government brought Prince Napoleon and his adherents to trial before the Court of Peers, the highest tribunal of the realm. A middle-class jury had acquitted the conspirators of Strasburg ; but the Court knew itself safe in the hands of the Peers, although most of them owed their honours to the great uncle of the chief of the accused. The illustrious Berryer undertook the defence of the Prince, and the trial was begun on Sept. 28. Much curiosity was evinced as the Prince, followed by Berryer and the venerable Montholon and wearing the highest order of the Legion of Honour, passed to his seat a little apart from his adherents.

The Chancellor, addressing him as ' First Accused,' bade the Prince stand up. He gave his name and age ; his profession he described as 'a French Prince in exile.' Then, having obtained permission, he read the interesting statement from which here only extracts can be made. ' For the first time in my life,' said he in a firm voice, ' I am at last able to make my voice heard in France and to speak freely to Frenchmen. . . . In the midst of you, gentlemen, whom I know, I cannot think that I need justify myself or that you can be my judges.

If, without pride as without weakness, I recall the rights deposited by the nation in the hands of my family, it is only to explain the duties which those rights have imposed on us all. For the fifty years during which the principle of the sovereignty of the people has been consecrated in France by the most powerful revolution the world has ever seen, the national will has never been so solemnly proclaimed as in the adoption of the Constitutions of the Empire. The nation has never revoked this great act of her sovereignty, and the Emperor has said, " All that has been done without her is illegal." . . . The cruel and undeserved proscription which for twenty-five years has dragged my life from the steps of a throne to the prison which I have just left, has not been able to impair the courage of my heart. It has not made me for a day a stranger to the dignity, the glory, and the rights and interests of France. . . . As regards the recent enterprise for which I stand arraigned, I have had no accomplices. Nobody knew beforehand my projects, my resources, my hopes. If I be guilty towards anyone, it is only towards my friends. They will understand the motives of honour that prevent me from divulging even to them, how widespread and powerful were my reasons for anticipating success. . . . A last word, gentlemen. I represent before you a principle, a cause, a defeat. The principle is the sovereignty of the people ; the cause is that of the Empire ; the defeat is Waterloo. . . . The representative of a political cause, I cannot accept as the judge of my acts and aspirations a political jurisdiction. In the struggle about to open there is only the conqueror and the conquered. If you be the men of the conqueror, I have no justice to expect from you and I repudiate your generosity.'

This address made a strong impression on the Court.

The Prince's subsequent examination was brief, since he refused to criminate others and kept his own counsel. He declared that the discharge of his pistol was a casual mischance—an accident of excitement.

The trial lasted until Oct. 6th, the time for the most part occupied by the pleadings and evidence on behalf of the conspirators. The sentence to which the Prince was finally condemned was perpetual imprisonment in a fortress of France. Montholon, Parquin, Lombard, and Persigny were doomed to twenty years' 'detention,' and Mésonan to fifteen. Three more were sentenced to ten years', and three more to five; all to be under surveillance of the police for life, and to be deprived of their titles, rank, and decorations. Conneau and Laborde were sentenced to five years' imprisonment.

The sentences were delivered by the Court in the absence of the prisoners. At four P.M. of Oct. 6th, 1840, the officers of the Court of Peers entered the cell of Prince Louis Napoleon, and in a broken voice M. Cauchy read the decree condemning the nephew of Napoleon to imprisonment for life. 'At least, sir,' was the calm reply of Prince Louis, 'I shall die in France.' In response to a rather heartless question he asked with a quiet smile, 'How long does "perpetuity" last in France, monsieur?' Eight years later, and then again eighteen years later still, he was to answer that question as the result of his own personal experience.

CHAPTER VI

FROM PRISONER TO PRESIDENT

BEFORE Prince Louis Napoleon received his sentence of perpetual imprisonment he had already completed his preparations for the worst. He arranged his property in such wise that the pensions bequeathed by his mother to her entourage should be safely settled. No claim was disregarded. For the benefit of those dependent on him he held it necessary so to dispose of his property that it should be beyond the reach of the law. This was accomplished, and when on Oct. 6th, 1840 he left Paris for his prison he was, in the words of the faithful Thélin, 'as poor as Job.' It was something of a coincidence that on the day on which Louis Napoleon quitted the Conciergerie for Ham the *Belle Poule* arrived at St. Helena to receive the remains of his great uncle and restore them to the France which he had loved.

Accompanied by the venerable General Montholon on the evening of the 6th he was put into a carriage without being permitted to see any of his friends, and under the charge of a colonel of the municipal guard he was escorted to Ham, where he arrived at midnight of the 7th. Dr. Conneau, who was allowed to share the imprisonment of the Prince, followed in a few days, and with the faithful Thélin the little coterie was complete.

Ham is an obsolete fortress situated in the marshy
region through which flows the sullen Somme.   It had
been long used as a State prison.   At the commencement
of his enforced sojourn in Ham the Prince occupied the
rooms which had been previously appropriated to M. de
Polignac the Minister of Charles X. ; and he was later
transferred to those which had been occupied by the
Comte de Peyronnet the colleague of Polignac.   Those
apartments were simply in a state of utter dilapidation,
and comfort was as carefully excluded from this melancholy abode as was liberty.   The ceilings were full of
holes, the paper on the walls was torn, the brick flooring
was badly laid and rotten, the doors and windows could
be neither closed nor opened.   To remedy in some
measure this condition of matters which was sensibly
injuring the Prince's health and against which the
doctor had remonstrated with vigour, the Minister of the
Interior placed 600 francs at the disposal of the commandant for the purposes of repairs.   The pittance of
24*l.* was ridiculously inadequate, for new floors, ceilings,
windows, and doors were needed.   Nevertheless no
supplementary amount was forthcoming, and the Prince
was actually asked to complete the repairs from his own
resources.   'It is not for me,' he quietly answered, 'to
keep a State prison in repair.'   He certainly was not
of an exceptionally querulous nature.   The Chevalier
Wikoff, an American who visited him in his prison, thus
writes : 'From his person my glance wandered over the
room, which surprised me by its extreme rudeness.   It
was very small, the walls were bare, and the floor was
without covering.   Three or four wooden chairs, and a
single table on which among other objects stood a plain

student's lamp, constituted its principal furniture. In recesses on either side of the chimney were shelves carried up to the ceiling, filled with books; and here and there round the apartment were suspended several engravings with some miniatures of the Prince's family. On the low wooden mantelpiece stood a common clock and a small plain looking-glass above it. The whole had very much the appearance of a common kitchen in some unpretending private house.' When Wikoff observed that nothing could well be more vindictive and illiberal than the spirit which had assigned him those miserable quarters, the Prince answered, ' Oh! I am very well off now, I assure you, since they have ordered the removal of the damp brick floor, which in this wet climate and decayed old building was seriously impairing my health. I am afflicted with a violent rheumatism which, you see, has lamed me; but I trust it will pass off with time.'

The garrison of Ham consisted of 400 men, of whom at least sixty were constantly on duty. In addition to the military guard which properly speaking formed the guard of the fortress, there was within those gloomy walls a brigade of warders, turnkeys, and keepers, to whom the constant watch on the person and movements of the Prince was more particularly entrusted. Besides this mass of espionage, the commandant of the place zealously performed the duties of high surveillance. Sentries there were in all directions; on the stairs, in the corridors, at the doors, keepers were stationed whose duty it was never for a moment to lose close sight of the prisoner, and who dogged his footsteps even when he took his walk upon the ramparts within a space of forty yards long by twenty broad.

As regarded the interior arrangements the Prince's household consisted of a very modest establishment. The expenses of his table had been regulated by M. Lardenois, Lieutenant-Colonel of Gendarmerie, the officer who had escorted the Prince from Boulogne to Paris and from Paris to Ham. The sum paid to the canteen was fixed by this officer at seven francs a head per day. The Prince arranged his mode of life to the best possible advantage. He rose early and worked until ten ; after breakfast he walked on the ramparts or cultivated the flowers for which he had made a sloping parterre along the parapet ; he then retired to read his correspondence, to write to his friends, or to take up his reading ; and he thus continued to occupy himself till dinner, which was served at half-past five. After dinner he conversed with his friends and received the formal daily visit on the part of the Commandant of the fortress ; and in the evening a game of whist in which General Montholon, the Commandant, and Dr. Conneau joined, completed the somewhat dreary day.

In the further right-hand corner of the main court-yard of the fortress were the watched and barred windows of the building in which the Prince and his companions were confined. The main entrance was by a narrow door opening to a white-washed passage at the extremity of which was the guard-room. On the ground floor to the right of the passage were the two rooms occupied by General Montholon ; on the other side of the passage were the bath-room and chapel. The Prince's quarters consisted of two rooms on the first floor, the windows of which were closely barred. One of those was the work-room, the other the salon, which

was the first on entering. Its principal furniture consisted of a great mahogany bureau, an old commode, a
couch, an easy-chair, four straw-bottomed chairs, a deal
table converted into a card-table, and a screen hung with
designs from 'The Charivari.' Little by little the Prince
had added several engravings connected with the historic
epic of the Empire, a portrait of his mother, busts of
the Emperor and the Empress Josephine by Chaudet,
statuettes of soldiers of the Imperial Guard, and lastly,
on the shelves fixed against the walls a number of books
—in particular a file of the 'Moniteur' and fifty volumes
of the 'Journal des Débats.' The second room served
as a bedroom, in which was a bed of painted deal, a
toilette table in white wood, a jar of earthenware,
several chairs, and two small deal tables on which
was a toilette service in silver bearing the Imperial
arms. The Prince habitually wore either a military
great-coat and forage-cap or a blue frockcoat buttoned
up with a red *képi* trimmed with gold cord. The
presence of the three men, Montholon, Conneau, and
the valet Thélin, who were always, so to speak, at his
side, very greatly ameliorated the bitterness and sorrows
of the Prince's captivity, all the more because they loved
him devotedly.

Nevertheless Louis Napoleon chafed under the petty
and continual vexations of which he was the victim.
He had calculated that he should be able to refrain from
making complaints until he had endured nine months of
suffering ; but then he considered that he was called on
no longer to endure in silence an intolerable situation,
and he consequently addressed the following protest to
the French Government :

'Accustomed from my youth,' he wrote, 'to a strict rule of life, I do not complain of the inconvenient simplicity of my dwelling; but that of which I do complain is being made the victim of vexatious measures by no means necessary to my safe-guarding. . . . During the first months of my captivity every kind of communication from without was forbidden and within I was kept in the most rigorous confinement; since, however, several persons have been admitted to me, these internal restrictions can have no longer an object, yet they are the more rigorously enforced. . . . The attentions of my single faithful servant who has been permitted to follow me are encumbered by obstacles of every description. . . . The insulting inquisition which pursues me into my very chamber, and which follows my footsteps when I breathe the fresh air in a retired corner of the fort, is not limited to my person alone but extends even to my thoughts. My letters to my family are submitted to the strictest scrutiny; and if a letter to me should contain any expression of too lively a sympathy, the letter is sequestrated and the writer is denounced to the Government. . . . The treatment which I endure is neither just, legal, nor humane. If it is to be supposed that such measures will subdue me, it is a mistake; it is not outrage, but marks of kindness which subdue the hearts of those who suffer.

'(Signed) NAPOLEON LOUIS BONAPARTE.

'Citadel of Ham, May 22, 1841.'

The result of this protest was that the Prince's valet Thélin obtained permission to go out into the town of Ham, and that the authorities were induced to adopt measures more conformable to their true dignity. The future of the Prince was accepted by him as that of one who notwithstanding numerous offers of devotedness to his cause, chose to remain a stranger to any thought of escape. Indeed, this acceptance of an indefinitely prolonged imprisonment had a certain serene pleasure for the exiled. 'Recovered,' he wrote, 'from all the illusions of youth, I find in my native air which I breathe, in the studies which I sedulously pursue in the quiet of my prison, a charm which I have never before felt even when partaking of the pleasures of foreign lands.'

Apparently he was in earnest. Writing to Lady Blessington in 1841, he said: 'I have no desire to go beyond the limits within which I am enclosed, because here I am in my place. With the name I bear, for me is either the gloom of a dungeon or the glare of power. My life passes here monotonously enough because the rigour of authority is unbending; nevertheless I cannot say that I find myself bored, because I can create for myself occupations which interest me. I am just now engaged in writing some reflections on the history of England, and then also I am planting a little garden in a corner of my rampart by way of change. But I must own that these things merely pass away the time without stirring the heart and that sometimes I do recognise a vacuity of thought. But I make no complaint of the position I have made for myself, and I am completely resigned.'

The Prince carried on a large correspondence; but that by itself did not occupy his active mind. In the course of the five years from 1840 to 1845 he wrote and published articles on a curious variety of subjects.

It was while in Ham that he wrote his 'Historical
Fragments'; where he treated on the 'Analysis of the
Sugar Question' published in the local journals; where
he published a treatise on the 'Extinction of Pauperism';
and where he drew up a memorial which he sent to
Arago, on the 'Production of Electric Currents.' He
wrote a memoir of his uncle Joseph Bonaparte, who
died in July, 1844. Among his other works were
'Opinions on Various Political and Administrative
Questions,' 'Of Governments and their Supporters,' 'A
Reply to M. de Lamartine,' 'The Past and Future of
Artillery,' and 'The Revision of the French Constitution,' as well as a series of 'Miscellaneous Papers.' In
1844 he schemed out a history of Charlemagne; and in
1845 he occupied himself with the question of the possibility of the junction of the Pacific and Atlantic Oceans
by means of a canal. The Minister Plenipotentiary of
Guatemala offered him the presidency of the construction
of the Nicaragua Canal, as the sole person who could
fulfil the diverse conditions which might bring success to
that important undertaking.

In April, 1845 Lord Malmesbury visited the Prince
in Ham, at the request of the latter. The Prince stated
that a deputation from Ecuador had come to him,
offering him the Presidency of that Republic if Louis
Philippe would release him, and in that case he would
give the King his parole never to return to Europe.
He was anxious that Sir Robert Peel, then Prime
Minister of England, should intercede with the French
King to comply with his wishes, promising every possible
guarantee for his good faith. The Prince assured Lord
Malmesbury that the soldiers had for the most part been

gained over, and that the prestige of his name was universal in the French army. 'You see that sentry under my window?' asked the Prince. 'I know not whether he is one of mine or not; if he is, he will cross his arms; if not, he will do nothing when I make a sign.' He went to the window and stroked his moustache; there was no response until three sentries had been relieved, when the fourth answered by crossing his arms over his musket. 'You see,' said the Prince, 'that my partisans are unknown to me, as I to them. My power is in an immortal name, and in that only; but I have waited long enough and cannot endure imprisonment any longer.' Lord Malmesbury returned to London deeply impressed with the calm resolution—or rather philosophy—of Prince Louis, but putting little faith in his ever renouncing his pretensions to the throne of France. Sir Robert Peel was not averse to apply to the French Government in favour of the Prince on certain conditions; but Lord Aberdeen, then Foreign Secretary, 'would not hear' of the Ecuador proposition.

In the end of 1845 Louis Napoleon had been a prisoner in the fortress of Ham for over five years. His father, the ex-King of Holland, was lying dangerously ill in Florence; and he sent an emissary to beg of the French Government that he might have the presence of his only son at his approaching death. The Council of Ministers, however, decided that 'it could not accede to the Prince's request, because it would be contrary to law and because it would be granting a full and free pardon without the King having the merit of it.' The Prince then wrote direct to his Majesty. On receiving the letter Louis Philippe seemed satisfied, and without

breaking the seal, said that he thought 'the guarantee
previously offered by the Prisoner of Ham—"his
honour"—was sufficient.' But the Council held that the
acceptance of the letter would amount to a pardon by
indirect means ; and that ' in order to maintain the proper
exercise of the King's clemency, it was necessary that
this act of grace should be deserved and frankly avowed.'
M. Odilon Barrot proposed to M. Duchâtel the drawing-
up of a new letter to the King containing the following
passage : ' I had hoped that your Majesty's Government
would see in that engagement' (of returning to prison)
' one guarantee more and a new obligation in addition
to those which gratitude should have imposed on me.'
The Prince, however, refused to go further. ' I may die
in prison,' he exclaimed, ' if unexampled severity con-
demns me to such a lot, but nothing shall induce me
to degrade my character. My father, I am convinced,
would regard my liberty as over-dearly purchased at the
expense of my dignity and of the respect I owe to my
name.'

Yet the Prince, being anxious to go as far as possible
without failing in what he owed to the dignity of his
name, authorised his English friend Lord Londonderry
to assure the French Government that if the Prince
were set free from his imprisonment in Ham, he would
undertake, after spending a year with his father in Italy,
to betake himself into exile in America there to reside
permanently. But to this proposal no reply was
accorded ; and then it was that the Prince resolved to
attempt making an escape from his imprisonment in
Ham. This resolve was finally made only ten days
before the plan was put into execution, and at a time

when at length some workmen had appeared to repair the dilapidated rooms and staircases. Dr. Conneau has described the preparations and the Prince's escape :

'Every morning we rose betimes, to watch the movements and habits of the workmen as they entered the prison, and to ascertain whether there had occurred any alterations in the usual orders. We noticed that the Commandant was more vigilant than ever and that he was constantly superintending the workmen ; but as he was then suffering from a severe rheumatic attack, we found that he did not rise before eight o'clock and we therefore determined to carry out our project before that hour. On May 25 we rose early, by six o'clock. The Prince put on his workman's disguise consisting of a coarse shirt, a blue blouse, a pair of blue trousers with an apron, and a pair of sabots over his boots. As his face was naturally pale, he coloured it with some dye which gave him a ruddy complexion. He also painted his eyebrows and put on a black wig which completely disguised him and covered his ears. Shortly after seven he shaved off his thick whiskers and moustache ; and I should certainly not have recognised him notwithstanding my familiarity with his person. Thélin invited the workmen to have something to drink ; and when the Prince knew that they were all partaking of a morning dram he went downstairs with a plank carried on his shoulder, convinced that he would not be recognised. I assured him that he might go forth in safety. The workmen came out one by one and I saw that none of them recognised the Prince. He went out into the courtyard followed by the workmen. It had been arranged that Thélin should hold the guards in converse,

in order to keep them engaged while the Prince passed
out.   I ran to the window to watch what was occurring
and I had a few moments of anxious doubt ; but presently
I saw the Prince with the plank on his shoulder advance
towards the officer who was on guard, and who was
reading a letter and paying no attention to the workmen.
I observed the engineer officer and the director of the
works come into the court separating the prison from the
guard.   As both were well acquainted with the persons
of all the workmen I dreaded lest they should recognise
the Prince ; but they were both reading papers and did
not notice the Prince.   He then advanced towards the
gate ; the guard opened the wicket, and to my inexpress-
ible relief I saw his Highness go forth.'

In a letter written from London a few days after his
escape the Prince thus described his adventures to the
editor of a Calais newspaper :

' The gate of my prison was kept by three warders, two
of whom were always on duty.   It was therefore necessary
to pass them first, and then to traverse the whole interior
court ; at the gate it was necessary to pass the wicket
kept by an orderly, and afterwards to pass in succession
a sergeant, a turnkey, a sentry, and finally a post of thirty
men.   I had cut off my moustache and taken a plank on
my shoulder.   Scarcely had I left my room when I was
accosted by a workman who took me for one of his
companions.   Face to face with the keeper at the foot of
the stairs I screened myself with the plank and reached
the court, always keeping the plank towards the sentries.
As I passed in front of the first sentry I let my pipe fall ;
I stopped, however, to pick up the fragments.   The
soldiers at the wicket seemed surprised at my figure ;

meantime, however, the orderly of the guard opened the gate and I found myself outside the fortress. There I met two workmen, who looked at me with attention. I shifted the plank to the side next them ; they appeared, nevertheless, so curious that I thought I should not be able to escape them, when I heard them say : " Oh, it's Berton."

' Once beyond the walls, I walked rapidly towards the St. Quentin road. Shortly afterwards Thélin, who on the previous evening had engaged a cabriolet, joined me and we reached St. Quentin. I crossed the town on foot, having got rid of my blouse. Thélin having procured a post-chaise under pretence of a drive to Cambray, we arrived without hindrance at Valenciennes, whence I took the railroad through Belgium to Ostend, and thence crossed to England.'

The faithful Conneau made great efforts to conceal the escape of the Prince ; his anxiety was to gain at least twenty-four hours for the escape of his Highness. He gave out that the Prince was ill in bed and had taken medicine. Conneau took the medicine himself ; then he mixed coffee and nitric acid to produce a disagreeable smell, so that his men-of-all-work might be assured that the Prince was really ill. At noon came the Commandant, whom Conneau informed that his patient was somewhat easier. He came again at seven in the evening, with an air of some suspicion. ' If,' said he, ' the Prince is still ill I must speak to him!' Conneau had prepared a large stuffed figure which he had laid in the Prince's bed, the head resting on the pillow. He called the Prince, from whom naturally came no reply. It was then indicated by a sign to the Commandant that the Prince was asleep. This did not

satisfy the suspicious officer; he sat down in the salon
with the observation, 'The Prince will not sleep always;
I shall wait.' The hours passed and the evening drum
beat. At length the Commandant rose and said, 'The
Prince has moved; he is waking up.' The Commandant
strained his ears, but heard no sound of breathing from
the form in the bed. Conneau pleaded, 'Let him sleep
on.' But the suspicions of the Commandant had
reached a climax. He approached the bed, to find there
the stuffed figure. Turning to Conneau he angrily
exclaimed, 'The Prince has gone! At what hour?'
Conneau answered, 'At seven this morning.' 'Who
were the persons on guard?' asked the irate Commandant. 'I know nothing,' replied Conneau. 'These,'
Conneau has said, 'were the only words which were
exchanged between us; and the Commandant went
out.' Conneau was sentenced to three months' imprisonment, the Commandant and keepers were
acquitted, and Thélin was condemned *in absentiâ* to
six months' imprisonment.

On his arrival in England Prince Louis wrote to the
British Foreign Minister, assuring him of his peaceable intentions. Lord Aberdeen replied that on this
assurance the Prince's residence in England would
not be objectionable to the Queen or her Government.
The Prince publicly i. timated to the French Ambassador to the British Court his escape from Ham and his
arrival in England, stating formally that he had no
intention 'to enter on the political scene nor to attempt
to disturb the peace of Europe, but solely to fulfil a sacred
duty.' His endeavours, however, to procure passports
which would admit of his reaching his father's death-bed

met with no success. The Austrian Minister refused
his request, the reason alleged being deference to the
expressed desire of the French Government. The
Grand Duke of Tuscany refused to allow him to pass
even twenty-four hours within his territory, on the
pretext that French influence blocked the way. The
French Government remained pitiless ; and the ex-King
Louis died at Florence on July 25, 1846, without having
had the solace of having been permitted to embrace his
only surviving son.

From May, 1846 until February, 1848, Prince Louis
Napoleon lived quietly in England. In the beginning
of 1847 he installed himself in a newly-built house in
King Street, St. James's, where he occupied himself in
collecting his books, portfolios, and family portraits. It
was while living in this house—which was originally numbered 10, King Street but which is now
numbered 'I.C.,' in that street, and on the front of
which is the blue plaque commemorating the residence
there of Louis Napoleon from 1846 to 1848—that,
according to Mr. Jerrold, 'he saw his days of comparative poverty.' Yet the rent of his house amounted
to 300*l.* a year ; and although he incurred heavy losses
on the Turf and needed to have recourse to the help of
friends, he probably never was in the straits to which he
has been said to have been reduced. He had many
staunch and true friends, although it seems unquestion-
able that when he went to Paris in February, 1848 he
was 'almost moneyless.' The subject is not one on
which there is any necessity to dwell ; it remains that in
his worst days Prince Louis Napoleon was always able
to pay his way with more or less promptitude.

The Prince was living his usual life in London, waiting and watching with alertness yet without impatience, when the Revolution of February, 1848 suddenly opened for him a vista of which he did not delay to take advantage. He had departed for Paris as soon as the tidings of the flight of Louis Philippe reached London, and on Feb. 28 he addressed the following letter to the Provisional Government :

'Gentlemen,—The people of Paris having destroyed by their heroism the final vestiges of the recent foreign invasion, I hasten from exile to place myself under the flag of the Republic just proclaimed. With no other ambition than that of serving my country, I announce my arrival to the Provisional Government, and beg to assure them of my devotion to the cause which they represent, and my sympathy for them personally.

'L. N. BONAPARTE.'

The Government, however, promptly requested him to withdraw from France, thus acknowledging the danger in which his presence would involve them. He answered courteously, 'You think that my presence at this time would be an embarrassment ; I therefore retire for the present.' He returned to England, to serve in London on April 30 on his beat in Park Lane, armed with the truncheon of a special constable. Although strongly pressed he declined to be nominated for the Constituent Assembly elected on April 23, but was elected in June in three Departments and in Paris ; in each case, however, he declined the honour. He was well out of the ferocious and bloody insurrection of June, during which tremendous conflict between the Red

Republicans and the guardians of society more than 300 barricades were erected, 16,000 persons were killed or wounded, 8,000 prisoners were taken, and the loss incurred by it to the nation was estimated at 300,000,000 francs.

At length, in his fortieth year, after a life of exile and captivity, of danger and trouble, the nephew and heir of Napoleon the Great entered the capital of France, called thither, in spite of the animosity of hostile factions in the Assembly, as the representative of five Departments, offering him a total of over 200,000 votes. He elected to sit for Paris, which was his place of birth ; and he went quietly to the Hôtel du Rhin in the Place Vendôme, from the windows of which he could see towering over the capital the figure of the great man whose genius had been the guiding star of his life.

On Sept. 26, 1848, the heir of Napoleon made his first appearance in the National Assembly. On his way he had been heralded by irrepressible shouts of ' *Vive Louis Napoléon !*' ' *Vive l'Empereur !*' Inside the Assembly he was received in deep silence. Under the gaze of his enemies his bearing was quiet, composed, and resolute ; when he mounted the tribune the audience listened to the firm voice and marked the soldierly attitude. He wasted no words :

' After thirty-four years of proscription and exile,' he said, ' I have returned to my country and to my rights as a citizen. The Republic has given me this blessing ; let it receive my vow of gratitude and devotion, and let the generous compatriots who have returned me to this Assembly be assured that they will always see me devoted to the noble task which devolves on all of us—

that of securing order and tranquillity, and the development of the institutions of the State which the people have a right to demand.

'For a long time, gentlemen, I have been able to give to my country only the meditations of exile and captivity. To-day the career which you follow is opened to me also. Receive me into your ranks, dear colleagues, with the affectionate sympathy I myself feel. You need not doubt that my conduct will always be inspired by respectful adherence to the law ; it will prove to all who have endeavoured to traduce me with the design of proscribing me still, that no one is more devoted than I to the defence of order and the consolidation of the Republic.'

On Oct. 13 the Republican Constitution of 1848, which Marrast, President of the Assembly, had prepared, was carried ; on Oct. 9 the Assembly decided by a vote of 627 against 130 that the President of the Republic should be elected by a direct universal vote of the nation ; and on Nov. 4 the famous Constitution of 1848 was finally carried by 739 votes against 30. On Nov. 12 was held the national *fête* of the promulgation of the Constitution. Venetian masts from which tricolour banners waved and from the base of which incense rose into the air, adorned the Place de la Concorde. By the gates of the Tuileries rose a gorgeous altar all velvet and gold, and surmounted with the sacred legend ' Love one another.' Armand Marrast, the President of the Assembly, with General Cavaignac on his right, and Marie, Keeper of the Seals, on his left, stood bareheaded in the wind and snow of the bitter winter day and read the Constitution in a loud voice. The Archbishop of

Paris celebrated high mass followed by a *Te Deum*, and on the morrow the ' Moniteur' approved this grand and simple manner of promulgating the new code of laws ' in the face of Heaven.'

The method of the election of the President of the Republic was the battle-ground of parties in the Assembly, the Republican democrats fully conscious that election by universal suffrage meant the return of Prince Louis Napoleon. In the ballot of Dec. 10 the great class of small owners and small manufacturers voted in a body for the Prince. They voted for law, order, and authority, for settled times and quiet streets, because they wanted to be at work and to renew the old happiness of saving. And the result was decisive, for Prince Louis Napoleon had a majority of three and a half millions over all his rivals combined. The election was held on Dec. 20. No opposition was presented against the colossal majority which the Prince had obtained. As he entered the thronged Assembly all eyes were turned upon him. M. Marrast rose from the Presidential chair, and announced that Citizen Louis Bonaparte having obtained an absolute majority of votes, was proclaimed by the National Assembly President of the French Republic from that day until the second Sunday of May, 1852 ; and he was invited to ascend the tribune and take the oath. The spectacle was sombre in the dimly lighted chamber as M. Marrast read aloud the oath :

' In the presence of God and before the French people I swear to remain faithful to the democratic Republic, and to defend the Constitution.'

The Prince raised his right hand, and said, ' I swear.' M. Marrast again spoke in a solemn voice : ' I take God to witness the oath that has been sworn.   It will be inserted in the *procès-verbal* in the " Moniteur," and will be published in the form prescribed for public oaths.'

The scene ended with the measured withdrawal of the Prince-President, escorted by questors nominated to conduct him to the Élysée Palace with the ceremonies due to his exalted position.   So hurriedly had the function been prepared that not a single room in the Élysée had been arranged for his reception.   A bed, a table, a chair, and a washhand-stand sufficed for the new occupant of the Élysée, who had returned to one of the haunts of his childhood after forty years of wandering and exile.

CHAPTER VII

THE *COUP D'ÉTAT*

ON Dec. 20, 1848, Prince Louis Napoleon had sworn in the presence of God and before the French people 'to remain faithful to the democratic Republic and to defend the Constitution.' Then, asking leave to address a few words to the Assembly, he said : ' I shall regard as enemies to the country all who should attempt to subvert the Constitution, and between me and the Assembly will exist the most perfect harmony of views. The policy of France should be peace abroad and a spirit of conciliation at home. I have called to my Council honourable men who, sprung from varied origin, are a guarantee of conciliation. . . . The Government will be neither Utopian nor reactionary. We will strive to give happiness to the country ; and we hope that, with the blessing of God, if we do not accomplish great things we shall endeavour to do good things.'

The Citizen-President had three years before him in which to make good these words ; but, as it turned out, they were mere words and nothing more. He soon gave the 'men distinguished for talent and patriotism' whom he had called to his Councils to understand that he had little regard for their advice, and he did not delay to apprise them that he had no intention of according to them the responsibilities which etiquette ascribes to high official functionaries. When he demanded of the Minister of the Interior the delivery to him of the papers and evidence relating to the Strasburg and Boulogne affairs, M. de Malleville, 'refusing to be a purloiner of public documents,' resigned from the Ministry. This first and most respectable of the half-dozen Ministries which, with intervals of no Ministry at all, the Prince-President formed and dismissed in the course of the three years from December, 1848 to December, 1851, had Odilon Barrot for its chief and it had to be reconstructed almost as soon as formed. When, after sundry chops and changes, it went to pieces in October, 1849, the Prince-President fell back on his devoted adherents Persigny and Ferdinand Barrot to form a Ministry. They constructed one of men independent of party ties, but in the main devoted to the policy of the Élysée. From this time commenced that system of puppet administration, in which neither genius, experience, nor patriotism, neither honesty nor personal honour, could intervene to check or modify the absolute will of the Prince-President. To follow the Ministerial history of the subsequent periods would be a humiliating and unprofitable task. In the course of three years Louis Napoleon had some eighty or ninety Ministers—the Cabinet generally consisting of ten members—to not one of whom did he accord an unreserved confidence except to Saint-Arnaud and de Maupas, members of the Ministry during which the *Coup d'État* occurred.

The Prince-President held on his way to the ultimate goal. In his domestic policy his first acts were to suspend universal suffrage, now that it had served his turn ; to shackle the press ; to suppress associations of all kinds—in a word, to crush the expression of public opinion. The Church Party having been propitiated and military ardour having been gratified by the bombardment of Rome, the systematic corruption of the army was undertaken. Champagne, sausages, and cigars were distributed lavishly among whole regiments on the plains of St. Maur and Satory, the recompense for which was shouts of '*Vive Napoléon!*' and '*Vive l'Empereur!*' Those proceedings, which stank in the nostrils of all Europe, justly alarmed the Constitutional party in France. This alarm was the more justifiable because the Constitution had jealously provided that the President should never have any personal command of the army. Yet Louis Napoleon, with no other military rank than that of a captain of artillery in the Swiss service, wore the uniform of a French general officer and surrounded himself with an *état-major*, aides-de-camp, and orderly officers. He reviewed troops, distributed orders and honours with all the forms employed by soldier-sovereigns, and in all respects deported himself as the General-in-Chief of the army. Then followed those demonstrations, ostentatious progresses through the provinces, feasting and speech-making, in which 'the consolidation of the new institutions of the country' were phrases which were mingled with allusions to a 'great name' and the policy and institutions of a 'great ancestor.'

Nothing proved more fully the conciliatory character of the Assembly as a body than the manner in which, though its members were justly jealous of Imperial banquets and Imperial progresses among the troops and through the provinces, they abstained from cutting short those extravagances by refusing the supplies expended in paying for them. The Assembly made allowance for the hereditary vanity of the President ; and deemed it the wisest policy to allow the period of his rule as limited by the Constitution to elapse without insisting on a rigid adherence to justice and public honesty.

The Constitution had contemplated, on the principle of economy, a President without a Court. It had provided that 'he should be lodged at the public expense, and that he should receive a stipend of 600,000 francs (24,000*l.*) per annum.' This sum the Assembly with a certain liberality consented to double by an additional vote under the pretext of 'expenses of display,' with 150,000 francs extra for charities, &c. ; making the President's total official income about 1,625,000 francs in addition to the expenses of his palace, being above a million francs more than the sum specified in the Constitution. But even this amount proved insufficient for the Prince's occasions, surrounded as he was by an entourage of courtiers and maintaining a semi-Imperial luxury—to say nothing of roast fowls and champagne to 20,000 men at St. Maur and to 30,000 more a week later at Satory. Previous to those expenditures the President had asked through his Ministers for a large supplementary addition to these sums—indeed, for no less than 1,400,000 francs. The Assembly with some reluctance voted this extraordinary allowance also, chiefly at the persuasion of General Changarnier. But when after the reviews of St. Maur and Satory the President in February 1851 made yet another demand for 1,800,000 francs, and intimated that he expected his annual income should be fixed at 3,425,000 francs (about

140,000*l*.), being about five times the amount specified
in the Constitution, in spite of the eloquent protest of
M. de Montalembert the Assembly refused the credit by
a majority of 102. Indiscreet friends of the President
proposed a national subscription to furnish the moneys
which the Assembly had declined to grant; but the
Prince, to do him justice, promptly suppressed this project. His reply to the defeat of his Minister of Finance,
according to Mr. Jerrold, was the reduction of his establishment and the sale of some of his horses and
carriages.

Louis Napoleon, it must be owned, was profuse rather
than avaricious. His hand was ever open, however
unworthy was the suppliant. He sincerely loved France
and was zealous for her welfare. In his message to the
Assembly in the session of 1850 he dwelt on plans
prepared for the completion of the main lines of railway, for the construction of canals and highroads, and
the improvement of rivers. Attention had been given
to the introduction of agricultural machinery, the improvements in breeds of cattle and horses, the application of scientific farming and cultivation, and the establishment of model farms. Other measures affecting the
development of arts, manufacture, and industry were
in progress. The President was already projecting the
embellishments and drainage of the capital. The prolongation of the Rue de Rivoli and the demolition of
the old stalls and tenements which had long disfigured
the Place du Carrousel were voted ; but the completion
of the Louvre had to be temporarily postponed, although
the measure would have given work to the unemployed.

In the same message the Prince referred significantly

to the future. ' If,' said he, 'you decide in favour of a
revision of the Constitution, a Constituent Assembly will
recast our fundamental laws and will regulate the future
of the Executive power. If you do not, the people in
1852 will give expression to its will. Rest assured that
what preoccupies me is not who will govern France in
1852, but how so to employ the time at my command
that the transition be effected without disturbance.'
When the Legislative Assembly on May 25, 1851,
entered on its final year of existence, the two burning
questions were the revision of the Constitution and the
prolongation of the President's tenure of office. The
question of the revision was lost by a considerable
majority. But the vital portion of the Presidential
message of Nov. 6 was that in reference to the restoration of universal suffrage, upon which the Prince
had now fixed his hopes of re-election. This measure,
however, like that of the revision, was lost ; and with it
the last hope of an accommodation between the President and the Assembly.

The President had displayed firmness in the crisis of
January, 1851, by boldly dismissing General Changarnier
from the command of the army. On Oct. 26 was
announced the formation of a new Ministry, the most
important members of which were General Saint-Arnaud
the hero of the recent campaign against the Kabyles,
who was appointed Minister of War; and M. de Maupas,
recently a provincial Prefect and now holding the office
of Prefect of Police. Colonel Fleury it was who
answered for Saint-Arnaud's entire devotion to the cause
of the President and whose mission it had been to bring
him from Algeria to a higher sphere in Paris. General

Magnan during the *Coup d'État* was Saint-Arnaud's second in command. He had not cared to be informed as to the events in which he was to participate ; he chose to remain the soldier who simply obeyed his chief and confined himself to his military *rôle*. The other African generals who came to command divisions in the army of Paris were for the most part soldiers of whom the country had reason to be proud, and who were later to add to the glory of France in the Crimea and in Italy. De Maupas was something of a busybody and his self-complacency was amusing ; but he was a loyal and devoted creature of the Prince-President, knew his duty as assigned to him, and carried it out with a characteristic thoroughness, and, it may be added, with a characteristic fussiness.

To the officers of the regiments newly arrived in Paris, who were received on Nov. 9 by the Prince-President in the Élysée, he thus spoke : ' In receiving the officers of the various regiments who succeed each other in the Paris garrison, I congratulate myself that I ee them animated by the military spirit which was once our glory and which to-day provides our security. Your duties you have ever discharged with honour, whether on African or on French soil, and you have always amidst trials preserved discipline intact. I trust that those trials will not recur ; but should grave circumstances ever bring their return and compel me to appeal to your devotion, it would not fail me I am sure, because you know that I would not ask you to do aught incompatible with my rights, with the honour of a soldier, with the welfare of the country ; because I have placed at your head men who possess all my confidence and deserve yours ; and

because, if ever the hour of danger should strike, I
should not do as did the Governments which preceded
me and say to you "Go! I will follow you"; but "I go!
follow me."'

The Prince was addicted to procrastination.
Nov. 20 was the first chosen date for the *Coup d'État*;
then he preferred the 25th; then again he was for
the 28th; presently he asked for a fresh delay and proposed Dec. 2; and finally he proposed to alter that
day for one in the next week but one. Dec. 2
was finally fixed on, and only just not too late. 'The
question is,' said Changarnier to Odilon Barrot, 'which
of us two, Louis Napoleon or myself, will take the
initiative.' When Odilon Barrot asked him bluntly
whether he was in a position to arrest the President,
Changarnier replied that whenever he received an order
to do so, he would put him in a *panier à salade* and
drive him to Vincennes without more ado.

On the evening of Dec. 1, 1851, the Prince-
President held his customary reception in the Élysée,
at which were present a throng of officers, Deputies,
diplomates, and distinguished foreigners. Hostile
Deputies who were on the watch went away in the
conviction that nothing extraordinary was in the
immediate future. About nine the Prince went into his
private room for a short time, remarking to his secretary
that 'nobody had the least suspicion'; and he went carefully over the proclamations which he had prepared, and
which in a few hours were to be posted on the walls of
Paris. Then, returning to his guests, he made a leisurely
tour of the suite of apartments, conversing with groups
of ladies and exchanging a passing word with a General or

Ambassador. At ten o'clock, as usual, he retired to his private room, remarking cheerfully to his secretary, 'Do you know what is being said in the salons? There is a general talk of an imminent *Coup d'État*, but it is not ours; it is a *Coup d'État* which the Assembly is preparing against me!' Presently Persigny entered, soon followed by the other three members of the intimate Cabinet— de Maupas, Prefect of Police; de Morny, Minister of the Interior; and Saint-Arnaud, Minister of War. The proclamations which in a few hours were to alter the destinies of France were carefully re-read and finally settled. Saint-Arnaud and de Maupas recapitulated the measures each had to carry into effect, and expressed their confidence that no hitch would be allowed to occur. Then the Prince bade his friends good-night and retired to his bedroom. Morny went to play whist at the Jockey Club until he should come on duty at the Ministry of the Interior at seven on the following morning, by which time such difficulties as Saint-Arnaud and de Maupas might encounter would have been surmounted. Saint-Arnaud went to instruct General Magnan regarding the duties assigned to him; he carefully detailed the military strength at the disposal of the latter to meet the contingency of a possible conflict on the morrow; and in concert with Magnan, on whom he could implicitly rely, he took every precaution as if in an enemy's country. Colonel Espinasse was directed to surround the Assembly with a military cordon.

When de Maupas left the Élysée he was accompanied by Colonel Béville, who was entrusted with the proclamations for the printers of the Imprimerie Nationale. A company of Mobile gendarmerie entered the printing establishment along with the Colonel, sentries were posted at doors and windows, and the strictest orders were given to prevent all communication with the outside. The work was performed with expedition, and at the appointed hour the printed proclamations of the President, the Minister of War, and the Prefect of Police were in the hands of M. de Maupas for distribution among his men, for whom conveyances were waiting; and they started for every quarter of Paris and the suburban communes. At half-past seven the work of placarding was finished in Paris, between eight and half-past in the outskirts.

A grave responsibility rested on de Maupas—nothing less than the success or failure of the *Coup d'État*. If a single arrest should fail the alarm might be given and would spread. But de Maupas was equal to the occasion. Every arrest was to be personally directed by a commissary of police. He had chosen from among his subordinates for the most important missions the men whom he judged to be the most energetic and most devoted. The selected functionaries received at two o'clock in the morning instructions to present themselves at the Prefecture of Police at a given moment and within short intervals, between three and half-past four A.M. On arrival they were absolutely isolated one from the other. Each was introduced into the Prefect's room by himself, and received every detail of his instructions from him alone. To each commissary the astute de Maupas confined himself to an announcement of the arrest with which he was entrusted, leaving him in ignorance that he was participating in a collective measure. No doubt, nevertheless, intelligent as they all were, those men understood that they were co-operating in the long-spoken-of *Coup d'État*. 'To each,' in de Maupas's words, ' I recalled in brief terms what his duty required of him, the perils courage and energy can brave when the soul is inspired ; I enjoined each one to shrink from no measure in the execution of his mission, but above all to protect and to respect, at the risk of his own life, those men whom he was detailed to arrest. Every few minutes, and without as yet communicating with any of his colleagues, a commissary left my room and repaired to an indicated spot, where he found the staff necessary to an arrest which had to be made under such conditions that failure was almost impossible.'

The prison of Mazas was chosen as the place of confinement for the State prisoners. To the Governor of Mazas was appointed a commissioner in extraordinary of superior rank in the person of Colonel Thiérion, a man of approved energy, tact, and devotion. The persons who were to be arrested by the police were of different categories ; members of the Assembly more or less implicated in a counter-plot, the heads of the secret societies, and the noted commanders of barricades. For the last fortnight they had all been watched and had never been lost sight of by invisible agents. The total number of persons to be arrested amounted to seventy-eight, among whom were eighteen members of the Assembly and sixty heads of secret societies and of barricades. It had been arranged by the Prefect of Police and the Minister of War that the several arrests should be made a quarter of an hour before the arrival of the troops at their respective destinations. The arrests were to take place simultaneously at a quarter-past six, and the agents were ordered to be at the doors of the persons specified at five minutes after six. Everything was effected with astonishing punctuality, and no arrest occupied a longer time than twenty minutes. Some of the details of those arrests presented traits so characteristic as to be worth narrating. Some had resisted; some had made solemn protests; and some had frankly acknowledged that they had been outwitted.

The commissary detailed to arrest General Changarnier found a difficulty in obtaining entrance; but his assistant got into the courtyard by passing through an immediately adjacent grocer's shop and so opening the door to his principal. The General was found in his shirt in the doorway of his room, with a pistol in each hand; but he surrendered immediately, only saying, ' I expected the *Coup d'État*, and now here it is.' He was promptly carried to Mazas. The commissaries entrusted with the task of arresting the two quæstors residing in the Palace of the Assembly, M. Baze and General Le Flo, found the latter sound asleep; but he hurriedly dressed while vehemently protesting against his arrest. He attempted to bully the commissary and threatened to have him shot; then he poured abuse on the Prince-President, General Saint-Arnaud, and the Prefect of Police; and it was only after some lively resistance that he consented to leave his apartment. M. Baze showed still greater irritation and was even more violent than General Le Flo. He resorted to every means of resistance, refused to dress himself, and had to be carried almost by force to the carriage waiting for him. The arrests of Generals de Lamoricière, of Bedeau, and of Colonel Charras gave rise to incidents similar to those in the case of M. Baze—the same fruitless resistance and the same abortive attempts to address the troops on the way to Mazas. General Cavaignac was more guarded in the expression of his anger, and remained very dignified. M. Thiers was seized with a genuine terror when informed that he was arrested. He became quite incoherent—'He did not want to die, did not conspire, for the future he would abstain from politics and would retire abroad.' On discovering that his life was not in danger the illustrious orator, sitting down on his bed, proceeded to harangue the commissaries. When requested to rise and dress he responded by a very unceremonious act, from which it would have been more decent to refrain. Then, still undressed he produced a brace of pistols, remarking to the commissary, 'I might blow your brains out; I am armed; and would have every justification for treating you as a malefactor.' The commissary quietly remarked that he, too, could shoot, and at the instance of M. Thiers that topic of remark was not continued. When at length dressed and in the carriage, terror once again assailed M. Thiers. 'You are going to have me shot,' he exclaimed—'I see clearly that I am being led to execution.' Reassured on that point, he then tried to bribe the commissary into letting him escape by promise of a large reward. At Mazas M. Thiers fell into a state of complete prostration; his strength wholly forsook him. M. Lagrange, who had come home in the morning thoroughly inebriated, indulged in the most violent imprecations. M. Cholat, powerless at first in the dread of being shot, regained fictitious courage by drinking a quantity of absinthe. The arrests of the various other representatives were not marked by any incident worthy of notice. When the arrested persons found themselves congregated in Mazas there were many greetings of recognition; bitter smiles and as bitter words were exchanged. 'See how he treats us,' said General Changarnier to General Cavaignac. 'Well, he makes a mistake, because he would certainly have been re-elected next May, but now . . . ' By half-past eight the last of the arrests were over. No attempts had been made to escape; nor were there any attempts at rescue from outside. De Maupas's instructions had been carried out to the letter. No precautions had been neglected to secure the guardianship of his prisoners against any attempt on the part of foes and friends; and every possible measure had been taken to soften the severities inseparable from the situation. General Changarnier sent the following note to his sister: 'Set your mind at rest; I am treated with the greatest consideration. M. de Maupas treats me like a gentleman.'

On the 3rd Generals Bedeau, Eugène Cavaignac, Changarnier, Lamoricière, and Le Flo, Colonel Charras, and MM. Royer and Baze were despatched by General Saint-Arnaud to the fortress of Ham, where they were treated with great leniency, had access to their families, and within a month were set at liberty. M. Thiers after a few days at Mazas where he was treated with great consideration, was conducted beyond the Rhine frontier and set at liberty. The representatives who had been sent to Mont Valérien and Vincennes were liberated within a few days, many within a few hours, of their arrest.

Early on the morning of the 2nd Persigny arrived

at the Élysée with his report of the nocturnal proceedings. The Prince presently appeared, calm and
cool as was his wont. De Morny was at the Ministry
of the Interior, telegraphing assiduously to the provinces. Saint-Arnaud was at work at the War Ministry.
General Magnan had occupied all points with bodies of
troops. De Maupas had sent out his emissaries far and
wide, tracking insurrectionists and rioters. Changarnier's
counterplot had been foiled utterly by the arrest of himself and that of his principal accomplices. Among the
earliest visitors to the Élysée were the Princess Mathilde,
King Jerome, and Marshal Exelmans. At nine o'clock
the Prince mounted his horse, and as he rode out from
the courtyard of the Élysée followed by his friends, his
staff, and his mounted escort, handkerchiefs fluttered
from every window, welcoming the cortège as it deployed into the street. He rode on to the Place de
la Concorde, vociferous adherents scattering copies of
the proclamations among the crowd. Shouts of ' *Vive
Napoléon !*' ' *Vive l'Empereur !*' came from the massed
soldiery; and the excitement was intensified when the
Prince rode towards the Tuileries and entered the
gardens of the palace. ' He is going to take possession
of the palace,' a workman was heard to say—' *Il a fait
son coup*. Well, all the better ; work will be slack no
longer.' The Prince, however, was not going to the
palace. He rode into the Place du Carrousel, where he
reviewed the regiments of the line stationed there.
His reception along the quays and boulevards was
diversified ; at some points in sombre silence, at others
with hostile manifestations, at many with ebullitions of
welcome. He returned to the Elysée in good spirits, for

his adventure seemed to have the approval of the masses, and on the whole he considered that he had been well received.

Mr. Kinglake has asserted that the Prince remained gloomy and solitary during those eventful days. After his ride along the boulevards on the morning of the 2nd, according to that brilliant but bitter writer, the Prince 'thenceforth, for the most part, remained close shut up in the Élysée. There, in an inner room, still decked in red trousers, but with his back to the daylight, they say he sat bending over a fireplace for hours and hours together, resting his elbows on his knees, and burying his face in his hands. . . . What is better known is, that in general, during this period of danger, tidings were not suffered to go to him straight. It seems that, either in obedience to his own dismal instinct, or else because his associates had determined to prevent him from ruining them by his gloom, he was kept sheltered from immediate contact with alarming messengers. It was thought more wholesome for him to hear what Persigny or the resolute Fleury might think it safe to tell him, than to see with his own eyes an aide-de-camp fresh come from Saint-Arnaud or Magnan, or a commissary full fraught with the sensations which were shaking the health of Maupas.' Captain Gronow, who witnessed what he described, says, on the other hand, that the Prince during his ride through the streets maintained his wonted equanimity, and was not more grave and silent than usual; that he never for an instant flinched from possible danger, but was always quietly prepared to meet it. 'The Élysée,' continues Captain Gronow, 'was not closed to any visitors entitled to present themselves.

Those who were received found the Prince calm, collected, and urbane ; he addressed all with his customary affability and kindness, and conversed freely upon various topics. He thinks and weighs before he speaks, and what he says is concise and to the point. His manner is certainly quiet and reticent—that of a grave and thoughtful man ; but this quiet is amply made up for by the flattering attention which he gives to the words of all with whom he speaks. He listens intelligently to everything that is said, and his replies and observations seem to evince a wish, not to express his own opinion, but to learn that of others. He never fails to appreciate with courtesy the views and opinions brought before him.'

Notwithstanding the decree pronouncing the dissolution of the National Assembly, the re-establishment of universal suffrage, the repeal of the law of May 31, the announcement of the forthcoming elections, and the proclamation of the state of siege, groups of members of the dissolved Assembly met in the Palais Bourbon on the morning of the 2nd, with the object of pronouncing the downfall of the Prince-President. The Deputies insisted on seeing their President, M. Dupin, who for hours had recognised the futility of resistance. When at length he made his appearance, he wasted no words. ' It is evident,' said he, ' that the Constitution is being violated. Right is with us ; but as we are the weaker party, I suggest your withdrawal. I have the honour to bid you adieu ' ; and M. Dupin summarily took his departure. A noisy demonstration was being prepared, when a battalion of gendarmes abruptly cleared the chamber. A later meeting, at which were present about

300 Monarchist and Republican Deputies, was held at the Mairie of the 10th Arrondissement. In this assemblage M. Benoist d'Azy occupied the presidential chair and M. Berryer was the principal speaker. The orator addressed from the window the groups of Deputies gathered in the outer courtyard. A decree was unanimously carried removing Louis Napoleon Bonaparte from the Presidency of the Republic, and declaring that the Executive power had passed by right into the hands of the National Assembly—an institution which no longer existed. In the midst of the confusion two of de Maupas' commissaries entered the arena with soldiers at their backs, and summoned the gathering immediately to disperse. After a wrangle the commissaries seized by the collar the president and vice-president; and when the representatives vehemently declared that they would yield only to force they were marched arm-in-arm by twos, through the streets to the barracks of the Quai d'Orsay where they were shut up until later in the day, when they were driven away in omnibuses to a brief incarceration in Forts Valérien and Vincennes. Thus ended the Parliamentary resistance to the *Coup d'État*. The legal opposition was yet more feeble. The High Court of Justice dispersed abruptly at the sight of commissaries of police backed by soldiers, leaving behind them futile decrees declaring Louis Napoleon guilty of high treason and convoking a national jury to proceed to judgment on him.

Paris had rested perfectly quiet throughout the critical day of Dec. 2. But shrewd critics of the situation recognised the improbability that the calm would last. The Reds were not the men to refrain from taking advantage of an opportunity so tempting. Before midnight Baudin, Schoelcher, Esquiros, and Madian de Montjau, the chosen leaders of insurrection, were already on the warpath. De Maupas had averted the ominous tolling of the tocsin by the expedient of cutting the bell-ropes and guarding the belfries. But the work of barricade-building was begun late in the evening on the old familiar fighting ground of the Temple, and of the St. Antoine, St. Martin, and St. Marceau quarters. The masses, however, were not forthcoming in their thousands ; and the leaders of anarchy postponed their activity until the early morning of the 3rd. It was to be a half-hearted insurrection—a very feeble repetition of the terrible days of June, 1848, when the gutters ran with human blood. Behind the barricades there now stood but a puny minority of malcontents ; opposed to them was a great mass of soldiery commanded by able chiefs, and the vast preponderance of contented Parisians, who stood for order and social security.

During the 3rd there were for the most part mere desultory conflicts, in the course of one of which Baudin the insurrectionist was killed. A great part of the eastern quarters of Paris was a scene of riot, but as yet no general movement on the part of the troops was made. Magnan kept the gross of his soldiers in barracks, holding them fresh till the time for converging and overwhelming action should arrive. The two brigades which he sent out to deal with the insurrectionists of the Faubourgs St. Antoine and St. Jacques swept the barricades and scattered their defenders ; elsewhere also detachments of chasseurs prevented barricade-building in and about the

Rue du Temple; but the day closed without serious fighting. Magnan's orders to his subordinate commanders for the 4th were firm and precise : ' The troops mostly are to have their night's rest; the barricade-building is not to be interrupted. To-morrow at ten the army of Paris will proceed to carry the barricades with artillery.'

During the forenoon of the 4th Magnan was at the Place du Carrousel, while his army was steadily converging on the strongholds of the insurrection. At the appointed hour of two P.M. the Carrelet and Levasseur brigades headed for the centre of the insurgent Faubourgs. The Bourgon brigade swept into position between the Portes St. Martin and St. Denis. Canrobert carried the great barricades thrown up in the Rue Faubourg St. Martin and adjacent streets, his chasseurs attacking fiercely at the bayonet-point. Dulac's brigade supported by artillery cleared the Rue Rambuteau and its vicinity ; Levasseur and Marulaz struck at the heart of the insurrection in the Rues du Temple, de Rambuteau, and the region of the Rue St. Denis ; and Courtigis, from the Faubourg St. Antoine, took the barricades in reverse and scattered their defenders in all directions. Desultory fighting still continued about the Montmartre region, where Colonel Lourmel destroyed five barricades after dark, killing forty insurgents in carrying one of the five. There was no more actual fighting after that. On the 5th Magnan displayed in a sort of parade to the people, the entire army of Paris ; detailing all arms to scour the streets in flying columns and destroy all obstacles to free circulation. Thus ended the short-lived insurrection following on the *Coup d'État ;* Paris beheld no longer an array of troops in her streets and promptly resumed her business and her pleasures. The casualties of the *Coup d'État* were never accurately computed. De Maupas gives them as about 600 killed and wounded. But those figures do not include the Jacquerie in the Provinces, which in many Departments was virulent, bloody, and prolonged. Abominable atrocities were perpetrated in the Jura, Provence, and Languedoc, where pillage and assassination were rife for days. At Clamency the insurgents had their will of the town for a day, and horrible cruelties were committed, while the Reds shouted, '*Vive Barbés!* Death to the rich!' Those bands of miscreants were ultimately dispersed by flying columns of regular troops, and the ringleaders of the insurrection were gradually secured. They were dealt with sternly, but justly. A large proportion of the sentences inflicted by the fixed commissions were remitted by commissioners charged with powers to remit punishments on an extensive scale. 'Compare,' wrote M. Chéron de Villiers, 'the results of those mixed commissions with the condemnations pronounced against the insurgents of 1848, and the list of transportations to Cayenne at that period—and it will be easy to judge in which case moderation was shown.' Well, however severe were the punitive measures carried out against the insurgents of 1848, and however long the lists of transportations to Cayenne and elsewhere at that period, moderation was scarcely the strong enough term in relation to the punishments following on the *Coup d'État*. The total number of persons arrested and prosecuted in France after that event amounted to 26,642. The number of the convicted reached a total of 15,033. The *déportés* to Cayenne numbered 239, to Algeria 9,536 ; those sentenced to exile or expulsion 1,545, to imprisonment 2,804—making a total of 14,124. Apart from those figures, up to Jan. 27, 1852 the following punishments on persons already under sentence by mixed commissions were inflicted : to Cayenne, 173; to Algeria, 4,042 ; exile or expulsion, 614 ; internment, 1,324—a total of 6,153. Persons subjected simply to police surveillance, 5,108.

Yet there can be no question that the French nation as a whole approved of the action, stern as it was, by which the Prince-President had done away with a factious Assembly and had disconcerted the Bourbon, Orleanist, and Socialist factions. Of the 8,116,773 persons who voted on Dec. 20 1851, no fewer than 7,439,216 indicated by their votes their approval of the deeds of Dec. 2 ; and it was apparent that the tide of public opinion in regard to the *Coup d État* set strongly in its favour throughout Continental Europe.

CHAPTER VIII

EMPEROR OF THE FRENCH

PRINCE LOUIS NAPOLEON emerged from the *Coup d'État* the absolute ruler of France. From Dec. 2, 1851 until March 29, 1852, the date of the first meeting of the governing bodies which he called into existence as the elected Chief of the State, his position was that of Dictator. In his proclamation of Dec. 8, 1851, he called on the people to refrain from bloodshed but to make their will known at the ballot-boxes on the 20th. 'Our troubles,' said he, 'are at an end. Be the decision of the people what it may, society is saved. I was convinced that an appeal to the nation to put an end to party conflicts would not put public tranquillity seriously in danger. But until the nation has spoken I shall spare no effort to put down factions.' On Dec. 31, M. Billault, president of the Consultative Commission, presented himself at the Élysée as head of the Commission, when he formally informed the Prince-President that his election was acclaimed by seven million four hundred and fifty suffrages. In his reply the Prince used the famous phrase, '*Je n'étais sorti de la légalité que pour rentrer dans le droit.*' 'More than seven million suffrages,' he added, 'have absolved me, by justifying an act which had but one object—that of saving France

from years of disorder and misery. I thank you for
having officially declared this manifestation to have been
thoroughly national and spontaneous.'

In the midst of his legislative activity and while
taking every precaution for the maintenance of order,
the Prince-President lost not a day in putting in execution measures of public utility. So early as Dec. 10
he gave the concession for the line of railway from
Lyons to Avignon, decreed the immediate construction
of the Ceinture Railway round Paris, ordered the prompt
renewal of the interrupted public works in the capital,
and issued instructions for the demolition of the ugly
structures between the Tuileries and the Louvre. On
Jan. 1, 1852 the Prince went in state to Notre
Dame to pray, as he said, for God's protection for the
fulfilment of the duties and undertakings to which he
was to devote himself. 'Invested by France,' so he
expressed himself solemnly, 'with the right which
emanates from the people,' he prayed for 'the power
which is derived from God.' On the same occasion he
decreed the restoration of the Imperial Eagle to the
French flag and of the Cross of the Legion of Honour.
In an introductory explanation of the details of the
Constitution of 1852, which was about to be promulgated,
the Prince on Jan. 14 addressed to the people a
synopsis of the principles which had weighed with him
in its preparation, but of which only a mere *résumé* can
be here given. The 'first wheel in our new organisation,' to use his own term, was to be the Council of
State—the real Council of the Government—which
should prepare and debate laws in a General Assembly
with closed doors before presenting them for the accept-

ance of the Corps Législatif. Of the two Assemblies, the Chamber styled the Corps Législatif was to vote the laws and taxes, be elected by universal suffrage, and to consist of about two hundred and sixty members. The other Assembly, to be styled the Senate, was to be composed of 'elements which in all countries are legitimate influences—illustrious names, fortune, talent, services rendered to the country.' Its character was to be that of ' supreme moderator,' intervening to solve any difficulty that might arise in the absence of the Corps Législatif, or to define any point of the Constitution and regulate its operation. 'The Constitution outlined cursorily had been fixed,' said its specious author, ' only in places that could not be left doubtful. It had not closed in an iron circle the destinies of a freed people. Space enough had been left for chance, so that in any great crisis there might be means of safety other than the disastrous expedient of revolution.'

Mr. Jerrold remarks truly that the power vested in Prince Louis Napoleon by the Constitution of 1852, as formed on his own model, was such as had scarcely ever devolved on mortal man. He was absolute master of a great people standing in the van of modern civilisation, master of the foremost nation of Continental Europe, and he could boast that he was Dictator by the free assent of the millions whose fate lay in his hands. The political institutions which he had called into existence, from the Senate downwards, centred in him ; all the public servants of France derived their authority from him. For from the prison of Ham he had reached at length the Tuileries, and the eyes of the civilised world were bent intently on the man who, after having surmounted vicissitudes so strange and so varied, was now the absolute ruler of a great nation, and who, whenever he chose, might mount the steps of an Imperial throne.

One of the first cares of the Prince was to surround himself with as many men of high character and good birth as possible. His anxiety in this respect, it was true, was scarcely evidenced in his hurried appointments to the Consultative Commission at the time of the *Coup d'État*, but it was fairly manifested in regard to his nominations to the Senate and the Council of State. Of the seventy-two Senators appointed by him in January there were eighteen generals, three admirals, fourteen ex-Ministers, and five Judges, the rest being ex-peers of France and ex-representatives. Ex-King Jerome Bonaparte, Marshal of France, was created President of the Senate. The Council of State had for Vice-President M. Baroche (presiding in the absence of the Chief of the State); and besides the Presidents of Sections there were thirty-four Councillors in addition to forty Masters of Requests and thirty Auditors. In those two bodies of supporters and advisers the Prince-President secured all the political wisdom, the administrative experience, and the personal devotion which he could command.

The famous decree of Jan. 22nd, in virtue of which the landed property of the House of Orleans was to be confiscated within a year, was denounced with great severity and brought on Louis Napoleon no small odium. But he was not destitute of justification for this sweeping measure; indeed, there was a precedent which it was not likely that he should forget. It was but natural that the Prince should have regarded as a matter of fair reprisals against Louis Philippe the confiscation or sale of their property in France which Louis XVIII. inflicted on the members of the Bonaparte family in January, 1816. And there was another precedent to his hand in the circumstance that the head of the House of Orleans had deprived the elder branch of his own family —his own flesh and blood—of the right to hold property within French territory. 'The decree of Jan. 22 declared that measures of realisation and removal of property belonging to the Orleans family with the alternative of confiscation on default, were needful to public order and for the public good; and that it was all the more necessary to take drastic measures with regard to the property of the House of Orleans, since that property was computed to have a value of over twelve millions sterling., The political influence which a princely family although in exile yet endowed with possessions so vast, could sway, was in the nature of a standing menace to the assured quietude of the reigning Sovereign; and the necessity for diminishing so vast a property, if intrigue were not to be constantly fomented, was beyond question. It appeared that the property dealt with by the decree of Jan. 22, 1852, had been put under provisional sequestration immediately after the Revolution of 1848, when Jules Favre had proposed that it should be confiscated to the State since it had been secured to Louis Philippe fraudulently, who had been confirmed in the possession of it by an obsequious Parliament and a servile Ministry. That proposition had been negatived on the counter-representations of M. Berryer; and so late as Feb. 1850 M. Fould argued against confiscation. But within a month after the *Coup d'État* the decree promulgating the confiscation of the

Orleans properties was issued, it having been prepared without the knowledge of the Prince's closest friends. Several of the most important Ministers resigned in token of their disapprobation, and a number of men of influence who had accepted the Government of the *Coup d'État*—such men, for instance, as the Duke Pasquier, M. de Montalembert, several Senators of note; and most of the new Councillors of State—now resigned their functions. M. Dupin sent in his resignation in protest against the violation of the rights of property, and those of the Ministers who retained their portfolios did their utmost to dissuade the Prince from carrying out the measure. But the feeling thus expressed did not move him from his resolution. He seems, indeed, to have considered himself generous when it was stated in the decree that the Orleans family would still have left to its members some four millions of private property, on which, as the decree curtly stated, 'they could maintain their rank abroad.' No dissuasion could conquer the obstinacy of the Prince in regard to this subject, although his attitude was almost universally considered a great mistake.

The reader, however, should not disregard the fact that the confiscated property was wholly devoted to the benefit of the French public. The property which would come into the possession of the State when realised was to be devoted to the carrying-out of such measures as subventions to mutual benefit societies, to the improvement of artisans' homes in great cities, to credit societies in agricultural districts, and to other kindred purposes which will presently be detailed. The decrees affecting the rank and file of the old soldiers of the Republic and the Empire called for an inquiry into their numbers and condition. A Commission had examined the papers of the veterans, had recognised the claims of 11,200 ancient warriors who had fought for France on many fields and were now in indigent circumstances, and had claimed for them pensions ranging from 200 to 325 francs per annum. The conditions were that the pensioner should be eighty years of age, have soldiered for twenty years, and have received at least six wounds. The Prince recognised the obligations to France of the old soldiers by opening a credit of 2,700,000 francs to be disbursed in pensions to the 'glorious veterans.' He also decided that services performed within the realm in the suppression of insurrection or disorder should confer equal privileges; and he therefore recognised the claims of the gendarmerie, those 'martyrs of the demagogues.' A number of military reforms, such as the institution of the military medal and the restoration of the eagle to the national flags, were warmly welcomed by the army. On the occasion of the first distribution of the military medal on March 1, the Prince-President explained to the troops its intention. It was to be supplementary to the Legion of Honour; and it would be awarded to men re-engaging after having served their first term with honour, and to soldiers who had made four campaigns, been wounded, or had especially distinguished themselves. 'The medal,' said the Prince, 'would carry a pension of a hundred francs— no great sum—but it will mark your character as a worthy soldier.' And the military medal would lead too, with good fortune, to the higher decoration of the Legion of Honour, which latter was at the same time being reorganised.

No sooner had order been established after the *Coup d'État* than the Prince manifested remarkable vigour in causing work and resultant prosperity in every part of France.   In Mr. Jerrold's fanciful but expressive phrase, ' the sound of workmen's hammers was the music of his triumph.' Between December, 1851 and March, 1852 public works of various kinds were authorised ; in the great provincial towns improvements were set on foot, municipalities were empowered to raise loans of magnitude ; canal and railway systems received a vigorous and well-judged impetus ; and private enterprise, stirred by the strength and resolution of the new Government, took heart to expand itself with courage in commercial and financial adventures.   Credits were early offered for the improvement of the navigation of the rivers Seine and Rhone, and for the construction of important departmental highways.   In virtue of an agreement between the Government and a private company the long-delayed line of railway communication from Calais to Marseilles by way of Lyons was to be completed within four years, a measure which would connect by the most direct way the English Channel with the Mediterranean.   Decrees conceded railway lines from Dijon to Besançon, and from Mulhouse to Lyons ; and presently was sanctioned another line connecting Strasburg with the territory on the right bank of the Rhine, by which France should acquire a railway route to southern Germany.   The Northern Railway Company obtained concessions for branches which should link it with the eastern system of lines, so shortening the route to northern Germany.   Thus the great network of French railroads was in course of completion, and

that, too, without subventions from the State. The
only advantage obtained by the Government was the
extension of the concessions to a period of ninety-nine
years, at the expiration of which time they were to
become the property of the community. Following on
the outline of a system of telegraph wires linking with
the capital the principal provincial cities—a scheme
sketched by M. de Morny in a clear and comprehensive
report—a decree authorised that Minister to proceed at
once to the construction of the system and a large credit
was opened for this purpose.

The financial reforms of the short Dictatorship were
not less important than the commercial and industrial
activities with which the period was rife. The principal
operation was the conversion of the 5 per cent. Rentes into
$4\frac{1}{2}$ per cents., with the equitable condition that objectors
should be reimbursed at the rate of 100 francs for every
five francs of Rentes, provided the demand were made
within twenty days from the date of the decree. The
proof that this measure was reasonable was shown by
the fact that the State creditors evinced no wish
to withdraw their investments, while the saving to
the Government by the transaction amounted to
720,000*l*. The last of the important financial operations during the Dictatorship was the authorisation
of Crédit Foncier societies in agricultural loan or
mortgage banks, the first funds placed at their disposal
being a subsidy of ten million francs to be derived from
the Orleans property, an equal sum to be furnished by
the State, and two hundred million francs to be advanced
as required by the Bank of France to the departmental
branches of the central society established in Paris.

Finally, the finances of the Dictatorship as embodied in the Budget for 1852 showed an increase for extraordinary public works of fourteen million francs. And wonderful to relate, although the army estimates were increased by a million francs and the navy estimates by thirty-two millions, the Finance Minister could still present a surplus of about eighteen million francs.

Mr. Jerrold has pointed out that the above was not all the work of the Dictatorship, and he has referred to other salient features of the Prince-President's policy: 'Sanitary measures for the improvement of the homes of the working poor, regulations for the prevention of food adulteration, the transfer of taxes from necessaries to luxuries, the assurance of Christian burial to the poorest, increase of pay and honour to the lower ranks of the army, railway works withdrawn from Government patronage, extended, and confided to private enterprise, town improvements set in operation all over the country, Sunday labour discountenanced, and the provident habits of the people promoted by a vast system of mutual benefit societies, the National Guard remodelled, and the educational machinery of the State reformed and withdrawn from party political influences.' Some of the measures of the Dictatorship must, no doubt, have been rash and crude; some questionless evinced a love of show and splendour; some were bids for the favour of the masses or for the favourable disposition of the army, and others deserved to be condemned as concentrating over-much power in the hands of the Chief of the State. But it is not possible to regard the measures of the Dictatorship as a whole without arriving at the conviction that they were well meant, full of consideration for the public weal, and conceived by a man of a firm but of a kindly and sympathetic nature.

The term of the Dictatorship came to an end on March 29, 1852 ; and on the same day the Chambers met in the Hall of Marshals in the Palace of the Tuileries. In this noble hall there was nothing of Republican simplicity or severity. It was hung with crimson hangings. Its galleries were filled with the ladies of the Diplomatic Corps and the high functionaries of State ; its floor was thronged with diplomatists, Senators, and Deputies in rich and varied costumes. The scene was dominated by the canopy overhanging the daïs, on which was the State chair of the Prince-President ; near by, on a lower elevation, was that of ex-King Jerome, President of the Senate. To the sound of cannon and the beating of drums the Prince entered the hall, preceded and followed by his staff and household. Courteously desiring the company to be seated, he proceeded forthwith to read his speech :

' The Dictatorship which the people entrusted to me ceases to-day. Public affairs are about to resume their regular course. My constant care has been to re-establish order. . . . Often discouraged, I admit that I have thought of giving up a power so persistently disputed. I held on because I saw that there was only anarchy to take my place. . . . When, through the assistance of a few men of courage and the energetic attitude of the army all those perils were swept away in a few hours, my first care was to ask the people for institutions. Universal suffrage was re-established, authority was restored. France having adopted the

principal features of the Constitution which I submitted
to her, I was enabled to create political bodies, the influence and prestige of which will be great because their
functions have been carefully regulated. . . . While
watching me re-establish the institutions and re-awaken
the memories of the Empire, people have repeated again
and again that I wished to reconstitute the Empire itself.
If this had been so the transformation would have been
accomplished long ago ; neither the means nor the opportunities would have been wanting. . . . But I have
remained content with that which I had. Resolved now,
as heretofore, to do all in my power for France and
nothing for myself, I would accept any modification of
the present state of things only if forced by necessity.
. . . If parties remain quiet, nothing shall be changed.
But if they endeavour to sap the foundations of my
Government ; if they deny the legitimacy of the result of
the popular vote ; if, in short, they continually put the
future of the country in jeopardy—then, but only then,
it might be prudent to ask the people for a new title
which should irrevocably fix on my head the power with
which they have already clothed me. But let us not
anticipate difficulties ; let us preserve the Republic.
Under its banner I am anxious to inaugurate once more
an epoch of reconciliation and of pardon ; and I call on
all without distinction, who will frankly co-operate with
me for the public good.'

But, as was inevitable, the Prince was urged on all
sides to put an end to what was obviously a provisional
form of government, by boldly assuming the Imperial
dignity. Yet he continued steadfastly to refrain from
taking this final step until he should have ascertained as a

certainty that it was the desire of the great majority
of the French nation. He professed that he would
accept the Imperial elevation only when the sovereign
people should have definitely signified its united will that
he should mount the throne. Meantime the State balls
in the Tuileries, the organisation of a magnificent
hunting establishment, the Prince's name heading all
public documents and his head on the coinage, the oath
of personal fidelity, the restoration of the eagles to the
standards, and the selection of Aug. 15—Napoleon's
fête day—as the national holiday of the year; those
were all so many circumstances and events tending
significantly in the direction of the Empire. It seemed
that any day the Empire might suddenly arrive. It
was in the air when, on May 10, the Prince-President
distributed eagles to an army of 60,000 men on the
Champ de Mars; eagles which were blessed by the
Archbishop of Paris and handed back by the Prince
to the standard-bearers with the words, 'Take back
these eagles which so long led our fathers to victory,
and swear to die, if need be, in defence of them.' It
was in the air when the first celebration of the Fête
Napoléon was marked by an amnesty granted to
1,200 political prisoners; and men held it as good
as accomplished when Thiers, Rémusat, and other
prominent politicians who had been fugitives from
France were allowed to re-enter their native land on
Aug. 7.

In the autumn of 1852, having earlier in the year
made a progress to Strasburg, the Prince-President set
forth on a journey through the provinces of southern
France, in order to ascertain for himself the sentiment of

the people on the subject of the accession to the Imperial
throne, which was recognised by all about him as the
condition precedent to the consolidation of his Government.   He had been suffering from mental and physical
overstrain ; and at the outset of his tour he begged the
authorities of the towns which he intended to visit not to
waste money on his reception, desiring that where large
sums had been voted for this object at least part of the
fund should go to the poor.   His progress was one long
triumph.   All along the route from Paris to Lyons, from
Lyons to Marseilles, from Marseilles to Bordeaux, and
from Bordeaux back to Paris, his way lay through regions
the inhabitants of which crowded around him with shouts
of ' *Vive Napoléon III.* ! *Vive l'Empereur* !'   In the old
seats of Socialism, as, for instance, in Lyons, the workmen gathered *en masse* to greet their future Emperor.
When, in the midst of a vast throng of spectators in the
great square of that city he unveiled an equestrian
statue of Napoleon I., he frankly mentioned that all the
way from Paris he had been hailed with shouts of
' *Vive l'Empereur* !'; and he added, ' This greeting
awakens a memory which goes straight to my heart,
rather than a hope which flatters my pride.'   At
Montpellier, a place in which Socialism had taken deep
root, cries of ' *Vive l'amnistie* !' arose during a workmen's *fête* in honour of the Prince, and as he was leaving
the sinister cry was repeated.   The Prince was equal
to the occasion.   Facing the turbulent throng with
untroubled mien, he signed to the people to listen.   ' I
hear,' said he, ' calls for an amnesty.   An amnesty is
more in my heart than it is on your lips.   If you really
desire it, become worthy of it by your good conduct and

patriotism.' The tour culminated at Bordeaux ; and it was there, at a dinner in his honour given by the Chamber of that city, that he at length announced his resolution to accept the Throne. In the course of his speech the Prince said : 'I have conquests to make, but they are conquests of peace. We have vast waste territories to drain and cultivate, roads to open, ports to be deepened, canals to be completed, rivers to be made navigable, railways to be connected. . . . This is how I shall interpret the Empire, if the Empire is to be re-established. These are the conquests which I meditate ; and you who surround me, who desire the good of your country, you are my warriors.'

Prince Louis Napoleon returned to Paris a week later, in effect Emperor of the French. From the railway station he was conducted with great military pomp and under triumphal arches to the Tuileries, where the municipal and other official metropolitan and provincial bodies presented addresses conjuring him to accept the Imperial Crown and so assure to France a secure and permanent future. On Nov. 7 the Senate pronounced the Imperial dignity re-established in the persons of Louis Napoleon Bonaparte and his heirs male, and the Constitution of Jan. 14, 1852, maintained in all its parts except those which referred to the Chief of the State. But this decision was not to take effect until ratified by the vote of the nation ; the Prince would accept only a sovereignty proceeding from the direct voice of the people. This vote was obtained on Nov. 21 and 22, and on the 25th the Corps Législatif was convoked to receive and declare the result of the plebiscite. That result was overwhelmingly conclusive.

' I am anxious,' said the Prince-President addressing the Corps Législatif, 'that you should formally put on record the freedom with which the voting has taken place, and the number of suffrages stated, so that the legitimacy of my position may be established beyond dispute.' The result of the scrutiny had proved the fact that 7,824,129 Frenchmen had replied 'Aye' to the question whether or not the Imperial dignity should be re-established in the person of Prince Louis Napoleon. The 'Noes' were 253,149.

On the night of Dec. 1 the dignitaries of the new Empire went to St. Cloud, carrying to the Prince the Imperial Crown. The imposing ceremony was held in the Gallery of Apollo, where, surrounded by his household, Louis Napoleon took his seat on the throne. Addressed as 'Sire' by M. Billault on the part of the Corps Législatif and by M. Mesnard on that of the Senate, the Emperor said : 'The new reign which you now inaugurate has not originated in violence, conquest, or conspiracy. You have just declared it the legal result of the suffrages of almost an entire people, who have consolidated in the midst of peace that which they had founded in a period of agitation. I am full of gratitude to the nation which three times in four years has supported me with its suffrages, and which on each occasion has increased its majority to add to my power. . . . I assume from to-day with the Crown the name of Napoleon III., because the logic of the people in their acclamations has already given it to me, because the Senate has legally proposed it, and because the entire nation has ratified it.'

On the following morning the Emperor Napoleon III. rode from St. Cloud to the Tuileries, the Palace of

successive French dynasties. The procession marched
between lines of soldiers with arms at the 'present'; the
cannon roared, the bells rang gaily, and the military bands
played ' Partant pour la Syrie,' the stirring air composed
by Queen Hortense. The three marshals, Saint-Arnaud,
Magnan, and Castellane, created that morning, rode with
Persigny at the head of the brilliant staff; and at the
entrance of the ancient Palace the members of the House
of Bonaparte waited the arrival of their head. What a
contrast from the prison to the Throne of a great nation!
Cynics had sneered at the man's faith in his destiny ; but
thus far at least his destiny had fulfilled itself. He who
had been the mock and gibe of France was now the
omnipotent master of that France.

The proclamation of the Empire was made with
stately ceremony on the Place de l'Hôtel de Ville, on the
Place de la Concorde, and in the Court of the Tuileries.
In the midst of his state the Emperor did not omit to
mark the opening of his reign by many gracious acts of
charity. He could afford to be charitable, for his income
was fixed at a million sterling per annum. The settle-
ments on the several branches of the Imperial family,
comprehending twenty-one persons, were very munifi-
cent. Rich salaries were bestowed on the dignitaries of
the Imperial household. None of his adherents of the
evil days were forgotten in this time of lavish prosperity.
Thélin, for instance, the devoted valet, became Treasurer
of the Privy Purse. It was the aspiration of the Head
of the State that the Imperial Court should reflect the
pride and full-handedness of the nation, in contrast with
the affected simplicity of the Republic and the meanness
of the Monarchy of July. England hastened to recognise

the new Emperor under the title of Napoleon III., and the other Great Powers followed with less warmth, but promptly.

In his matrimonial enterprises Napoleon III. was scarcely so successful as had been his great uncle. Immediately after he became Emperor he despatched Walewski to enter into negotiations. A proposal for the hand of Princess Vasa, the present Queen of Saxony, did not prosper. Then, on Dec. 13, Walewski came to England to ask for the Princess Adelaide of Hohenlohe, a niece of Queen Victoria, in marriage for the Emperor. The Queen did not object to the marriage, but on Dec. 28 came a letter from the lady's father declining the marriage in consequence of objections of religion and morals. Three weeks later, on Jan. 22, 1853, the Emperor summoned to the Tuileries deputations of the Senate, the Corps Législatif, the Council of State, and the great dignitaries of the Empire, to hear an address from the Throne announcing his approaching marriage, of which the following is an extract : 'When,' said his Majesty, 'in the face of ancient Europe, one is carried by the force of a new principle to the level of the old dynasties, it is not by affecting an ancient descent or endeavouring to push into the families of Kings that one claims recognition. It is rather by remembering one's origin, by preserving one's own character, and by assuming frankly towards Europe the position of a *parvenu*—a glorious title when one rises by the free suffrages of a great people. Thus, compelled to part from precedents, my marriage becomes but a private matter. It has remained for me to choose my wife. She who has become the object of my choice is of lofty birth. French in heart, by education she has as a Spaniard the advantage of not having a family in France to whom it would be necessary to give honours and dignities. Gifted with every quality of the heart, she will be the ornament of the Throne as in the hour of danger she would be one of its most courageous defenders. A pious Catholic, she will pray with me for the happiness of France. . . . . I come to-day, gentlemen, to say to France : " I have preferred a woman whom I love and respect to an unknown woman, an alliance with whom would have brought advantages mixed with sacrifices." . . . Soon, on my way to Notre Dame, I shall present the Empress to the people and the army. The confidence which they repose in me secures their sympathies towards her whom I have chosen ; and you, gentlemen, when you have learned to know her will be convinced that once again I have been inspired by Providence.'

Next day the ' Moniteur' announced what was already an open secret, that the lady whom the Emperor had chosen for his wife was Mademoiselle de Montijo, Countess of Teba. The Emperor's address was universally regarded as being in admirable taste and dignified by a high tone of self-respect. ' Nothing,' said ' The Times '—and it said well—' could be better than the phrase in which the Emperor adopts the position of *parvenu*, keeping his origin clearly before him, and emancipating himself from the traditions of States in which the bases of society have not been destroyed nor monarchical institutions suffered ruin.'

The Emperor watched with joy the rapid progress which his beautiful betrothed made in the hearts of his countrymen. When the Imperial bride declined to

accept the costly diamond necklace presented to her by
the Municipal Council of the Seine, desiring that its
value should be devoted to charitable purposes, the
kind-hearted action was received throughout France with
warm appreciation.   Her husband's wedding-gift of
250,000 francs she distributed among maternal societies
and to beds in the hospitals.   On the evening of
Jan. 29 she was received on the threshold of the
Tuileries by the Court dignitaries, who ushered her into
the drawing-room in which the Emperor and his Court
awaited her coming.   Then Napoleon led his bride to
the Hall of Marshals, where the civil ceremony was
performed by the Minister of State.   When, after the
signature of the marriage contract the wedding party
assembled in the theatre to listen to Auber's cantata, the
scene presaged the splendour that was to belong to the
new *régime*.   On the conclusion of the cantata the
Grand Master of the Ceremonies conducted her Majesty
back to the Élysée.

Next morning the pair set forth for Notre Dame in
great pomp, the Empress wearing the crown which
Napoleon I. had placed on the head of Marie Louise.
Before the high altar in the crowded cathedral were the
State chairs of their Majesties on a raised platform under
a lofty canopy.   The procession of the clergy moved
slowly from the porch towards the altar, and the notes of
the 'Wedding March' swelled as the vast congregation
rose; then the Emperor appeared, leading his bride
with the Regent diamond on her bosom.   The marriage
rites were performed by the Archbishop, the Bishop of
Nancy presenting the pieces of gold and the ring upon a
gold salver for the blessing.   The Empress moved from

the throne to the altar, and after the benediction she crossed her brow, her lips, and her heart with her thumb in the Spanish fashion. At the end of the gorgeous ceremony the Archbishop conducted the bride and bridegroom back to the cathedral porch, and Napoleon and his Consort returned along the quays to the Tuileries.

CHAPTER IX

THE CRIMEAN WAR

It was at the Bordeaux dinner, on Nov. 9, 1852, that
Louis Napoleon, not yet Emperor of the French, said:
' Distrustful people say to themselves and to one another
that the Empire means war. I say that the Empire
means peace. It means peace, because France desires
it ; and when France is satisfied, the world is tranquil.'
There had been a time when the pessimists were
permitting themselves to believe that France was
becoming isolated in Europe, but the advent of Lord
Derby to power in England had improved the relations
of the two countries, and the Prince-President found an
old and true friend in Lord Malmesbury, who was now
the English Foreign Secretary. Under the gloomy
influence of the brooding Eastern Question England
and France had been drawing together more and more
closely : and the British Court and Cabinet had fully
accepted the sincerity of the Emperor's anxiety for the
continuance of peace and for a firm and stable alliance
with England. On Aug. 8, 1853, the Queen's Speech
said : 'The Emperor of the French has united with her
Majesty in earnest endeavours to reconcile differences,
the continuation of which would involve Europe in war.'
The Prince Consort wrote to Stockmar that ' Louis

Napoleon wishes for peace, enjoyment, and cheap corn.' Later he wrote to the same correspondent that the relations between England and France had 'settled into an *entente cordiale*' ; and in November he added that ' Louis Napoleon shows by far the greatest statesmanship, which is easier for the individual than for the many ; he is moderate, but firm : gives way to us even when his plan is better than ours, and revels in the advantages he derives from the alliance with us.' This testimony from such a source cannot be gainsaid ; and it may be taken for certain that the French Emperor faithfully co-operated with the British Government throughout in its endeavours to settle the great quarrel by diplomatic pressure backed by a display of force.

A Russian force crossed the Pruth on July 2, 1853, and proceeded to occupy the Danubian Principalities ; and on the 3rd the Czar issued a manifesto to the effect that 'it was not his intention to begin war, but to have such security as would ensure the restoration of Russian rights.' This invasion, for invasion in effect it was, might justly have been met by the Sultan with a counter-declaration of war, for which the Turkish soldiers were burning with impatience. But the Western Powers, anxious for the maintenance of peace, resorted to a conference at Vienna. That measure had no result and the Porte demanded the evacuation of the Principalities within fifteen days, with the alternative of war. This summons being disregarded a state of nominal war occurred on Oct. 23, but for some time no actual hostilities took place. Up to this period the Western Powers were not involved. It has often been said that England ' drifted ' into the Crimean War. In a sense

this was true ; no actual convulsion of national emotion
stirred us. In the perspicuous terms of Hamley : 'Our
part in the war was the result of a state of feeling
gradually aroused by observation of what was passing in
the East, and of the steps which the British Government, with intentions anything but warlike, had slowly
taken, tending to commit it to the active support of
Turkey. Up to the period when the Western fleets were
ordered to the Bosphorus, it had been possible for
England to restrict herself to diplomacy.' But she had
abandoned her attitude of mediator when Nicholas in
his blind arrogance chose to show his hand to the
British Ambassador in the following terms : 'We have
on our hands a very sick man. If your Government has
been led to believe that Turkey retains any elements
of existence your Government must have received incorrect information. I repeat to you that the sick man
is dying, and we can never allow such an event to take
us by surprise. We must come to some understanding.
. . . I can only say that if, in the event of a distribution
of the Ottoman succession upon the fall of the Empire,
you should take possession of Egypt, I shall have no
objection to offer. I would say the same thing of Candia ;
that island might suit you, and I do not know why it
should not become an English possession.' Nicholas
seemed the chronic victim of illusions. Even when he
was at actual war with Turkey he sent an autograph
letter to the Queen expressing surprise that there should be
any misunderstanding between her Government and his
own in regard to Turkey, and appealing to her Majesty's
'good faith' and 'wisdom' in the character of arbiter.
It would thus seem that Russia was the Power which had

drifted into war, rather than England ; this being owing to the false and narrow views held by the Autocrat.

When, however, the Allied Governments despatched their fleets to the Bosphorus, the control of events passed out of their hands. Should Russia disregard the moral pressure of the Allied fleets and resenting their entry into the Bosphorus avenge that measure on the Turks, the Allies could no longer preserve a mediatory attitude but had to become active principals. This was foreseen with singular prescience when her Majesty wrote to Lord Clarendon : 'We seem to have taken on ourselves in conjunction with France all the risks of an European war without having bound Turkey to any conditions with regard to provoking it.' The Turks, while keeping most of their fleet in the Bosphorus, had left a squadron of light warships in the Black Sea. On Nov. 30 it was found at anchor in the roadstead of Sinope by the Russian admiral Nackimoff, who signalled the Ottoman squadron to surrender. The superiority of the Russian force would have justified compliance, since Nackimoff had six line-of-battle ships against the Turkish flotilla of seven frigates and three corvettes ; but nevertheless the stubborn Ottoman seamen answered the summons by opening fire. With obstinate gallantry they fought on until their ships blew up under them or burned to the water's edge. When the sun went down there remained nothing of the Turkish squadron in the bay but the blazing wrecks and the mangled and powder-scorched bodies of the sailors. Nearly 4,000 men perished ; one steamer only escaped to bring to Constantinople the tidings of the awful disaster.

It is not necessary to argue that the Russians were

exceeding their rights as belligerents in order to prove the impolicy of this stroke. The disparity of force in the encounter deprived it of any glory; but it roused public feeling in England, already by no means favourable to Russia, to a degree which could only be appeased by reprisals. For months and indeed years, the English people had been chafing at the wrongs inflicted by the Russians on the Turks. The seizure of the Principalities had evinced a contempt for public law and common justice so gross that the popular mind could not but become alive to it. The manifestoes of Nicholas, haughty and insolent in tone and matter, had aggravated the bitter feeling; and now the catastrophe of Sinope was of a character thoroughly to exasperate a nation whose greatest triumphs have been won on the sea. The French people had hitherto been somewhat supine, since the impending war was not popular; but now they were to be deeply stirred.

It seemed in the nature of things that the French Emperor should desire to engage in war, at once to divert attention from the circumstances attending the origin of his elevation and to find employment for an army which could not always be depended on. Both for himself and for his people it was distinctly expedient that he should make the influence of France promptly and markedly felt. But that in allying himself with Great Britain on the Eastern Question the French Emperor was seizing an opportunity for war is a surmise in favour of which there was no pronounced evidence. The advantage was obvious of ranking himself alongside of the great Sea Power his neighbour on the other side of the narrow strait; and he had lived long enough in

England to have acquired a warm esteem for British
people, British institutions, and British habits.   As a
contrast to the cordiality of his insular neighbour, which
none appreciated more than he, was the haughty
arrogance by which Nicholas of Russia had given just
offence both to him and to the French nation in refusing
to address him as ' *Mon Frère* ' ; as if he, the elected of
France, was not entitled to enter the brotherhood of
Sovereigns.   That treatment, which stung the French
sensibilities, still did not prevent the French Emperor
from addressing to the Russian potentate, as a final
attempt at accommodation, a letter suggesting a possible
scheme of general pacification ; assuring him, however,
at the same time that if it were rejected the Western
Powers must declare war.   The answer of the Czar was
a bitter taunt.   ' Menaces,' he wrote, ' will not induce me
to recede.   My confidence is in God ; and Russia will
prove herself in 1854 what she was in 1812.'   This
allusion to the French disasters in the humiliating
campaign of 1812 effectually dispelled the apathy of
the French people.   It was accepted as a challenge ;
and when the insulting terms were disseminated peace
became impossible, even if the outrageous conditions
which Nicholas had sent to Vienna and to which he
haughtily referred the Emperor Napoleon, had been
admissible.   At the instance of the French monarch the
Allied fleets promptly entered the Black Sea, driving all
Russian ships into refuge in the harbour of Sevastopol.
England and France declared war against Russia in the
end of March.   The Allied troops gradually moved up
from Gallipoli to Scutari and from Scutari to Varna.
At the summons of Austria the Czar began the evacua-

tion of the Principalities, in which his arms had not prospered; and the Pruth was recrossed in the beginning of August, the Austrian troops occupying the territories abandoned by Russia. But English resolutions had long gone further than the acceptance of a mere drawn game. On the first declaration of war the French Emperor had sketched and our Ministry had approved, a plan for the attack of Sevastopol. The feeling was all but unanimous. ' In no event,' said the venerable Lord Lyndhurst in June, 'except that of extreme necessity, ought we to make peace without previously destroying the Russian fleet in the Black Sea and laying prostrate the fortifications by which it is defended.' In July ' The Times ' spoke with decision : ' The broad policy of the war consists in striking at the heart of the Russian power in the East ; and that heart is in Sevastopol.' And the Queen in dealing with the causes of the war wrote : ' It is the selfishness, the ambition, and the want of principle of one man which has done it.'

In the middle of Sept. 1854, there landed on the coast of the Crimea within a few marches of Sevastopol, an Allied force consisting, all told, of somewhat more than 60,000 men with 128 guns.

War once entered upon, the French Emperor acted with prudence and promptitude in amassing a reserve force to meet the casualties of probable battles and certain losses by disease in his army on active service in the field. Unlike England, France was, as she still is, a military nation ; and although the Emperor had materially reduced the strength of the army it still amounted to about 600,000 men. The camp at Boulogne which was formed as soon as the army which Marshal Saint-

Arnaud commanded had been despatched to the East
proved to Europe, that without weakening the garrisons
of the French frontiers and of the interior, no difficulty
was experienced in assembling an army of 100,000 men
between Cherbourg, St. Omer, and Boulogne, which
should yield relays of reserves to the field army, while
instalments of reinforcements should be forthcoming to
supply the drain which otherwise would diminish the
standing strength of the forces in the camp.   The
Emperor in one of his addresses to the soldiers specified
yet another *raison d'être* for the camp at Boulogne.
'The creation,' said he, ' of the Camp of the North was
intended to bring our troops nearer to those of England,
so that they might go swiftly whithersoever the honour
of the two nations might call them.'

The Duke of Saxe-Coburg-Gotha, the elder brother
of the Prince Consort, had paid a visit to the Emperor
in the spring of 1854; and in the summer Napoleon
asked the British Ambassador in Paris whether an invitation to the Boulogne camp would be acceptable to the
Prince Consort.   The result was a cordial letter from
the Emperor to the Prince.   'Wishing,' wrote Napoleon,
' to prove my determination to carry out to the end the
struggle we have begun together, I have formed a camp
between Boulogne and St. Omer.   I need not tell your
Highness how pleased I should be to receive you and
how happy I should be to show you my soldiers.   I am
convinced, moreover, that personal ties will contribute to
strengthen the union so happily established between
two great nations.   I beg you to present my respectful
homage to the Queen, and to receive the expression of
the esteem and affection I have conceived for you.'

The Prince's reply was even warmer than was the Emperor's invitation. Napoleon was addressed as ' *Sire et cher Frère*,' and the Prince signed himself ' *le bon Frère* ' of his host to be. The visit lasted four days. It was remarked that during the first greetings there were tears in Louis Napoleon's eyes while he expressed to the Prince his pleasure at ' this fresh proof of the cordiality of the alliance which England proffered him.' An autograph letter from the Queen was couched in terms which delighted him. When the Prince and the Emperor were together by themselves their conversation, as reported to the Queen by her husband, was very frank and cordial. Napoleon questioned the Prince very closely as to the details of the administration of the English Government, the Queen's relations with her Ministers, and her supervision of the whole of the diplomatic correspondence. He was astonished when the Prince told the Emperor that every despatch went through the Queen's hands and was read by her. He, it seemed, merely received extracts made from the despatches ; and he appeared to have little time or inclination to read. Napoleon frankly stated that he did not allow his Ministers to meet or discuss matters together, each of whom transacted business solely with him. He rarely told the one Minister what he had settled with the other. In other words, it seemed, he was an absolute monarch—a despot, if, for the most part, a genial and benign despot. In regard to military matters he was quite frank as to the condition in which the outbreak of the war found the French army. He owned that France was not yet ready for the struggle. In his own words, He had to refurnish almost his whole material, but was going on satisfactorily, and would be quite ready next year.' And then he described how he intended to keep up the camps and season his troops for the field.

According to the Prince Consort, the Emperor was almost the only individual among the French military men who had any real hope of the success of the expedition against Sevastopol. Before the Prince left Boulogne the decision was announced to advance to the Crimea ; Saint-Arnaud writing of himself, '*Je suis plein de confiance et plein d'ardeur.*' 'On the whole,' the Prince Consort wrote to the Queen, 'the impression which my stay at Boulogne left upon me was that by nature the Emperor would neither in home nor in foreign politics take any violent steps ; but that he appears in distress for means of governing, and is obliged to look about for them from day to day. Having deprived the people of any active participation in the government, and having reduced them to passive spectators, he is bound to keep up the "spectacle" ; and as at fireworks whenever a pause occurs between the displays, the public immediately grows impatient, forgetting that new preparations require time. Still,' the Prince continued, 'he appears to be the only man who has any hold on France, relying on the "*nom de Napoléon,*" the last thing left to a Frenchman's faith.'

In the midst of war the Emperor was pursuing his projects for the embellishment of Paris, and especially for the first International Exhibition of Industry in France to be held in the summer of 1855. About the same time he re-established the Imperial Guard, assigning to it a force of 20,000 men, a *corps d'élite* consisting of soldiers of good conduct who had completed seven

years' service. On Jan. 9, 1855, he addressed detachments of this fine force on their departure for the East,
bidding them plant their eagles on the ramparts of
Sevastopol. A levy of 140,000 men was demanded to fill
the gaps made by expirations of service and by the war.
The revenues of the years 1852 and 1853 had exceeded
expectations by 110 millions of francs—a wonderful
evidence of prosperity. But surpluses have an un-
pleasant habit of melting like snow in the face of huge
war-votes and more huge war-loans. During the first
year of the Crimean War the French expenditure in
that struggle amounted to $2\frac{1}{2}$ milliards of francs, just
one-half of the war indemnity exacted from France by
Germany in 1871.

The year 1855, although it was to be among the
most glorious of the Second Empire, opened gloomily.
The bitter winter weather on the Chersonese upland
told with awful effects on the Allied armies lying in
misery under the walls of Sevastopol. The delay in the
reduction of the great fortress caused the impatient
Parisians to chafe and murmur. The Emperor followed
every episode and every stage of the siege with the
closest attention. In his slow methodical manner he
gradually conceived a plan for the spring campaign ;
and then there arose within him the resolve to go
himself to the Crimea, and take position at the head of
his army. Many reasons combated the project. Scarcely
yet firm on the Throne, there was danger in prolonged
absence from his capital. His health was never strong.
While weighing the issues, Canrobert sent him a report
that the British army was sinking gradually under the
privations which maladministration had brought upon it.

He resolved to despatch large reinforcements to the Crimea immediately and he requested the British Admiralty to help him with ships since all the French ships were already engaged in transport service. The request was promptly complied with, and before the close of 1854 a French army was sailing from a British port on board a British fleet on the way to confront a common enemy.

Then the desire to go himself to the Crimea revived in Louis Napoleon. On Feb. 16, 1855, his cousin the Princess Mathilde argued long but ineffectually against his determination. The Empress, on the other hand, urged him to go, and, indeed, proposed to go part ot the way with him. On the 18th it was all but decided that he was to go, and the day of departure was actually fixed. The Council of Regency in his absence was provisionally formed. On the 20th the Emperor said, ' I am going to the Crimea in the interests of peace, which can only be secured at the scene of action. The incidents of the campaign will bring this about more effectually than any diplomatic conferences ; and moreover the Emperor Nicholas will also probably come to the Crimea.' A week later Nicholas was a dead man ; and on the 27th the journey of the Emperor to the Crimea was countermanded.

On Feb. 20th Napoleon had written to Lord Palmerston announcing his determination to go to the Crimea, where his presence, he believed, could alone save the expedition from disaster. He detailed his proposed plan of campaign, which need not here be recapitulated. ' Not only,' he wrote, ' would a mere General not be able to exert my influence, but time would no longer be wasted between Canrobert and Raglan and between Raglan and

Omar Pasha.' Lord Clarendon crossed the Channel to
discuss the subject with the Emperor. Fleury frankly
told the English statesman that although the French
army was loyal to Napoleon as Emperor, 'it did not like
to be commanded by anyone save a professional soldier,
while he was regarded as a civilian.' Lord Clarendon
brought forward argument after argument against the
Emperor's project; and although the latter did not at
once abandon it, the impression produced by the English
statesman's reasoning prepared the way for the *coup de
grâce* which the Queen gave it during the Windsor visit.

A fortnight later came a proposal on the part of the
Emperor that he and the Empress should pay a visit to
the Queen. Her Majesty cordially desired the visit;
and on April 16 the Imperial guests passed through
London on their way to Windsor. As they landed at
Dover a telegram announced to the Emperor that the
second bombardment of Sevastopol had opened on the
9th. All classes of the metropolis greeted the august
pair with cordial enthusiasm. He who had lived for
years in London a powerless exile and regarded as a
dreamy adventurer was now the master of France, the
honoured ally of England, the most powerful antagonist
of Russia. Louis Napoleon had many faults, but there
was no snobbery in his nature. As the cortège passed
along St. James's Street he halted the carriage that he
might point out to the Empress the modest dwelling in
King Street in which he had lived during his later exile
in England. At Windsor a reception not less gratifying
but of a quieter though not less cordial character awaited
the Imperial guests, and the visit was an unbroken
success. The Emperor at once charmed her Majesty.

Her diary is full of appreciation of her guests. She wrote : ' Nothing can be more amiable or more well-bred than the Emperor's manner—so full of tact.' Of the Empress the Queen noted : ' Her manner is the most perfect thing I have ever seen—so gentle, and graceful, and kind ; and the courtesy so charming, and so modest and retiring withal.'

On April 18 a Council of War was held at Windsor, at which was present the Prince Consort, Lords Palmerston, Panmure, Hardinge, and Cowley, Sir Charles Wood, Sir John Burgoyne, Count Walewski, and the French War Minister, Marshal Vaillant. All present unanimously declared against the Emperor's project of going himself to the Crimea ; but without obtaining from him the admission that he was shaken in his resolution. On his return to Paris the Emperor, however, found that while the Windsor visit had vastly increased his popularity in France, the failure of the Vienna negotiations had so greatly complicated events that he announced to the Queen the final abandonment of his intention to go to the Crimea. But his scheme for the conduct of the war was nevertheless persisted in.

While the cannons were roaring and men were dying in the trenches before Sevastopol, the Emperor on May 15 —the day before Canrobert's resignation of the chief command in the Crimea—was opening with pomp and circumstance the Universal Exhibition of 1855 ; in Napoleon's own words, ' a temple of peace which invites all nations to a gathering of concord.' Twenty-five thousand exhibitors had responded to the Emperor's appeal, and hosts of visitors from all parts of the world crowded to Paris during the summer and autumn. But below the gaiety and festivities of this brilliant period lay the solicitude incident to a state of war and the resultant strain. Among the exigencies were the calling-out of 140,000 conscripts as the contingent for 1856, the imposition of further taxation, and the conjunct guarantee with England of a Turkish war-loan of five millions sterling. The nation was loyal and eager, the Government asked for a war-contribution of thirty millions sterling, and the subscriptions came pouring in until the collective offers amounted to 146,000,000*l.* !

The battle of the Tchernaya fought on Aug. 16 and won so gallantly by French arms, heralded auspiciously the visit to France of the Queen of England, accompanied by her Consort and their two elder children. Received by the Emperor in person they landed at Boulogne on the afternoon of Aug. 18, under salutes from the batteries and a *feu de joie* maintained for miles along the edge of the cliffs, and later were escorted to the railway station by cavalry. The Queen has herself recorded her impressions of her ' first sight of Paris ' : ' The approaching twilight rather added to the beauty of the scene ; and it was still quite light enough when we passed down the Boulevard de Strasbourg (the Emperor's creation) and along the Boulevards, by the Porte St. Denis, the Madeleine, the Place de la Concorde, and the Arc de Triomphe.' Along the Champs Élysées and through the Bois de Boulogne the progress to St. Cloud was made in the twilight ; but all the way the troops kept the road, bands playing the National Anthem at intervals. The Queen was delighted with the splendour and brilliancy of the scene ; and as she approached the Palace she remarked the Zouaves as ' splendid troops in splendid dress, the friends of my dear Guards.' The Empress, who was in expectation of an heir and was suffering, met the Queen at the Palace. Sunday was a *dies non*; and what the Prince Consort called the Parisian Campaign, which lasted during the week, began on the Monday with hours spent in the Exhibition. Incognito drives through the quaint places of Paris, pilgrimages to the Tuileries, to the Invalides where lay the Great Captain, a visit to the old palace of the Stuarts at St. Germain, another to Versailles, and yet another to the grand final ball there, filled up a varied and busy week. On Monday the 27th the British royalties departed for home.

Having definitely abandoned the intention to go himself to the Crimea, the French Emperor determined, nevertheless, that the plan which he had matured should be carried out. Briefly that plan was as follows : the Allies were to divide themselves into three armies. One army was to continue to guard the trenches and push the siege. A second army, under Lord Raglan, was to assemble in the valley of Baidur (east of Balaclava), and to push its advanced post towards Bakshisarai. The third, under the French General-in-Chief, composed of troops from before Sevastopol and the reserve French army from Turkey, was to land at Alushta on the south-eastern face of the peninsula about abreast of Bakshisarai. This last army was to cross the Tchatur-dagh range and march on Simpheropol. Should the Russians have concentrated there their chief magazines and massed troops for their defence, Lord Raglan marching on Bakshisarai would threaten the Russian right or rear in combination with the other field army. But should the enemy abandon Simpheropol and concentrate in the vicinity of

Sevastopol, the French army from Simpheropol would advance on it by Bakshisarai while Lord Raglan in concert would attack the Mackenzie Farm heights. The Russian army if defeated, would be driven off the line of communication ; the Allies would sever it ; and Sevastopol, deprived of supplies and reinforcements, must speedily surrender.

No doubt to defeat the Russian field army and to sever the communication between Sevastopol and the interior of Russia would have speedily caused the surrender of the Russian stronghold. But there was another and a better alternative. There was the probability—indeed, the ultimate certainty—of capturing the south side of Sevastopol on the plan hitherto pursued. The besieging fire could always establish a superiority constantly increasing, over that of the place. The enemy's losses must continue to be immensely more severe than those of the Allies. It was certain, therefore, that perseverance in the siege would finally result in crushing the enemy's fire, in storming his works, and in rendering the south side untenable.

On this hypothesis Pélissier, who had succeeded Canrobert as Commander-in-Chief, resolved energetically to operate. Pélissier was a man of exceptionally resolute and determined character. After deliberate study of a difficult problem, he decided to ignore the Emperor's project and to devote all his forces to pushing the siege. He wasted no words, having once taken his resolution.

'The project,' he telegraphed to the Minister of War in Paris, 'of marching two armies from Alushta and Baidur is full of difficulty and risk. I have arranged with Lord Raglan for the storming of the advanced works, for the occupation of the Tchernaya, and finally for an operation on Kertch. All these movements are in train.' When it is remembered that Louis Napoleon was an absolute Sovereign who could pull this truculent general down just as he had chosen to set him up, it must be owned that in thus acting in direct and resolute opposition to the cherished scheme of his master Pélissier evinced himself to be an uncommonly strong man. There did come from the Emperor something in the nature of a rebuke to his doggedly determined subordinate. ' I have confidence in you,' the Emperor wired, ' and I don't pretend to command the army from here ; however, I must tell you my opinion and you ought to pay regard to it. A great effort must be made to beat the Russian army in order to invest the place. If you send 14,000 men to Kertch you weaken yourself uselessly. . . . Weigh all this carefully.'

The Emperor's arguments had no effect on Pélissier ; he went forward right in the teeth of his master. The expedition to Kertch was made, resulting in the complete destruction of everything that could aid the Russian forces in the Crimea throughout the shores of the Sea of Azov. Pélissier wrote to the War Minister : ' We have struck deep into the Russian resources : their chief line of supply is cut. I did well to carry out this expedition and I view with calm assurance the approach of the final act.' In full accord with Lord Raglan the French Commander-in-Chief resolutely prosecuted the siege operations, assailing in the first instance the principal outworks of the defence, the White Works, the Mamelon, and the ' Quarries.' The Emperor telegraphed : ' In conformity with the British Government which writes in the same sense to Lord Raglan, I give you a positive order not to devote yourself to the siege before having completed the investment.' But this message was crossed by the following telegram from Pélissier : ' Lord Raglan and I are settling the final dispositions for an attack by storm which should gain us the White Works, the Mamelon, and the " Quarries." I calculate on beginning this operation on the 7th (June) and on carrying it right through with the utmost vigour.'

The preliminary bombardment began on the after-noon of the 6th, and was maintained with tremendous energy until late on the following afternoon, when the Mamelon was silenced and the White Works were ruined. The latter were promptly captured and were presently connected with the French trenches. After desperate fighting the Mamelon was also captured and held, and ultimately the ' Quarries' remained in British possession. Pélissier had everywhere driven the enemy from their outworks of which he now had possession ; but during the bombardment and storm the total losses amounted to over 15,000 men.

Notwithstanding Pélissier's successes the Emperor would not relinquish his plan. It was not till a week after the action of the 6th and 7th that he telegraphed to Pélissier, saying that before congratulating him on his success he had wished to know the cost. ' I persist,' he wrote, ' in ordering you to make every effort to take the field.' Pélissier replied dauntlessly : ' The execution of your orders is impossible ; it would place me between insubordination and discredit. . . . I pray your Majesty either to free me from the straitened limits imposed on me, or to permit me to resign a command impossible to exercise in concert with my loyal allies, at the end, sometimes paralysing, of an electric wire.' No answer reached him ; and on the night of the 17th he telegraphed : ' I have waited all day for an answer to my important despatch of yesterday, but have received none. To-morrow at daybreak, in concert with the English I attack the Redan, the Malakoff, and their dependent batteries. I have firm hope.'

That hope was doomed to disappointment ; the 18th was marked by a series of blunders and misfortunes and the only gleam of good fortune was General Eyre's partial success. The total losses of those two bloody days, the 17th and 18th, were not short of 10,000, of which more than half were Russian casualties. Notwithstanding the reverses and bloodshed of those days of gloom Pélissier still held fast to the prosecution of the siege. He curtly reported : ' From causes which cannot now be discussed, our attack of to-day has not succeeded although part of our troops set foot in the Malakoff. Our allies not having attained a footing in the Redan in spite of their vigour, I ordered a withdrawal to the trenches. I cannot console myself for the failure otherwise than in repairing it by energy and, above all, by method.' After the lamented death of Lord Raglan Pélissier had no colleague and in effect was omnipotent over the Allied forces. The Emperor ceased from adverse criticism. On Sept. 8 the obstinate and bloody struggle was fought out, and at length Sevastopol fell.

The Emperor turned gladly to home affairs ; and the closing of the Paris Exhibition in November in the presence of a great assemblage of soldiers, statesmen, artists, and men of letters, gave him an opportunity of making his sentiments and wishes known, not only to France but to Europe. Presently he was welcoming on their return from the East bodies of the Guard and of the Line. As the heroes of the Crimea re-entered Paris amidst triumphant enthusiasm on Dec. 20, the Emperor accosted his home-coming soldiers in a stirring and appropriate address. The Guard and the Line, bearing with them their wounded and their shot-torn standards, marched along the Boulevard under triumphal arches and amid the loud acclamations of their fellow-citizens ; and this spectacle, now stirring to pride, now to sympathy as the wounded were borne by, closed what was one of the most eventful and most brilliant years of Napoleon's reign.

The feeling in favour of peace had always been much stronger in France than in England, for the war, save during the elation and excitement of its victories, was never popular with the French people ; and Sevastopol had no sooner fallen than public opinion demanded speedy peace with a voice which could not be disregarded. It was no small relief to Louis Napoleon when, on March 30, 1856, the Treaty of Paris was signed. After the signature of peace the Emperor addressed his congratulations to the Congress, and illuminations and a review of 50,000 men closed the scene. A letter from the Queen congratulated him on the peace concluded ' under his auspices ' ; and he in reply expressed his joy that the Alliance between France and England was as close and stable as when first it was ratified.

CHAPTER X

THE ITALIAN CAMPAIGN OF 1859

ON the morning of March 16, 1856, the guns of the Invalides informed Paris that a son had been born to the Emperor. The infant, for whom was in store a sad but heroic fate, received the names of Napoléon Eugène Louis Jean Joseph, the Pope and the Queen of Sweden being godfather and godmother. Paris wore a holiday aspect, and at noon the Emperor, radiant with joy, received the Diplomatic Body. The Pope's legate at a solemn service in the chapel of the Palace of St. Cloud, presented to the Empress the golden rose which the Pope had sent her. At length the dynasty seemed to be resting on a solid foundation. Such clouds as still lay on Napoleon's horizon appeared to be confined within the bounds of his realm, where a bad harvest, wild speculation, excessive expenditure, and extravagant public works threatened commercial disasters of the most perilous political character. Had he chosen then to adopt the methods of liberal and constitutional government to which he subsequently resorted when too late, he would have spent a calmer and a happier life and his end might have been both serene and glorious. But permitting himself to be influenced by evil and selfish advisers, he engaged in a course of political conduct

which embittered the resentment of his domestic
enemies and shook the confidence of his best friends
abroad.

In the winter of 1856 there passed through Paris
Prince Frederick William of Prussia (the late Emperor
Frederick II.), accompanied by his adjutant, Major von
Moltke, whom later the world was to know as the
greatest strategist of the age.   Of the French Emperor
the Prussian soldier wrote : ' He struck me by a sort
of immobility of features and the almost extinguished
look of his eyes.   The predominating characteristic of
his face is a friendly and good-humoured smile, which
has nothing Napoleonic about it.   He is a quite simple
and rather small man whose always tranquil countenance
gives a strong impression of good-natured amiability.
" Il ne se fâche jamais," say the people who are in most
frequent intercourse with him.   " Il est toujours poli et
bon envers nous ; ce n'est que la bonté de son cœur et
sa confiance qui pourront lui devenir dangereux." '   Of
the infant Prince Imperial Moltke remarked that ' he
seemed a strapping little fellow.'

The session of 1857 produced some useful measures.
A subvention of twelve million francs was voted for the
further embellishment of Paris, and another of fourteen
millions for the establishment of three great transatlantic
lines of French steamers.   The privileges of the Bank
of France were prolonged and extended, and its capital
was doubled.   The plebiscite of 1857 proved that the
popularity of the Emperor and his Government was not
materially impaired, although in comparison with the
plebiscite of 1852 that of 1857 showed fewer ' Ayes '
and more ' Noes.'   ' Nevertheless this election did not

pass off without menacing manifestations.   Probably the
life of no man of modern times was ever attempted by
the hand of the assassin so frequently as that of Louis
Napoleon.   He may be said to have habitually carried
his life in his hand ; but in that strange faith of his in his
' star ' his cool courage never faltered, save, perhaps, on
one occasion ; and the charge of want of personal courage
averred against him has only brought discredit on a
bitter enemy.   ' When,' in the words of Lord Cowper,
' we consider that the same charge was brought against
Marlborough and Cromwell, and the great Napoleon
himself, we may dismiss it with the words used by the
object of it when he read Kinglake's chapter—" C'est
indigne." '   The Emperor was hoping that the time was
approaching when the iron hand of absolute rule might
be relaxed as an act of favour as well as of prudence and
of safety.   But now the names of well-known revolutionary leaders were coupled with rumours of a widespread organisation for the advancement of the Republican
banner in the red hand of the regicide ; and Napoleon
found himself the mark of men who sought his life in the
name of the very cause he had always had at heart.

The restlessness of the French Emperor had created
by degrees a very dangerous state of public feeling in
Germany, Austria, and England ; and Persigny, then
French Ambassador in England, went to Paris to
describe to the Emperor the attitude of profound suspicion regarding him which England had assumed in
consequence of his disturbing and adventurous foreign
policy.   Napoleon suggested that the mutual misappre-
hensions would be best dispelled by a personal interview
with the Queen.   The proposal was accepted ; and the

Emperor and Empress reached Osborne on Aug. 6, where they spent three days. The meeting of the Sovereigns was still cordial; and the visit, with the assistance of Lords Clarendon and Palmerston and MM. Walewski and Persigny, was turned to the best account, since it brought into cordial contact the rulers of both realms and enabled them to settle the question of the Principalities and other matters of importance. But the cordial impressions which the Osborne visit had produced in the minds of Queen Victoria and her Consort were all but effaced by the subsequent excursion made by them a few days later to inspect the forts, basins, and breakwater of Cherbourg. 'It makes me very unhappy to see what is done here,' wrote the Queen in her diary, 'and how well protected the works are.' The Cherbourg breakwater was 'treble the size of the Plymouth one,' and 8,000 men were at work upon it. The Prince Consort wrote to Stockmar, 'Cherbourg is a gigantic work and gives one grave cause for reflection. The counter-defences at Alderney are childish in comparison.' The Queen and her husband did not care to accompany the Emperor to the camp of Châlons for the opening of the great school of war on that vast plain whereon the Imperial Guard was assembled. The great camp of Châlons, together with the vast works of Cherbourg and the prodigious growth of the French armour-plated naval force, served not unnaturally to foster that mistrust which, in spite of their personal regard for the French Sovereign, was taking hold of the minds of the Queen and Prince. Yet at the meeting of monarchs at Stuttgart in September, 1857, the French Emperor was found to be loyally impervious to all

inducements to a breach of the English Alliance. Of
Napoleon's conduct at Stuttgart Sir Theodore Martin
remarks : ' The *parvenu* Emperor, thrown for the first
time into the midst of the royalties of the " Almanach de
Gotha," had distinguished himself by great self-possession
and dignity, bearing himself, as said a shrewd observer,
" like a thorough gentleman, holding his own, and
showing no eagerness to seize at the advances made to
him which might well have turned the steadiest head."'

On the evening of Jan. 14, 1858, the Emperor
and Empress were driving to the Opera House in the
Rue Lepelletier to hear the opera of ' Le Bal de
Gustave,' which culminates in the assassination of
Gustavus III., when Felix Orsini and his accomplice
threw three explosive bombs under the carriage of their
Majesties. The Emperor received a slight wound on
the nose and the Empress a blow on the eye—her dress
was spotted with blood from the wounded surrounding the
carriage. Both Emperor and Empress appeared wonder-
fully composed and courageous—she, indeed, rather more
so than he. They remained all through the performance in
ignorance of the bloody tragedy enacted outside, where
eight persons had been killed and a hundred and fifty-
six wounded. Orsini was an Italian revolutionist of the
most reckless and uncompromising type. From the
fortress of Mantua he had escaped to England in 1856,
whence in 1857 he had repaired to Paris, having formed
a conspiracy with Pieri, Rudio, and Gomez the aim of
which was the assassination of the French Emperor.

For once the ' habitual calm ' of Napoleon was not
maintained. He has, indeed, been accused of having
sunk for the time into the position of a political poltroon,

trembling under the threats of the Carbonari, to whom
he was believed with truth to have belonged in his own
early revolutionary days, and quaking under the terror
of such another lesson as Orsini had administered. His
ill-wishers declared that his prestige was gone and that
his cool courage had forsaken him ; it was even averred
that his time was occupied in devising precautions for
his own safety. He was said to wear a cuirass under
his coat ; to have had wires fixed over the chimneys of
the Tuileries so that explosive substances should not
reach him at his hearth ; to have bought the houses
opposite the Tuileries lest grenades should be dropped
from their windows into his carriage ; and that a cohort
of spies mingled with the guests at Lady Cowley's ball
to assure his protection.

Whether it was by significant pressure or by strenuous
entreaty that in 1858 Cavour obtained from Louis Napoleon his promise to support Italy with armed force, may
never be known. The bargain was struck—the com-
pact of Plombières was ratified between the French
Emperor and the Sardinian Prime Minister. That
Italy made a good bargain is long since beyond dispute.
She leaped by two or three great bounds into a new and
free liberal national life. An united Italy was not in the
Plombières agreement, nor did Cavour expect to find it
there. What he did hope for and obtained was a free
northern kingdom to begin with, which should absorb
the Italian nation ' from the Alps to the Adriatic.' But
the impulse which his genius and patriotism gave to his
countrymen's destinies has carried the seat of the Italian
Government from Turin to Florence and from Florence
to Rome.

In November, 1858, Vincenzo Salvagnuoli presented a memorial to the Emperor at Compiègne, in which the expulsion of Austria from Italy with the assistance of France was assumed as a question already agreed upon. The Emperor undertook to throw 200,000 troops into Italy and to command them in person in the following summer. On New Year's morning of 1859, when the Emperor was receiving the customary greetings of the Diplomatic Body at the Tuileries, he turned to M. Hübner the Austrian Ambassador and said to him abruptly in the hearing of his colleagues, ' I regret that our relations with your Government are not so good as they have been hitherto ; but I beg you to assure the Emperor that my personal feelings towards him are unchanged.' Those simple words fell upon Europe like the shock of an earthquake. The ' Moniteur ' was instructed to declare that there was nothing in the diplomatic relations of the two Courts to warrant the prevailing rumours of war. But this pacific assurance was counteracted by the tone of Victor Emanuel's speech in opening the Sardinian Chambers on Jan. 10. It was generally believed that a secret alliance had been formed between the French Emperor and the King of Sardinia, although its precise nature remained unknown. That it was to the advantage of France was inferred from the marriage of Prince Napoleon to the Princess Clothilde, eldest daughter of Victor Emanuel. Her hand by proxy was demanded by General Niel on Jan. 23, and the marriage was celebrated a week later. Those and other indications of the designs of the French Emperor warned the Austrian Government to make energetic preparations for the defence of its Italian possessions ; and an appeal was made to the German Confederation to act as an united power if Austria by an attack on her Italian provinces should be called upon to take up arms against France and Sardinia combined. While thus appealing for support to the other German Powers, Austria was pushing forward great armaments along the Ticino and the Po. Strong masses of troops were quartered in Cremona, Placenza, and Pavia, assuming an aggressive aspect against Piedmont; and a loan of 150 million francs had been contracted in Vienna.

Louis Napoleon had given his pledges to Cavour, but it seemed as if he were fain that they would not be exacted. He was disconcerted by the precipitate march of events. He was not ready for action. He had been told that his words to M. Hübner would cost France a milliard. The French people were not at all eager to make heavy sacrifices for the deliverance of Italy. The Ministers, whose policy frequently clashed with that of the Emperor, were opposed to Italian independence and disliked Cavour—Walewski even hated him. The attitude of France towards Austria and Italy was the subject of much discussion and great difference of opinion throughout Europe when the question of war or peace was seemingly hanging in the balance. Notwithstanding the emphatic declaration of Louis Napoleon that the Empire meant peace, there was a strong and widespread suspicion that the Imperial policy would be guided by a spirit of war and conquest. The Emperor took great pains to effect the removal of this impression, especially from the minds of English statesmen ; but with slight success. The Congress, in the assemblage of which at the desire of the French Emperor Russia took the initiative, seemed to meet with general acquiescence but ultimately came to nothing. All efforts at conciliation proved unavailing. Each of the three Powers most concerned seemed animated by the conviction that the questions at issue could be settled only by an appeal to the sword. Each, in fact, was impatient for the opening of hostilities.

Before departing for the seat of war the Emperor addressed a proclamation to his subjects from which a few sentences may be extracted : ' I desire no conquests, but I resolve firmly to maintain my national and traditional policy. I observe treaties on the condition that no one shall violate them to my disadvantage. I respect the territory and rights of neutral Powers ; but I boldly avow my sympathy for a people whose history is mingled with our own and who groan under foreign oppression. . . . I am about to place myself at the head of the army. I leave in France the Empress and my son. Aided by the experience and enlightenment of the last surviving brother of the Great Emperor the Empress, who will be the head of the Regency during my absence, will understand how to show herself equal to the grandeur of her mission.'

The Franco-Austrian War of 1859, so unpopular when first rumoured, became so popular when actually engaged in that the French people watched the military movements with eager enthusiasm and crowded eagerly to subscribe to the war-loan.

Just before the opening of the war Victor Emanuel summoned Garibaldi to take the command of the little army of noble Volunteers. ' We want you,' said Cavour. ' I am always ready to serve my country,' said Garibaldi simply. 'My first duty is to offer my sword to my country. My war-cry therefore shall be, " Italian Unity under the constitutional rule of Victor Emanuel." Remember, however, that the aid of foreign arms must be paid for dearly. As for the man who has promised to help us, I ardently wish he may redeem himself in the eyes of posterity by achieving the noble task of Italian liberation.' By the end of April Garibaldi was in command of three fine regiments of Cacciatori delle Alpi, a company of Genoese sharpshooters, and a small squadron of Guides. The little force, slight in numerical strength, was formed from the best elements of Lombardy, the Romagna and the minor Duchies ; and it did gallant service in the war.

On May 2 King Victor Emanuel called his warriors to arms. He was himself Commander-in-Chief. He had five divisions of regular infantry, amounting to about 13,000 men. Each division had two battalions of Bersaglieri, a regiment of cavalry, three batteries, and a company of sappers. The cavalry division consisted of sixteen squadrons, with twelve field-guns and two batteries of horse artillery. The third and fourth French corps were on the march before the declaration of war ; they crossed the Alps and hastened from the slopes of Mont Cenis and Mont Genèvre toward the scene of action in the great Italian plain. The first and second corps with the *matériel* of the army had sailed from Toulon to Genoa, and having crossed the Apennines were hurrying northward to occupy the valley of the Scrivia. On May 12 the French Emperor made his entry into Genoa under arches, draperies, and flowers. At Alessandria he rode under an arch on which was emblazoned the legend, 'To the descendant of the Conqueror of Marengo!' And when he entered the Palace he found on his table the map on which his great uncle had traced the movements of his army before the battle of Marengo.

Space forbids any attempt to give the details of the battles of this short but bloody campaign. The first engagement occurred at Genestrello on May 20; from which place after some hard fighting the Austrians were driven out. They then made a stand at Montebello, where, although 20,000 strong, they were routed by some 6,000 Sardinians. The Austrian general was completely outmanœuvred by the Emperor and the King. By a wide turning movement the Allied commanders forced the Austrians to cross the Po and then to retire behind the Sesia. On the 30th General Cialdini crossed the Sesia and drove the Austrians from the fortified positions of Palestro, Venzaglio, and Casalino, having carried each position at the bayonet-point. Next day the Austrian general strove hard to retake Palestro; but Victor Emanuel threw himself into the heart of the struggle and carried everything before him. The 3rd French Zouaves performed prodigies of valour and French and Sardinian soldiers vied with each other in gallant deeds.

The battles of the war followed each other with extraordinary rapidity. Magenta was a splendid if a bloody triumph. The brilliant march of MacMahon from Turbigo on Buffalora and Magenta, and the prodigies of valour performed by his soldiers; the deeds of the Grenadiers of the Guard at the bridge of Buffalora; the splendid fight at the Ponte Vecchio; the fierce bayonet charges under Wimpffen; the hand-to-hand struggle in the streets of Magenta; all were achievements of unsurpassed valour. The Emperor remained under fire on the bridge of Buffalora during the fighting. Many times during the day came messages that the commander of the Imperial Guard could no longer hold his ground. ' He must hold it ' was the Emperor's answer; and the Guard held on.

The Austrians left 6,000 dead and wounded on the battlefield, and 4,000 were taken prisoners. The losses of the victors were almost as heavy as those of the vanquished; but the great triumphant result of the day was that the hated Austrian had been once and for all driven out of Piedmont. On the early morning after the battle the Emperor and Victor Emanuel entered Milan; and the Emperor went to the Villa Buonaparte which for him was full of associations. His great uncle and Eugène Beauharnais had inhabited it. Queen Hortense had spent within its walls many happy days. Louis Napoleon pointed out to his aide-de-camp the very room in which he had slept in, 1813 : and he sent to ask whether the fine tall porter whom he remembered of those days was still alive. When the Emperor and Victor Emanuel appeared together in the streets of Milan their progress was a triumphal march. The King did not try to conceal the deep emotion which his face betrayed; and the Emperor himself, notwithstanding his phlegmatic temperament, could not control the joy which he exhibited. The enthusiastic Italians who then kissed his feet could not anticipate that five weeks later the discredit of Villafranca would follow the victory of Magenta.

After their defeat at Magenta the Austrians had abandoned Milan in haste, leaving at Malegnano, half-way between Milan and Lodi, a strong rearguard for the protection of their main army in its retreat. It was determined to attack this force and to attempt to cut off its retreat across the Adda. The commanders assigned to this undertaking were Baraguay d'Hilliers, MacMahon, and L'Admirault; the divisional generals were Bazaine, Forey, and Goz. Bazaine's division of Baraguay d'Hilliers' corps arrived before Malegnano at five P.M. of June 8. An Austrian division was in possession of the town, the entrance to which was barricaded and defended by four guns. Bazaine's troops suffered severely while exposed to the enemy's cross fire. Bullets rained down from the windows; shells, round-shot, and grape poured in showers on the road; bayonets and butt-ends of muskets were freely used; but the French storming parties were repulsed. Suddenly, however, the sound of artillery was heard from the other end of the town, indicating that Forey had turned the Austrian position. Then Bazaine's Zouaves dashed at the barricade with a fury which nothing could withstand. The first line of the Austrian defence consisted wholly of officers who fought with desperate valour; but nevertheless the obstacle was carried and the French sappers cleared the way for the artillery. The cemetery on the left of the road, defended by the Austrians with great obstinacy, was at length carried by General Goz and Colonel Paulze d'Ivry; and the fortune of the bitter fight manifestly began to turn against the Austrians. L'Admirault struck in at the double upon the massed troops of the enemy in the streets and piazzas of the town. The Zouaves at length reached the square, after having stormed every house, every church, every portico. As darkness set in torrents of rain covered the bloody ground and the noise of the fighting was responded to in peals of thunder. During the night the Austrian army succeeded in effecting the passage of the Adda, whence it fell back sullenly towards the Chiese, the Oglio, and the Mincio.

The Emperor and the King did not rest long on their laurels at Milan. The former fixed for the time his headquarters at Gorgonzola with the Imperial Guard, which thus acted as the reserve of the Allied armies. At Brescia the Emperor slept in the room which his great uncle had occupied, and wrote his despatches upon the table which the First Consul had used. From Brescia the Imperial headquarters were moved forward to Montechiaro, almost on the edge of the battlefield. On the day before the great battle the lines of the Allied armies reached from the shore of the Lake of Garda at Desenzano along the western edge of the hilly country from Lonato down to Castiglione; and bending back towards Caspenedolo touched thereabouts the river Chiese. During the 23rd and the early morning of the 24th the Austrian commander, General Hess, had caused the Austrian army to move out from Verona and Mantua; to recross the Mincio at Salionze, Valleggio, Ferri, and Goito; and to occupy Pozzolengo, Solferino, Cavriana, Volta, and Guidizzuolo—positions which had been abandoned by it only three days previously.

From the Imperial headquarters at Montechiaro there was issued on the evening of the 23rd a general order regulating the forward movements of the Allied armies, which were to begin by daylight of the morrow. To the left flank was assigned Victor Emanuel's army of which the 1st and 2nd divisions were in the hilly country about Lonato; the 3rd was at Desenzano and Rivoltella; the 4th in advance of Lonato; and the cavalry at Biddizole. The instructions were that his Sardinian Majesty should advance with his army on Pozzolengo; Marshal Baraguay d'Hilliers, whose left was in touch with the Piedmontese, was to march from Essenta on Solferino; and Marshal MacMahon was to advance from Castiglione on Cavriana. The two corps of Niel and Canrobert were to move across the plain, the former from Carpenedolo on Guidizzuolo, the latter from Mezzano on Medole. The Imperial Guard was to move forward from Montechiaro on Castiglione, and two cavalry divisions were to manœuvre in the plain between Solferino and Medole.

Considerable fighting had already occurred when at five A.M. of the 24th urgent messengers from MacMahon and Baraguay d'Hilliers reached the Emperor in his headquarters at Montechiaro. He at once despatched his staff to precede him to Castiglione, while he himself, escorted by the Cent-Gardes, drove with all speed in the same direction. Alighting at Castiglione he ascended a lofty church-tower from which is visible a wide panorama. As he surveyed the scene, the smoke of the guns enabled him to form a distinct idea of the conditions of the battle then being fought. From his elevated position he could see the masses of the enemy swarming along the heights uniting Cavriana with Solferino. The distant cannon-roar indicated that Canrobert had passed Castel Goffredo and was hurrying towards

Medole. Nearer to Castiglione could be seen the head
of the Imperial Guard marching forward in the direction
of Guidizzuolo. The Piedmontese cannon on the extreme left announced to the Emperor that the legions
of Victor Emanuel were fighting hard ; but the distance
and the undulations of the ground hindered the view
in that direction.

High military ability has been rarely ascribed to
Louis Napoleon ; yet the directions he sent to his
Marshals as soon as he had descended from the steeple
of the church of Castiglione certainly evinced the pene-
tration and tactical sagacity of an experienced commander. He had immediately perceived that the object
of the Austrians was to divert the attack on Solferino—
the key of their position—by outflanking the right of the
French army, filling up the gap between the second and
fourth corps and thus cutting the enemy's forces in
two. The Emperor, therefore, commanded the cavalry
of the Imperial Guard to join MacMahon, to whom he
sent orders to dislodge the enemy from Morino's farm ;
he also directed that the Imperial Guard should march
forward in rear of the heights on which the first corps
was fighting. The plan of the Emperor appears to have
been clear and precise. In a word, his design was to
make himself master of Solferino at any cost ; and then,
by a flank movement to beat the enemy out of his
position at Cavriana.

Meanwhile death was ravaging the divisions of
Baraguay d'Hilliers, fighting on the heights which face
Solferino. From the plain the Emperor saw the smoke
enveloping the masses of his army, and he felt that his
place was with them. Galloping up on to the Monte

Fenile, he found that Dieu's brigade had reached the foot of the Cypress Mamelon and that d'Alton's was massed on the road from Castiglione to Solferino, edging the foot of the hill from which the Emperor was witnessing the tremendous drama then being acted out. Suddenly a thick phalanx of bayonets was seen glittering through the trees of the valley—a body of Austrian troops which Stadion had sent to cut the line of the French. D'Alton's brigade stood its ground like a wall of granite, but the odds of five to one were too great and d'Alton could not hold his own any longer. The artillery of the Austrians was brought to bear on his flank, and showers of shot, grape, and shell were poured into the brave but shattered brigade. Forey's division, and more especially d'Alton's brigade, would undoubtedly have been crushed by a fresh hostile column just then debouching from the road of Casal del Monte, had not succour been at hand. The crisis was imminent; there was not a moment to be lost. From the heights of Monte Fenile Louis Napoleon had perceived the danger and saw that the instant had arrived when to engage his reserve. He may have remembered the exclamation so often used by his great uncle, '*A moi la Garde!*' He sent orders to General Manèque of the Guard to advance at once against the Austrian columns and give support to d'Alton. The movement was executed with the rapidity which is one of the finest qualities of the French army, and the Austrians were beaten back.

Hours of desperate fighting and of horrid slaughter passed before Solferino fell into the possession of the French. At length the Cypress Mount was carried and the Austrian artillery was captured. The long-expected moment had now come. Forey gave orders to storm the Tower Hill of Solferino. The drums beat, the trumpets sounded; shouts of ' *Vive l'Empereur !* ' rent the air; voltigeurs of the Imperial Guard, chasseurs, and linesmen rushed to the assault with an impetuosity which the Austrians could not withstand. The heights of Solferino were covered in a moment by thousands of French troops. The Tower Hill was carried, and General Forey then halted his victorious columns for a few moments; while Lebœuf brought up his powerful artillery to bear upon the defeated masses of the Austrians now retiring through the narrow streets of the village of Solferino towards Cavriana.

Long hours of hard fighting followed the great success just recorded, and the final issue was wholly in favour of the French. The Austrian retreat, though orderly, was so rapid that the Kaiser himself had barely time to gain the cross-road from Cavriana to Valeggio. Two hours later Cavriana was filled by the victorious adversaries of Francis Joseph; and the Casa Pastore which had been his temporary quarters, now opened its doors to receive the rival Emperor.

The valorous deeds performed by the Italian troops fighting on the extreme left of the Allied armies cannot be here detailed. After having beaten back the enemy from Monte Manca and forced him to retreat in disorder to the village of Pozzolengo, they were able to expel the Austrian masses from the strong positions of San Martino and Contracania. Those achievements proved that the Piedmontese were no whit inferior to their gallant allies; for they had to deal with Benedek, who certainly was a more skilful soldier and resolute fighting man than any of his colleagues.

The Allied armies had achieved a splendid victory but at a most serious cost. The French had 12,000 *hors de combat*; 150 officers killed, and 570 wounded. The Italian losses were 5,521 men killed, wounded, and missing. The casualties among the Austrians were stupendous—there were from 20,000 to 25,000 men *hors de combat* and the 'missing' reached a total of 4,000. The Austrians left thirty guns on the field as well as several regimental colours. The battlefield was a horrible and shuddering spectacle.

A strange and startling series of events followed the battle of Solferino. Two days after the victory Cavour had a long interview with the French Emperor. Napoleon was disgusted with the quarrels of his generals and shocked by the horrible scenes of war he had just witnessed, but proud and delighted that the military glory of France had been once again splendidly asserted. Cavour left the Imperial headquarters at Valeggio in high spirits and full of assurance that the Emperor was determined to prosecute the war with vigour to its conclusion. But rumours were presently rife in the camp that a French General had been sent to Verona on some mysterious mission to the Austrian Emperor. Those reports proved well founded. Since daybreak of July 6 the several corps of the Allied armies had been formed up in position for the battle which was believed to be imminent. On the early evening of the same day General Fleury left Valeggio with a letter from the French Emperor to the Austrian Kaiser, making direct proposals for an armistice. This step was taken without any communication with Victor Emanuel and without the knowledge of anyone except the bearer of the message. By eleven o'clock of the following morning Fleury was back in Valeggio, announcing the success of his mission. The result was the conclusion of an armistice for one month. The announcement spread consternation in the Sardinian camp and excited the deepest disappointment and indignation throughout Italy. Coming upon the Italians while still in the flush of victory and buoyant with hope, the tidings were felt not only as a terrible shock but as a betrayal of the cause and a national humiliation.

The two Emperors met at Villafranca on the morning of the 11th, and were closeted alone for an hour. Of what passed between them there is no record. When they came forth the Austrian looked pale and embarrassed, the Frenchman gay and at his ease. The proud descendant of the Hapsburgs doubtless felt bitterly the humiliation of that moment. Louis Napoleon, on the contrary, had satisfied his greatest desire—the dealing in person with a legitimate Emperor. Nothing had been committed to paper at that interview; but on his return to Valeggio the Emperor despatched his cousin Prince Napoleon to Verona, there to settle the preliminaries of that peace which was finally adjusted at Zurich after many delays and contentions. The same evening Napoleon informed Victor Emanuel that if the preliminaries of which Prince Napoleon was the bearer should be accepted, peace would be concluded. Victor Emanuel replied gravely and coldly, ' Whatever may be the decision of your Majesty I shall feel eternal gratitude for what you have done in behalf of Italian independ-

ence ; and I beg you to believe that you may reckon on
my fidelity.'   Cavour had less self-control.   He rushed
into the King's presence in great excitement, his face
scarlet with passion, and his manner, usually simple and
easy, marked by violent gesticulations.   He spoke of the
French Emperor in the most disrespectful language ; and
he advised his master to reject the terms of peace, to
withdraw his army from Lombardy, to abdicate, to do
anything to vindicate his dignity.   The great statesman
resigned rather than agree to a peace concluded without
his Sovereign or himself being considered, and Rattazzi
received instructions to form a new Ministry.

On the evening of July 12 the Emperor left the army
for France, passing through Milan and Turin, where he
had so recently been hailed with enthusiastic acclamations.   He must painfully have felt the contrast, when
the victor of Magenta and Solferino was allowed to
return from the scenes of his successes without a single
cheer from the people whose country he had promised to
free 'from the Alps to the Adriatic' ; but whom he was
now abruptly abandoning, leaving his 'mission' but half
accomplished.   On July 19 the Emperor received at
St. Cloud the great bodies of the State.   The Duc de
Morny addressed him in terms of lavish adulation.
Napoleon's reply was in effect an apology to the
French, the Italians, and the English for what he must
have felt to be a very imperfect fulfilment of the task he
had undertaken.   His reasons for stopping short were
very forcible in themselves, but they were susceptible of
this complete answer—that they should all have been
foreseen and should have entered into his calculations
when he published his programme of freedom to Italy

'from the Alps to the Adriatic.' Yet it appeared that even when he addressed the Italians at Milan as their deliverer the new light had not broken in upon him which revealed the strength of the Quadrilateral, the cost of expelling the Austrians from Venetia, and the conviction that further French successes would certainly bring mobilised Germany into the field. That new light seems to have flashed upon Napoleon for the first time from the stern Austrian ranks on the day of Solferino. It was then he realised that should he go forward, he would be obliged to attack in front an enemy entrenched behind great fortresses, and protected against any diversion on his flanks by the neutrality of the territories surrounding him. In short, to use the chagrined Emperor's own words, 'in commencing a long and sterile war of sieges I recognised in presence of me Europe in arms, ready either to dispute our success or to aggravate our reverses.' Admirable *à posteriori* reasoning, but curiously belated.

CHAPTER XI

THE MEXICAN TRAGEDY

LOUIS NAPOLEON was a man of very considerable ability, and it is possible enough that he would have been a stable Sovereign but for the restless ambition which possessed his soul. His life was one of constant plotting and scheming, occasionally, it is true—as in the cession to him by Victor Emanuel of Nice and Savoy—with substantial if unscrupulous results, but more often with a futile or disastrous outcome to his projects. At the outbreak of the Civil War in the United States in 1861 his impulse was to intervene in favour of the South, and to form of the Confederate States a separate Republic which, he dreamed, would become the ally of France. That inclination had been abandoned by a conviction of the force of the growing unanimity in the Northern States of the great American Union in favour of the abolition of slavery, and by the attitude of Great Britain. But Mexico presented to his sanguine disposition a tempting sphere of opportunity. The origin of the Mexican adventure has been said to have resulted from some scandalous financial operations on the joint parts of the Duc de Morny and a certain Jecker, a Swiss banker who was subsequently shot in the Paris Commune. The character of Morny in his financial relations and the pretensions of Jecker gave some colour to those charges. But as a matter of fact, the expedition to Mexico of 1861–62 was originally undertaken in consequence of the joint action of England and Spain under a convention signed in London on Nov. 20, 1861, to which France later became a party. Mexico had so long evaded her obligations to her English and Spanish creditors and had left unredressed so many outrages on individual Englishmen and Spaniards residing in Mexico, that the Governments of the two countries had at length resolved to resort to strenuous measures. France also claimed to have grievances ; and it was not in the first instance understood that the ultimate aims of the French Emperor were not in substantial accord with the objects of the other Powers.

The expedition sailed in December, 1861. Spain embarked 7,000 soldiers, France about 2,500, the English contingent consisted of but 700 Marines. In the early days of January, 1862, the troops landed at Vera Cruz without resistance, under the command of the Spanish General Prim. The Allied Commissioners presently published a manifesto addressed to the Mexican people, declaring that neither conquest nor political dictation was the object of the Allied Powers, which had long beheld with grief a noble people 'wasting its forces and extinguishing its vitality in the violence of civil war and perpetual convulsions'; and who had now landed on their shores to give them an opportunity of constituting themselves in a permanent and stable manner. Yet all this time the views of the French Emperor were extended to ulterior aims of which his Allies never dreamed. When, after the issuing of the manifesto, the

Commissioners of the Allied Powers began to exchange ideas and to communicate to each other the exact nature of the instructions emanating from their respective Governments, the divergence of views between the French and the other two Commissioners soon became apparent. The object of England and Spain was simply, by occupying a portion of the Mexican seaboard, to obtain a material guarantee for the redress of the wrongs of which their subjects had to complain. But the French Commissioner—evidently with an eye to the eventual introduction of an Imperial régime—refused, on the pleas of perverseness, renewed outrages, and general impracticability, to hold any communication with the Juarez Government; and insisted that the proper course of action on the part of the Allied forces was to march on Mexico, the capital. Regarding their views and those of their French colleague as utterly irreconcilable, General Prim and Sir Charles Wyke, the Spanish and British Commissioners, withdrew from the expedition on the parts of their respective Governments. The English and Spanish squadrons put to sea; and the French expeditionary forces, about 6,000 strong, remained by themselves in Mexico.

In February the Mexican Government and the Allied plenipotentiaries signed respectively a preliminary convention confirming the authority of the President Juarez and the maintenance of the Mexican flag. Two months elapsed while the draft of the treaty was being sent to and returned from Europe, during which time the Allied forces occupied the towns of Cordova, Orizaba, and Tehuacan, quarters favourable to the health of the troops. But when at length the return of the treaty was

signalled, it was notified that France declared she could
not accept the Convention, as being 'counter to the
national dignity.'

The French General Lorencez was then commissioned
to open an offensive campaign at the head of the French
expeditionary corps, then in march towards Mexico.
When approaching the strong city of Puebla, the light-
hearted Lorencez did not take the trouble to make a
preliminary reconnaissance, imagining that the city before
him was friendly, and he was rudely surprised by meeting
on May 5, 1862 with a vigorous resistance on the part of
the Mexican garrison commanded by General Zaragoza.
Lorencez sustained a disastrous check and was compelled
to retire on Orizaba, where he was joined by Marquez
a general of the Church Party at the head of 2,500
men. It was not, however, deemed advisable to attempt
a fresh advance until a reinforcement of troops should
have been obtained from France. When apprised of
the Puebla repulse the French Emperor promptly
appointed General Forey to the chief command in
Mexico, and hurried him across the Atlantic with an
army 30,000 strong. It was expected that a force so
powerful would immediately take the offensive and that
a vigorous and decisive campaign would result. In his
instructions to General Forey the French Emperor
wrote : 'Our military honour engaged, the necessities of
our policy, the interests of our industry and commerce,
all combine to make it our duty to march on Mexico,
boldly to plant our flag there, and to establish either a
monarchy, if not incompatible with the national feeling,
or at least a Government which may promise some
stability.' If, he added, the respectable portion of

Mexican society should choose to adopt monarchical institutions, so much the better for all concerned.

Alertness, however, was not Forey's strong point. He had landed in the end of September, 1862, with a fresh and imposing army. The winter months are those most suited for military operations on the lofty plateaux dividing Orizaba from Mexico. But Forey's proceedings were so dilatory that he gave the Juarists time to prepare their defence, to muster their contingents, and to shelter Puebla behind a double barrier of ramparts and cannon. Five months of futility passed, until at length in April, 1863, the French army advanced slowly on Puebla. It was considered necessary to undertake a siege in regular form. On March 29 Fort San Xavier, one of the principal defences of Puebla, had been attacked and taken by assault. ' For the first time,' wrote General Forey, ' the Mexicans felt the points of our bayonets ; they gave way before the impetuosity of our attack.' Puebla surrendered on May 18, in rather extraordinary circumstances. As the supplies of the place were running short, General Ortega, who commanded the garrison, proposed to capitulate, but on condition that the garrison should be allowed to march out with all the honours of war, and with arms, baggage, and artillery to withdraw to the city of Mexico. General Forey refused to accept this proposal ; but agreed that the garrison might leave with all the honours, on condition, however, that they must march past the French army and lay down their arms, remaining prisoners of war. ' These proposals,' says General Forey in his despatch, ' were not accepted by General Ortega, who in the night between May 16 and 17 disbanded his command, destroyed their weapons, spiked the guns, blew up the powder magazines, and sent me an envoy to say that the garrison had completed its defence, and surrendered at discretion. It was scarcely daylight when 12,000 men, most of them without arms or uniforms which they had cast away in the streets, surrendered as prisoners ; and the officers, numbering from 1,000 to 1,200, of whom 26 were generals and 200 superior officers, informed me that they waited at the palace of the Government!' Although the besieged had given way and fallen into panic-stricken confusion, the command nevertheless was given by Forey to retire and abandon the positions already taken. This wretched siege lasted three days longer than that of Saragossa ; and but for the fortunate attack on the fort of Totime-huacan which caused the fall of the town, preparations must have been made to undergo the winter in front of the entrenchments of Puebla. After the capitulation the French march on Mexico would certainly have been deferred but for the interposition of the generals of division. This sheer folly would have had the effect of causing another siege, for the city of Mexico was surrounded by works which were about to be armed. Suddenly attacked, the capital made no resistance.

With the adverse result of the defence of Puebla, on which he had expended all his resources and in the attempt to relieve which General Comonfort had been defeated, Juarez had played his last card for the time. He fell back on San Luis de Potosi and on June 10 the French army entered the capital. In spite of the fireworks and flowers scattered in the path of Forey, the enthusiasm was only factitious. Juarez had not been

expelled by the will of the population of the capital.
The Chief of the State had yielded to *force majeure*, but
without compromise. He was brought down, but he
never abdicated. He took with him into his retreat the
Republican power, nor did he ever allow it to slip from
his grasp.

On June 14 a Provisional Government was constituted in the first instance, which presently convened a
'Junta of Notables.' This assembly was desired at the
instance of General Forey and of course under French
auspices, to determine after due deliberation what form of
Government should be definitely established in Mexico—
the vote on the question to unite at least two-thirds of
the suffrages. The phantom of a Junta was got together
somehow, held a meeting, and duly voted, to the sound of
the cannon which proclaimed the birth of the Empire.
The decision was in favour of a monarchy and the proffer
of the Crown to the Archduke Maximilian. A Commission was appointed to proceed to Miramar, bearing the
requisite documents and proffering the Imperial sceptre.
When the deputation presented itself at Miramar Maximilian hesitated—and well he might ; for he could not
but be aware that a burning principle of resistance against
monarchical institutions was tenaciously maintained by
a large proportion of the population of Mexico, and that
the aversion of the people of the United States from this
masterful conversion of their Republican neighbours to
Imperialistic sentiments was notorious. On the very
day on which the French troops entered Mexico city
brave old Juarez published from his retirement in San
Luis de Potosi a proclamation bearing the sternest
defiance. 'Concentrated on one point,' so spoke Juarez,

'the enemy will be free on all others; if he divides his forces, he will be weak everywhere. He will find himself compelled to acknowledge that the Republic is not shut up in the towns of Mexico and Puebla; that life, the consciousness of right and power, the love of independence and democracy, the noble pride aroused by the invasion of our soil are sentiments common to all the Mexican people.' Señor Doblado, a man of high character, was not less outspoken. 'In the bloody struggle,' said he, 'in which we are now engaged, there are only two camps—Mexicans and Frenchmen— invaded and invaders.'

Maximilian, as has been said, was hesitating; he at length made the declaration that he would accept the proffered Throne only 'on the condition of its being tendered to him as the result of a truly popular vote and secured by European guarantees.' Mexico meanwhile waited. The French arms were everywhere successful. Juarez had been driven from San Luis de Potosi and his adherents were weak and scattered. The gallant General Comonfort had been slain in battle. The Provisional Government was styled the 'Regency'; it had a triumvirate consisting of Generals Almonte and Salas, and the Archbishop of Mexico.

In October, 1863, General Bazaine took the Command-in-Chief out of the hands of General Forey, who had been promoted to be Marshal and had been recalled to France; he also assumed the functions which had devolved on M. de Saligny, who did not long delay in following the cunctatory captor of Puebla. When succeeding to the command Bazaine was preceded by a reputation for bravery which had its influence over the

Mexicans, who besides were not indifferent to his good-humour, so full both of heartiness and polish. They also felt flattered by hearing the French Commander-in-Chief speak the Spanish language, which he had learned during the last Spanish war. He acted with great promptitude. In six weeks the enemy was overthrown by the rapidity of his advance. The Franco-Mexican flag waved on all the plateaux from Morelia to San Luis, towns which Marquez and Mejia won brilliantly for the future Crown; and from Mexico to Guadalajara, which Bazaine after six weeks' rapid marching entered without striking a blow. This was a campaign entirely of speed, happily planned and promptly terminated. Never since 1821, the date of its independence, had Mexico enjoyed a calm equal to that which it experienced during the four months following this campaign in the interior.

The Mexican adventure had been from the first unpopular with the French people, and it served the enemies of the Empire as a weapon against the Government. M. Rouher, indeed, called it 'the greatest enterprise of the reign'; but in spite of the reports of the splendours and wealth of Mexico it never found favour even with the majority of the Legislative Body which voted the expedition. Two sinister influences combined to damage the enterprise in public opinion. The speculators for whom Morny acted were its main supporters; and from the time when war was made to establish a Catholic Empire in a continent almost exclusively Republican the Clerical Party alone defended it.

Nevertheless Maximilian in an evil hour allowed himself to be persuaded into accepting the Mexican

Crown. A Mexican loan of fifteen millions sterling was
placed on the principal European bourses, but the conditions were so onerous that Maximilian carried with him
to Mexico only a small portion of that great sum. By
the terms of his convention with Louis Napoleon of
April 10, 1864, it was arranged that a French corps of
25,000 men was to remain in Mexico until Maximilian
should have organised an army of his own ; and that on
the withdrawal of the French corps there should still
remain in Mexico for six years longer a force of 8,000
men, forming a foreign legion in the service of that
Empire. The Emperor of Austria also gave permission
for officers of the Austrian army to volunteer into the
Mexican foreign legion, retaining for six years their
Austrian military rank. In accordance with the convention Maximilian on April 10, 1864 formally accepted
the Mexican Crown ; and a few days later he and the
Empress with a large suite embarked on board the
Novara frigate for their new destination, halting on
their way to pay a short visit to Rome, where they had
an interview with the Pope. On May 28, 1864 the
new Sovereigns landed at Vera Cruz, where their reception was not propitious. After a rough journey
from the coast they made their entry into the capital
on June 12, followed by a brilliant cortège, and subsequent to a short sojourn in the Palace took up
their permanent residence in the adjacent château of
Chapultepec.

On Maximilian's arrival an active Imperialist party,
sincere and full of enthusiasm, was freely and spon-
taneously formed, captivated by the personal charm of
their Majesties. There was then a time when the young

Empire, in spite of the difficulty which the task promised, had a good chance for a great future. It was a fortunate hour for Mexico; but neither the monarch nor his subjects knew how to take advantage of it. Despite the loyal efforts of a wife abounding in illusions which were subsequently to be so painfully dissolved, Maximilian committed numerous errors, because with his mingled chivalric and undecided character he persisted in fancying that he was seated as on an European Throne. He could not have expected to conquer a turbulent kingdom with a bulletin of laws as his weapon; he should have been always in the saddle, with sword in hand.

It cannot be said, however, that he was inactive. During the autumn of 1864 he made considerable progress in pacifying the country and in endeavouring to crush the partisans of Juarez, who were defeated in a pitched battle at Durango in September. But Maximilian had unfortunately incurred the hostility of the powerful ecclesiastical interests of the country. The settlement of the mortmain endowments still remained in suspense. The Court of Rome had not yet consented to declare its sentiments; and it appeared the less inclined to do so as Maximilian, determined to uphold the law of secularisation, had in effect repudiated the Clerical Party to which he mainly owed his Crown. This sudden *volte-face* had but little disposed the Pope to make any concessions, for his Holiness in assisting an Austrian Archduke to place himself on an old Spanish throne had expected that the result would be to bring those distant lands into the bosom of the Church. On the other hand the holders of the clerical property professed themselves anxious for a settlement favourable to their interests,

although to a great extent their right of property had
originated in fraud.

By the end of the year armed resistance was almost
wholly subdued, while the French troops were in possession of the country from the Atlantic to the Pacific. The
new Empire seemed, to be making progress towards a
condition of prosperity. But the Church question remained unsettled, and Maximilian's Liberal proclivities
gave no hope of a reversal of the policy of confiscation.
In December, 1864, the Papal Nuncio, Monsignor
Meglia, arrived from Rome, to whom Maximilian presented a settlement of religious questions on the basis
of (1) the supremacy of the Catholic religion in Mexico,
(2) gratuitous religious ministration, (3) the support of
the Church at the cost of the State, and (4) the confirma-
tion of the law under which the Church lands had been
confiscated. The Nuncio positively refused to negotiate
on those terms, asserting that when he left the Vatican
the belief prevailed that the confiscation of the Church
lands was to be reversed. Maximilian, with whom
haughtiness and irritability were constitutional, promptly
ordered his Minister to submit to him Bills founded on
the basis specified; and he presently issued a decree
reviving an obsolete law requiring that Pontifical Bulls
and rescripts should receive the *exequatur* of the Government before publication. The Nuncio, protesting strenu-
ously, quitted Mexico, whereupon diplomatic relations
between Rome and the new Empire were entirely broken
off. No real progress was made towards conciliating
the Liberal Party, and it was certain that the measures
specified effectually offended and estranged the great
majority of the Conservatives.

At the beginning of 1865 tranquillity was for the most part established, while, as has been said, the French troops remained in possession of the country from shore to shore. The national army had been organised on the basis of the schemes proposed and elaborated by the military chiefs. The whole territory had been divided into nine military departments. On Jan. 26 the Emperor signed the military code of laws; and two months later he released the French head-quarter staff from its duties in a complimentary letter thanking Marshal Bazaine for his services in the re-organisation of the Mexican army, which the Minister of War had thenceforth to administer. But Maximilian unfortunately seemed incapable of realising that he was making no effective advance in attaching to his person and Government the Mexican nation or any considerable portion of it, and that he was still, as from the first, entirely dependent on French bayonets. On Oct. 3 of that year he promulgated the ill-omened and sinister decree which in its consequences ultimately proved fatal to himself—the condemnation to outlawry of all persons who thenceforward should be taken with arms in their hands. In virtue of this sweeping and outrageous decree several Juarists were actually shot by drumhead courts-martial, and extreme indignation was not un-naturally aroused by those summary executions not only among Mexican Republicans but also in the con-tiguous States of the American Union. In the inten-tion of Maximilian the decree was directed only against persons whose object was to shelter their brigandage under the Republican flag; but nevertheless the original minutes of the fatal decree were wholly written in the

Emperor's own hand. The date of its publication marked the beginning of Maximilian's progressive ill-fortune. The Civil War in the United States was now at an end and the undisguised objection of the American people to the intermeddling of the French Emperor in Mexican affairs, hitherto in abeyance during the war period, was beginning to have vent. In the course of the winter of 1865–66 the American General Sheridan continued covertly to supply arms and ammunition to the Mexican Liberals—more than 30,000 muskets were sent from Baton Rouge Arsenal alone; and by midsummer of 1866 Juarez, having organised a considerable army thanks to the goodwill of the North, was in possession of the whole line of the Rio Grande, and in fact of nearly the whole of Mexico down to San Luis de Potosi. In his message to Congress of Dec. 4, 1865, President Johnson had animadverted strongly on the outrage to Republican feeling which the situation beyond the Rio Grande presented to American eyes. He pointed out that the American people refrained from intervening in the affairs of Europe on the express condition that the European Powers should not interfere in the concerns of the New World ; and he added with grave significance : ' I should regard it as a great calamity to the peace of the world that any European Power should throw down the gauntlet to the American nation, as if to challenge it to the defence of Republicanism against foreign intervention.' With continuous steady pressure and in terms more and more peremptory, the American Government in the latter months of 1865 and during 1866 kept urging upon the French Emperor the recall of the French troops from Mexico. Napoleon hesitated in face of the terms of the convention of April 10, 1864 ; then he threw to the wind his pledged word to Maximilian. Rendered anxious because of the ominous condition of affairs in Germany which threatened to involve Europe in war, and reluctant to force the United States to extremities, the French Emperor at length decided to withdraw his troops from Mexico as soon as he could consistently with decency.

The year 1866 began under sad auspices. In the early part of January disaffection began to manifest itself on all sides in the very heart of the Empire. The situation had become extremely critical. The State Treasury was completely exhausted and the Mexican army was calling loudly for its pay. Maximilian realised that his Throne was imperilled. The state of his mind was depicted in the following lines : ' I know,' he wrote, ' that I have accepted a singularly difficult task ; but my courage is equal to supporting the burden and I will go on to the end.' The French Government, anxious to recoup for itself a portion of the expenditure incurred by the Mexican adventure, was severely exacting in regard to the Imperial loans of which it retained considerable amounts. After the ill-advised decree of October, 1865, Juarez and his partisans had been driven out of the settled districts by the French troops and compelled to resort to brigandage ; but the United States continued to recognise Juarez as President of Mexico. Marshal Bazaine, no doubt informed of Napoleon's real intentions, treated Maximilian with almost open contempt and acted in utter disregard of his wishes. The insurgents were well aware that the French Emperor was tired of Maximilian and of Mexico, and they became

more daring than ever. In April, 1866, was promulgated the decision of Napoleon that the French
troops would be withdrawn from Mexico between
November 1866 and November 1867. This decision
was in utter violation of the convention of April 10, 1864,
by the terms of which it had been agreed that the
French regular forces were to quit Mexico only when
Maximilian should have organised an army of his own ;
and that after their recall France should still let Mexico
have the services of 8,000 men as a foreign legion.
Scarcely two years had elapsed when those engagements
were abruptly broken, and then Napoleon cynically left
Maximilian to his fate.

The shipwreck of the Mexican enterprise, deservedly
doomed from the hour of its inception, was now almost
within sight. The efforts to organise a home army
failed for want of money. Quarrels broke out among the
foreign adventurers in Maximilian's service. As a last
despairing resort the Empress herself went to Europe in
the summer of 1866, in the forlorn hope of attempting to
shake the determination of Napoleon in regard to the
recall of the French troops in Mexico. 'Vainly did the
unfortunate Empress urge the arguments of justice,
honour, and good faith. Louis Napoleon was in an
ignoble alarm for himself and his dynasty ; and neither
tears nor eloquence availed to alter the resolve to which
selfish terror had given rise. Not only did he refuse
to prolong the period within which the troops were to
be withdrawn ; he brusquely informed Charlotte that
their departure would be hastened and that they would
be withdrawn in the beginning of 1867. This cruel
announcement seemed to close out all hope ; the brain of

the poor brave woman reeled; she went to Rome, and there during an interview with the Pope her reason gave way.'

In the latter months of 1866 the malcontents made rapid progress. As Marshal Bazaine gradually concentrated his troops in the capital previous to quitting Mexican ground, the Juarists followed closely and occupied province after province. Napoleon having determined to leave Maximilian to his fate was desirous, on account of the heavy expenses of the expedition, of saving from the wreck as much as possible for the benefit of the French Treasury. In October General Castelnau, sent by Napoleon, arrived with instructions to urge Maximilian to abdicate ; and also to treat with some Mexican chief who, in return for the possession of supreme power, would undertake the financial engagements with the French Treasury in which Maximilian had failed. The arrival of Castelnau impressed on Maximilian the conviction that he was definitively to be abandoned, and he quitted the capital for Orizaba on Oct. 21, in order to avoid General Castelnau. When the courier from Europe brought him the heart-rending details of the sad condition of the Empress, he retired to the Hacienda la Jalapilla, a retreat adjacent to the town of Orizaba. A portion of the Imperial baggage had already actually been sent on board the Austrian frigate *Dandolo* anchored in the roadstead of Vera Cruz; but he was still a prey to hesitation. He could not make up his mind to take any decided course, so great was the vacillation of his character and the extent of his reluctance. Probably he was finally influenced in some measure by a despatch forwarded from Vienna to the Austrian Ambassador to Mexico, which forbade

the Archduke to set foot on Austrian soil if he returned
to Europe bearing the title of Emperor. Yet he was
preparing to set sail for Europe without intention of
return, when a letter from M. Eloïn, the Belgian Coun-
cillor, was handed to him. Its tenor was such that
Maximilian, disregarding all the perils before him and
obeying only the voice of ambition, again grasped the
reins of power ; and, having resolved to commit himself
into the hands of the Clerical Party who promised him
both men and money, he prepared to make an appeal
to the Mexican people.   On Dec. 8 Bazaine, Castelnau,
and Dano the French Minister presented themselves
to Maximilian, strongly urging him to abdicate ; but he
had taken his line and would not leave it. An instruction from the French Emperor to Castelnau proves that
Napoleon was utterly indifferent as to the fate of
Maximilian, and cynically thought only of saving appear-
ances. 'To treat with Juarez,' he wrote, 'would look
too much like a defeat. Arrange with Bazaine and
Dano in order to obtain promptly the abdication of
Maximilian. . . . . Make all necessary arrangements
to embark the troops in February or March (1867).
To sum up, I see by your letter that you have quite
understood my intentions, which are to leave Mexico as
soon as practicable, while protecting our dignity and
French interests as much as possible.'

On his return to the capital Maximilian abandoned
the Palace of Chapultepec for a modest villa just outside the city.   In November and December, 1866, the
French troops were all concentrated at Mexico and
Vera Cruz ; in January, 1867, the embarkation was
begun and it was completed in February. Now his

own master, Maximilian acted with energy. Early
in January he had sent General Miramon with 6,000
men into the northern provinces on the errand of
repelling the advancing Juarists. But Miramon was
utterly defeated in the battle of San Jacinto (Jan.
27), and with the remnants of his broken army he fell back
on Potosi, whence with about 3,000 men he withdrew
into the fortified city of Queretaro, distant about 130
miles north-west of the capital, already occupied by
General Mejia. Maximilian, advancing from Mexico
with 6,000 men, joined Miramon and Mejia in Queretaro,
having left the Austrian legion to hold and protect the
capital. On Feb. 19 he finally entered Queretaro, where
he was presently besieged by the Liberal forces under
the command of General Escobedo. Maximilian's
environed army stood stoutly on the defensive, and also
made many gallant sorties in which the Emperor took
part; but he did not succeed in compelling the Juarists
to relinquish the siege. Provisions began to fall short
and on March 17 Maximilian sent out a strong detachment commanded by General Marquez, Chief of the
Staff, with orders to return with reinforcements and
supplies. Marquez, indeed, cut his way through the
hostile lines, but he never returned to Queretaro.
Having occupied the capital and gathered to his standard
the garrison of that city, instead of hastening to the relief
of the beleaguered Maximilian, Marquez marched towards Puebla with the intention of raising the siege of
that place, which was being hard pressed by Porfirio
Diaz; but on learning that Puebla had fallen he retraced
his steps. Before he could reach Mexico he was
attacked by the Juarists at San Lorenzo on April 1, and

was defeated after three days of irregular fighting. With
the remains of his army he re-entered Mexico, where he
assumed supreme power as Lieutenant-General of the
Empire.

In Queretaro after March 24 there remained no
more meat. The garrison held out manfully; but scanty
rations, constant fighting, and the duty of continual
harassing watchfulness had cruelly reduced its strength.
On May 14 it was decided in a council of war presided
over by the Emperor that a general assault should be
made against the lines of the besiegers, that being the
only alternative to death by hunger. On the same night,
however, whether by negligence or, as was generally
believed, by the treason of Colonel Lopez, Juarist
soldiers gained admission within the town, which by
dawn of the following morning was in full possession
of the enemy. Maximilian, Miramon, and Mejia were
made prisoners. The fate of the fallen Emperor was
not long delayed. The representatives of the foreign
Powers at Washington entreated the intervention of the
United States to save the life of Maximilian ; and Mr.
Seward did intervene accordingly, but without favourable result. The Juarists observed duly the forms and
ceremony usual with civilised nations ; they appointed
with no indecent haste the day for the trial of the fallen
Emperor, and he had the advantage of the services of
two eminent Mexican advocates. His trial by court-
martial was held at Queretaro, and on June 13 he was
condemned to death. On the 19th the sentence was
carried into execution. Maximilian confronted the firing
party with calm fortitude, and met his death like a hero.
The following particulars taken from the diary of Prince

Salm-Salm, who was the Emperor's aide-de-camp and who later met a soldier's death in the battle of Gravelotte, may be read with interest : 'The Emperor had attended mass and received the last sacraments early in the morning, and had afterwards been brought up in a *fiacre*, attended only by the priest Father Soria and his Hungarian servant Tudos, to the place of execution, a rocky hill outside the town, called Cerro de la Campaña. Miramon and Mejia were placed beside him. An officer and seven men now stepped forward till within a few paces before each of the three condemned. The Emperor went up to those before him, gave each soldier his hand and a Maximilian louis d'or (twenty pesos), and said: "*Muchachos!* (boys!) aim well. Aim right here," pointing to his heart. Then he returned to his stand, took off his hat, and wiped his forehead with his handkerchief. This and his hat he gave to Tudos, with the order to take them to his mother the Archduchess Sophia. Then he spoke with a clear and firm voice the following words :

'"Mexicans! persons of my rank and origin are destined by God either to be benefactors of the people or to be martyrs. Called by a great part of you, I came hither for the good of the country. Ambition did not bring me here ; I came animated with the best wishes for the future of my adopted country and for that of my soldiers, whom I thank, before my death, for the sacrifices they have made for me. Mexicans! may my blood be the last which shall be spilt for the welfare of the country ; and if it be necessary that its sons should still shed their blood, may it flow for its good, but never for treason. *Viva independencia! Viva Mexico!*"

' Looking around, the Emperor noticed not far from him a group of men and women who sobbed aloud. He looked at them with a mild and friendly smile; then he laid both his hands on his breast and looked forward. Five shots were fired and the Emperor fell on his right side, whispering slowly the word " Hombre." All the bullets had pierced his body and each of them was deadly; but the Emperor still moved slightly. The officer laid him on his back and pointed with his sword to Maximilian's heart. A soldier then stepped forward and sent another bullet into the spot indicated.'

The resistance of Marquez could not be prolonged after Maximilian's death, and Mexico opened its gates to the Juarists on June 20. The Liberals used their victory with moderation. No excesses were committed, no vindictive excesses were authorised. The Europeans who had become prisoners of war were well treated and finally set at liberty. Juarez was definitively re-elected President of the Mexican Republic in October 1867.

The tidings of the execution of the Emperor Maximilian reached the Tuileries on July 2, while the distribution of awards at the Great Exhibition of 1867 was in progress. One authority states that the proceedings were interrupted and that the Emperor and Empress were stricken with deep sorrow. Another chronicler has it that the Court went into deep mourning; that on the 14th a mass was performed in the chapel of the Tuileries for the repose of the soul of Maximilian; and that on Aug. 4 the Emperor and Empress, having thrown off their mourning, went to the theatre to see Mr. Sothern play ' Lord Dundreary.'

Maximilian's body was embalmed by his friends and

adherents and sent to Europe on board the frigate
Novara, the same ship which three years previously
had conveyed him to this new Empire, the short-lived
possession of the Throne of which had cost him his life.
The remains reached his family in the following year
and were pompously buried in January 1868, in the
Imperial vault under the Church of the Capuchins in the
New Market of Vienna, among the metal coffins of the
dead Hapsburgs from Matthias (1619) to Maria Theresa,
the Emperor Joseph II., Marie Louise and her son the
Duke of Reichstadt, and many others. The Empress
Charlotte lives partly in the solitude of Laeken, partly
in her villa of Miramar near Trieste.

CHAPTER XII

CONSTITUTIONAL REFORMS—SADOWA AND LUXEMBURG

THE Treaty of Cession of Savoy and Nice was signed in March, 1860. Cavour signed it only on a threat that if he refused the French troops would occupy Bologna and Florence. In the same month the feeling against the French Emperor ran so high in English political circles that the Queen wrote to Lord John Russell that she feared lest ere long the union of Europe for safety against a common enemy might become a painful necessity. Lord Palmerston left no doubt in the minds of the people as to the quarter whence they might apprehend invasion. In demanding a subsidy of nine millions sterling for purposes of fortification he said (July 23): 'The horizon is charged with clouds which betoken the likelihood of a tempest. The Committee of course knows that, in the main, I am speaking of our immediate neighbours across the Channel, and there is no use in disguising it.' In view of England's defensive preparations, the increase of her navy, and the creation of a volunteer force—not to speak of an European coalition against the French Empire—all idea of lightening the burdens of France by the reduction of her military budget appeared impossible. The Emperor protested, but in vain, that he had no dreams of conquest and no intention of marching on the Rhine. But Lord John Russell delivered a strong anti-Gallican speech in the House of Commons, in which he described the annexation of Savoy as an aggression which might lead the warlike French nation 'to call on its Government to commit other acts of aggression,' and he declared that the policy of England should be to seek fresh alliances. Count Persigny the French Ambassador in London, and the Emperor's kinsman the Comte de Flahault, warned the English Government that this language might precipitate war by aggravating the mutual irritation between the two countries. The danger, however, was averted when Lord John stated later that as the French Emperor had undertaken to consult the European Powers regarding the neutralised portions of Savoy, the question might be regarded as satisfactorily settled. But although Lord Palmerston had written in January that 'there was no ground for imputing to Napoleon unsteadiness of purpose in regard to his views about Italy,' the idea had become fixed in the mind of the English Premier that the French Emperor was working his way to an opportunity for avenging Waterloo.

It was scarcely a favourable time, when the two nations were on unfriendly terms, for settling between them the terms of an international commercial treaty. But this great work, thanks to the devoted exertions of Mr. Cobden and to the patience and intelligence of the Emperor, became an accomplished fact in 1860. The broad lines of the famous treaty may be shortly stated. France undertook to reduce all duties on English manufactures 30 per cent. as a maximum and on English coal and coke to fifteen centimes the 100 kilo-

grammes.   England abolished duties on French manufactures, and reduced the duty on wines to one shilling
a gallon, rising to two in proportion to alcoholic strength.
The most-favoured-nation clause gave to each country
the benefit of any reduction or remission of duty either
might grant to a third Power.   The treaty was signed
for ten years, and within those ten years the value of
imports from France to England was more than
doubled.

A meeting of the French Emperor with the Prince-
Regent of Prussia (later Kaiser William I.) and with the
Sovereigns of Germany then at Baden-Baden, took place
there on June 16, 1860.   The Emperor at once explained
that he had sought the interview as an earnest of his
pacific intentions and to dispel the excitement which an
apprehension regarding his designs on a portion of their
country had given rise to among the Germans.   Nothing,
he said, could be further from his thoughts than to dis-
sever any territory from Germany and incorporate it with
France.   So clamorous, however, remarked the Emperor,
had been the outcry of the German Press, that something must be done to convince Germany of his sincerity.
What form should this take?   Nothing could be easier,
was the reply.   Most of the German Sovereigns were
then in Baden.   Let the Emperor tell them what he had
told the Prince-Regent, and the news of his desire to
refrain from disturbing Germany would speedily permeate
the country.   While the guest of the Grand Duke at
Baden the Emperor met in the course of a single day
the Kings of Würtemberg, Bavaria, Saxony and
Hanover, the Grand Dukes of Hesse-Darmstadt and
Saxe-Weimar, the Dukes of Nassau and Saxe-Coburg-

Gotha, and the Prince of Hohenzollern. It was quite a 'parterre of Princes.' When the Emperor returned to Paris on the 19th, the 'Moniteur' announced that 'his spontaneous mission of peace and goodwill would tend to consolidate the peace of Europe.'

On June 24 of this year died the ex-King Jerome, the last surviving brother of Napoleon the Great. In the autumn the Emperor made a progress through his recent acquisitions of Savoy and Nice and paid a visit to the cradle of his race in Corsica. The year ended sadly—in September the Empress lost her beloved sister, the Duchess of Alba; and in the winter, because of domestic disagreements the Empress made a journey to Scotland. She visited the Queen (Dec. 4), who recorded in her diary: 'She looked thin and pale . . . as amiable and natural as ever.'

In the autumn of 1860 the Emperor communicated to M. Rouher his resolution to liberalise the Parliamentary methods of the Empire. The important step by which he intended to institute debates on the Address, and to make other considerable advances towards a free Constitutional Government, was stubbornly resisted by the adviser in whom he had the fullest trust. M. Rouher believed that public opinion neither expected nor desired Constitutional Reform, and that the Sovereign in endeavouring to disarm the opposition of a few irreconcilables was running the risk of reducing that strength which the Imperial Government undoubtedly possessed with the consent of the immense majority of the country. The Emperor, on the other hand, insisted that the time had come to give the Senate and the Legislative Body liberty to reply frankly, after a free debate, to the speech of the Sovereign at the opening of the session ; and he resolved to select two Ministers who should act as the exponents of the Government policy. M. Billault was ultimately given the position of chief spokesman for the Government in both Chambers—a position filled by him with consummate tact and force until his death in October, 1863. The Government was unquestionably strong at the commencement of the new departure. Persigny was Minister of the Interior, Forcade la Roquette was Minister of Finance, Thouvenel was Foreign Minister, Baroche was president of the Council of State, Walewski was Minister of State, and Rouher held the portfolio of Agriculture and Commerce. Morny since 1854 had been the skilful and accomplished President of the Corps Législatif. Inclined by education in favour of Parliamentary Government he approved of the new order of things ; and Captain Bingham truly remarks that his commanding intellectual resources would have achieved for him lasting fame had his public services not been tarnished by the private vices causing his premature death, which occurred on March 10, 1865, after a brief illness. He had lived a profligate and reckless life, and when his end was near he had to choose between renouncing the pleasures and sins of the world and a sudden ending. He chose the latter. Shortly before he died he received a visit from the Emperor, who found the Comte de Flahault by the bedside of his wayward son. The Comte had been the lover of Queen Hortense, the mother of Napoleon III. ; Morny was therefore the half-brother of Louis Napoleon ; yet the brothers by the mother's side had never met until a short time before the *Coup d'État.* The Prince made Morny Minister of the Interior ; but he resigned that position when his half-brother the Prince-President confiscated the property of the Orleans family.   Subsequently he became President of the Chamber, where he was in his element.   He was not only a man of great natural politeness, but there was also an indefinable charm in his manner which disarmed faction.   His personal appearance was greatly in his favour ; he was distinguished rather than handsome. He was succeeded as President of the Chamber by Count Walewski, a natural son of the first Napoleon by a Polish lady.

The experiment of the license of speech permitted under the constitutional *régime* evoked the dangers which might have been anticipated.   The session of 1861 was marked by the violence of the active Parliamentary Opposition which the new prerogatives called into existence.   The Emperor was painfully impressed by the uncompromising tone of the Opposition speeches ; but, although disappointed, he was resolute to persevere in the policy of Liberalism.   Taking account of an Opposition numerically insignificant but formidable because of the distinguished men it included, the Emperor strengthened the hands of M. Billault by creating in him a Minister of State who should be in reality First Minister ; in whom the policy of the Government should be centralised, who should be responsible for all the departments of the Administration to the Emperor, and who should be able to speak with full authority for the Sovereign and the Government before the Senate and the Legislative Body.   At the same time M. Rouher was invested with the functions of President of the Council of State.   This arrangement, in effect, was the beginning of a system of Ministers responsible to the Chambers. But M. Billault did not live to assume the new functions confided to him. That strong and brilliant statesman died suddenly on Oct. 13, 1863. He was succeeded by M. Rouher, who thenceforth became the Emperor's most powerful subject and supporter.

The powerful Opposition of the new Chamber gave the Government an immediate indication of its hostile temper. In the opening speech of the session of 1865 the Emperor complained of the revolutionary harangues in the Corps Législatif and the agitation outside, by which his advances had been met. He exhorted the Senators and Deputies to oppose the supporters of changes suggested with the sole object of sapping the foundations of the edifice. In March, M. Ollivier appealed to the Government now that it was firmly established, to grant to the people political liberty as well as civil liberty. 'While,' said he, 'it was foolish to yield to clamour, it was dangerous to postpone concessions until popular anger had been aroused. Now was the right moment—neither too soon nor too late.' M. Thiers followed with a description of the liberties requisite for true national freedom. For himself, he required personal liberty, electoral liberty, free speech, and a free Press ; these constituted his 'missionaries of liberty.' Those phrases were caught up and bandied about. The time for the attack was ill-chosen ; for so complete was the freedom of the working classes to combine that Paris was without cabs owing to a strike of the cabmen. This episode occurred when the Emperor was making a tour in Algeria in 1865. The Empress, who was acting as Regent, was implored to interfere in order to compel the cabmen to resume work ; but she resolutely declined to meddle with the liberty which had just been granted. In the session of 1866 MM. Buffet and Thiers were the chief spokesmen of the Opposition ; and they asked for nothing that should not have been granted or which the Emperor was not anxious to grant to loyal men. But the six years of constitutional government had developed, not reform, but the sinister purposes of a masked revolutionary party. The result as a whole disappointed the Emperor, and he betrayed his chagrin when in his reply to the address of 1866 he said significantly : 'We are in quest of that liberty which enlightens and discusses the conduct of the Government, and not that which becomes an arm to undermine and destroy it.'

The part taken by France and England in the negotiations preceding and following the invasion of Denmark by the Austrians and Prussians was not creditable to either. It was proposed that the two Powers should offer mediation on the basis of the treaty engagements of 1852. A declinature on the part of Germany was to be met by a British squadron at Copenhagen and a French army corps on the Rhine frontier ; but to this proposal both France and Russia declined to agree. The Emperor Napoleon was in no mood to accept suggestions from the English Ministers, having in his mind the defeat of the Congress he had proposed—a defeat which was in the main their work. He met the proposal of England with cold reserve when she suddenly turned to him to co-operate with her. In June the British Government applied to the French

Emperor a second time to co-operate actively in defence
of the Danes. The Emperor again declined the terms
offered by England, but tendered his moral support.
The comparatively petty share of France in those
transactions must be attributed in great part to the state
of the Emperor's health, as well as to the condition
of perplexity and mistrust in which the failure of the
Congress had left him. When in June Lord Cowley
pressed him to go to war in alliance with England, the
Emperor was suffering acutely from the cruel disease
the character of which his physicians long misunder-
stood. He hesitated to commit the fortunes of his
country and his dynasty to the issues of a great war,
and the English Government took advantage of his
characteristic indecision to declare in Parliament that
since France would not fight for the treaty of 1852
England must decline to enter single-handed into the
fray.

The future of the Elbe Duchies was being played
pitch-and-toss with for the best part of a year ; but the
details of the nefarious game were too intricate to
be followed here. The Gastein Convention signed on
Aug. 14, 1865, provided that Austria should sell to Prussia
the Duchy of Lauenburg for 2,500,000 thalers ; thus
making market of rights of which she was but a trustee
for the German Confederation. The Confederation was
naturally offended by this trafficking ; and the Prussian
Parliament denounced the transaction for which it
assumed that Prussia would have to find the cash. But
King William drew this sting from his refractory
Commons ; he paid Austria for Lauenburg out of his
own private purse.

The Convention of Gastein was but a truce. Meanwhile, since Bismarck was not yet certain of the neutrality of France nor his alliance with Italy complete, he repaired to Biarritz to feel the pulse of the French Emperor.

Mr. Jerrold, in this matter, is not so accurate as usual. He says that 'the Emperor was in no mood to enter into fresh complications'; that 'the Emperor was favourable to the formation of a powerful Prussia'; that 'above all, he desired to finish his work as the emancipator of Italy'; and that 'it was on this desire that Bismarck worked to obtain his alliance with Victor Emanuel and to ensure the neutrality of France in the event of a war between Prussia and Austria.' He adds: 'The Emperor was sick in mind and body, and he was served by negotiators who were pigmies in the hands of the Minister of King William. He was a dreamer, of benevolent intentions; and he permitted an unscrupulous rival to outwit him, to use him, to cheat him, and at length to overcome him.'

As a matter of fact, it is difficult to particularise the dark, shifting, and tortuous policy pursued by the Emperor Napoleon during all this momentous time. The irritable jealousy of the French nation had been aroused by the success of the Prussian arms against Denmark; a Protestant Power was bidding fair to rally all Germany round itself, and to contest the palm of Continental supremacy with France. The speech of May 3, 1866, delivered by Thiers in the Corps Législatif betrayed an arrogant bitterness against the designs and ambition of Prussia which excited a wild hurricane of applause. The Emperor himself was not so effusive;

he even assumed a regard for the Power whose expansion he desired to limit. His policy, according to Louis Napoleon himself, aimed at ' the preservation of the European equilibrium and the maintenance of the work which we have helped to raise in Italy '—' Italy shall be free from the Alps to the Adriatic!'[1] And how did Napoleon proceed to attempt the preservation of the balance of power? By setting Prussia and Austria at daggers drawn and by attempting to reap the profits of their quarrel, in the shape, for instance, of the left bank of the Rhine. Should he aid Prussia to accomplish her purposes, that might be the price of his assistance. Should Prussia be beaten by Austria—and he sincerely hoped and believed she would—then he might claim the same or some such territory as the equivalent for his intervention in favour of the defeated. It was true that Napoleon, like another Iago feigning horror at the brawl between Cassio and Roderigo, made a show of proposing that they should submit their quarrel to a European Congress at Paris—a proposal which, though accepted by Prussia, was virtually rejected by her rival ; but he had previously plied Bismarck with offers of alliance against Austria, of which the main objects were the cession of the Elbe Duchies to Prussia, of Venetia to Italy, and of more than the left bank of the Rhine to France.

That there may be no question on this point, the text of the proposed treaty is quoted from Bismarck's famous Circular Despatch of July 29, 1870. Bismarck wrote : ' In May, 1866, those pretensions (of Napoleon) assumed the form of an offensive and defensive alliance, of which

[1] Memorandum by the Emperor to M. Drouyn de Lhuys, June 11, 1866.

the following extract has remained in my hands' : (1) In the event of a Congress, to arrange for the cession of Venetia to Italy and the annexation of the Elbe Duchies by Prussia. (2) If the Congress does not come off, an offensive and defensive alliance. (3) The King of Prussia to commence hostilities within ten days after the breaking-up of the Congress. (4) If the Congress does not meet, Prussia shall attack within thirty days after signature of the present treaty. (5) The Emperor of the French to declare war against Austria so soon as war shall have begun between Austria and Prussia. (6) No separate peace to be made with Austria. (7) Peace to be made under the following conditions :—Venetia to Italy ; to Prussia the following German territories, seven or eight million souls, as agreed on, in addition to federal reform in the Prussian sense ; to France the territory between the Moselle and the Rhine without Coblentz or Mayence, comprising 500,000 Prussian souls ; to Bavaria the left bank of the Rhine, Birkenfeld, Homburg, Darmstadt, 213,000 souls. (8) Military and Naval Convention between France and Prussia immediately on signature. (9) Adhesion of the King of Italy.

'The impossibility,' wrote Bismarck in the same despatch, 'of accepting any proposal of the kind was clear to me from the first ; but I thought it useful and in the interest of peace to leave to the French statesmen their favourite illusions as long as possible, without giving them even my verbal assent. I assumed that the destruction of hopes entertained by France would endanger peace, which it was the interest of Germany and Europe to maintain. . . . I kept silence regarding the demands made and pursued a dilatory course, without making any promises.' In denying charges brought against him by Benedetti and La Marmora he continued : ' I never pledged or promised anyone the cession of even so little as a German hayfield ; and I declare everything that has been said on this subject to be lies invented to blacken my character.'

It is a fact, although the thing seems incredible, that while Napoleon was tempting Bismarck with offers of an alliance against Austria he was simultaneously treating secretly with Francis Joseph for the cession of Venetia in return for Silesia, the province most prized by the Prussian monarch and his subjects.[1] And while negotiating separately and secretly with the two sworn enemies, he affected to prove his own disinterestedness by suggesting the submission of their quarrel to a European Congress. Bismarck, yielding to the inclination of the King, accepted the proposal of Napoleon ; but as he hoped and knew she would, Austria rejected it and the Congress was a failure.

On the morrow of Sadowa (July 4, 1866) the ' Moniteur' contained the following announcement :

' An important event has occurred.

' After having vindicated the honour of his arms in Italy the Emperor of Austria, acceding to the views of the Emperor Napoleon as expressed in his letter to his Minister of Foreign Affairs on June 11, cedes Venetia to the Emperor of the French, and accepts his mediation

[1] Professor von Sybel, Keeper of the Prussian State Archives, in his pamphlet on *Napoleon III.*, published 1873, says : ' While thus he (Napoleon) spoke openly for Prussia at Auxerre, he was carrying on profoundly secret negotiations with Austria. . . . And thus it was that Napoleon concluded with her (Austria, on June 9, 1866) a secret treaty, by which, in the event of a successful war, the Emperor Francis Joseph was to cede Venetia and receive for it Silesia, at the cost of Prussia.'

to arrange a peace between the belligerents. The Emperor Napoleon has hastened to respond to his appeal ; and has immediately addressed himself to the Kings of Prussia and Italy to arrange the terms of an armistice.'

After the battle of Sadowa, and onward to the signature of the Treaty of Prague on Aug. 23, the hesitations and discussions in the Imperial Councils were of the most lamentable kind. The Emperor was very ill, and anxious to find relief at Vichy from excruciating suffering. It was scarcely to be wondered at that a ruler who was grossly ignorant of the true state of his own army should have misjudged the military condition of his neighbour ; and his errors on this score had landed him in a most deplorable dilemma. In reply to a telegram from Napoleon, King William answered that 'we are prepared to accept your mediation, but of an armistice there can be talk only when we get from Austria the pledge of an acceptable peace.' 'What is your " pledge of an acceptable peace " ?' asked Napoleon, whose conception of the duty of a mediator was peculiar ; for he had undertaken to intervene on behalf of fallen Austria, and yet was willing, for a solid consideration, to mediate in favour of Prussia. The answer from Bismarck was : 'Exclusion of Austria from the German Confederation, erection of a new Federal State under Prussia, and her acquisition of certain lands previously interfering with her free and natural development.'

Monsieur Benedetti, the French Ambassador to Berlin, made his appearance at the Prussian headquarters and made himself cheerfully fussy in the business of mediation. After much journeying to and fro between the Prussian headquarters and Vienna he brought out to

Nikolsburg where the King and Bismarck were residing, the triumphant news that with infinite pains he had prevailed on Francis Joseph to accept the proposals of Napoleon as the basis of negotiations. With perfect frankness Bismarck declared that while the King was willing to accept the Napoleonic suggestions as the base of a five days' armistice, the main condition of a definite peace could only be the cession to Prussia of Hanover, Saxony, and Hesse. Benedetti affected to believe that in making such 'monstrous demands' Bismarck was not in earnest. Bismarck retorted that none of the European States would seriously oppose the designs of Prussia. 'What of France?' asked Benedetti. 'Your Emperor,' said Bismarck, 'cannot dispute our right to annex the territories specified.' 'Perhaps not,' answered Benedetti, slyly, 'on condition of your giving us Mayence and restoring us the Rhine frontier of 1814.' Bismarck quietly observed that the question of 'compensation' to France could best be settled after the conclusion of peace with Austria, which meanwhile was the most pressing matter in hand. Benedetti assented; and a week later Bismarck coolly informed him that the preliminaries of peace had been duly signed by himself and the two Austrian plenipotentiaries, without any participation on the part of the French representative.

The following is an extract from a speech of Bismarck in the Reichstag, May 2, 1871 : 'On Aug. 6, 1866, I was treated to a visit from the French Ambassador who in brief language delivered the ultimatum—Cede Mayence to France, or expect an immediate declaration of war. Of course I did not hesitate one second with my answer, and it was, "Very well, then ; let there be war !" With this reply M. Benedetti went back to Paris, where they thought over the matter and gave me to understand that his (Benedetti's) first instructions were extorted from the Emperor during his illness.'   A letter from Benedetti to Bismarck dated Aug. 5, 1866 enclosed the draft of a treaty in the handwriting of the former, the terms of which are as follows : ' France to regain the territory, at present belonging to Prussia, which was French in 1814 ; Prussia to obtain from the King of Bavaria and the Grand Duke of Hesse the cession of the territory which they possess on the left bank of the Rhine, and to transfer the same to France : All provisions which attached to the Germanic Confederation the territories placed under the Sovereignty of the King of the Netherlands, as well as those relative to the right of garrison in the fortress of Luxemburg.'   The South German States had already agreed to sign secret treaties conferring the command of their respective armies on the King of Prussia in the event of a national struggle.   Those treaties were signed on Aug. 22, the very day before the signature of the Treaty of Prague which secured to the Southern States ' an international and independent existence ' ; but the fact was kept secret until the following year, when it was divulged as a counter-stroke to the schemes of Louis Napoleon.

On his return from Vichy early in August the French Emperor found the situation very gloomy.   Benedetti had brought back to Paris the utter refusal on Bismarck's part to take into consideration the claims of France to obtain such an accession of territory as would redress the balance of power, disturbed by the immense conquests of Prussia.   France had been used by the Prussian states-

man while he needed her help ; but now he required her
no longer. When a negotiator was sent him from Paris
with a memorandum in which the establishment of a
neutral State on the Rhine frontier was submitted,
Bismarck declined to receive the French envoy and
referred him to an underling, who told him that Prussia
would listen neither to territorial compensations nor to
the neutralisation of German territory. Even the clause
which had been inserted in the peace preliminaries at the
instance of France in favour of North Sleswig was on
the point of having been omitted from the definitive
treaty, so defiant had the Iron Count become between
Nikolsburg and Prague under the influence of victory.
He bluntly declared that he owed no wages to France ;
he described her proceedings as a policy of *pour-boires* ;
and his countrymen, emulating his spirit, laughed at
caricatures in the shop-windows of Berlin which presented Napoleon in ridiculous and abject attitudes. A
Prussian member of the Paris Jockey Club angered the
young Frenchmen of society by laying a heavy bet that
Bismarck would not let France have the smallest German
village. He won his bet.

It would seem that the *rôle* of Benedetti was to
indite, *ipso manu*, draft treaties of a more or less
nefarious character, which were cynically dictated by
Bismarck and then locked up until a time should come
when they might advantageously see the light. The most
memorable of those drafts was revealed to an indignant
Europe in the columns of 'The Times' a few days after
the commencement of the Franco-German War. It was
pretended by Benedetti that this shameful abortive treaty
was the suggestion of Bismarck ; who, he said, offered

Belgium and Luxemburg to France in return for the latter's aid in 'crowning his work and extending the domination of Prussia from the Baltic to the Alps.' If Bismarck made such a proposal, it could only have been with the object of befooling the simple Benedetti, with whom he seems to have taken a cruel pleasure in amusing himself.

Sadowa stuck in the throat of France ; and the master-men of Prussia recognised from the hour of that victory that as the outcome of it Prussia would either have to fight France, or have to make some such concession to France as would smooth her national vanity ruffled by Sadowa. Less purposeful, less resolute, less gifted with the power of concentration, France foresaw war not less clearly than did Prussia. While the latter accepted the inevitable, the former created and maintained it. The French nation and its head acted and reacted in a curious mutually detrimental fashion. Napoleon might have preferred a quiet life ; but he had quite enough of acuteness to perceive how dangerous it was, unprepared, to create or confront serious contingencies. But if he would pursue an unaggressive policy and let France enjoy quiet, then France proceeded to give him trouble and endanger his personal position by clamouring for the concession of Liberal institutions. That kind of concession, he perfectly realised, led straight up to the end of him. But he could maintain his position only by diverting the nation from hankering after liberty and by concentrating its interest in a brilliant and flashy foreign policy. So he was always, to use a military simile, sapping up to a great *coup* in the effort to keep France in a state of excitement. But France did not find the engineering process sufficiently interesting to lure her from agitation for internal reforms ; and the Emperor had to be making concessions most of his time.

A fine opportunity seemed to offer itself to Napoleon in the beginning of 1867. The King of Holland was also Grand Duke of Luxemburg. When the Germanic Confederation broke up, the King of Holland acquired full sovereign rights over Luxemburg. It was against the policy of the new Confederation to have included in it possessions belonging to foreign rulers, and no pressure was exerted to bring Luxemburg within its pale. A Prussian garrison, however, still continued to occupy its fortress although that fortress had been defederalised ; and the right was not actively challenged by the King of Holland. He had no particular fondness for his Luxemburg possession, and he was a man to whom money was always peculiarly acceptable. He had no objection to enter into an arrangement with France whereby the latter was to acquire the Grand Duchy by purchase. On the French side there was anxiety that the negotiation should be kept secret from Prussia till the bargain had been carried out ; but the King of Holland did not see his way to this and formally notified Prussia of the transaction in progress. Prussia withheld her assent and further refused to withdraw the garrison. The Duchy was German soil and the public feeling of Germany ran high against any alienation of it. On the other hand France was in a state of acute excitement. Her national jealousy of Prussia lowering luridly ever since Sadowa, flashed out vehemently against the idea that an arrangement to which the Emperor of the French had agreed

was to be abandoned merely because Prussia thought fit
to forbid it.

War seemed imminent; yet the guiding forces on
neither side really desired war. It has been said that
Bismarck had great difficulty in restraining King
William from responding actively to the fervid demands
of his people; but this apparently was only gossip.
Prussia would fight if need were; but she was not yet
quite ready for war. On the other hand, Napoleon was
not eager for the fray. He would have been the reverse
of eager had he come to the knowledge of the condition
in which his army was; but he was not a man who
searched deeply into things. Both nations were nevertheless arming when the intervention of the European
Powers effected a settlement. The Duchy became a
neutral State under the guarantee of the Powers.
Luxemburg was to cease to be a fortified city and the
Prussian garrison was withdrawn. War, at least for the
moment, was averted; and there were sanguine people
who believed that an era of lasting peace had dawned on
Europe.

The ink of the treaty was scarcely dry when King
William accompanied by his great Minister arrived in
Paris on a visit to the Emperor Napoleon. It was the
summer of the Great Exhibition of 1867, when Napoleon
was on the summit of the great soap-bubble he had blown
and when he was able to vie with his illustrious relative
in the temporary possession of a 'parterre of Princes.'
The Tzar had arrived in advance of King William and
was residing in the Élysée. The Crown Prince and
Princess of Prussia were already in Paris before the King
arrived on June 5. Bismarck had fired his salute to

France before leaving Berlin, in the announcement that he had concluded with the South German States a full understanding between them and the North German Confederation. At the railway station his Majesty was received by the Emperor accompanied by the Ministers and Marshals of the Empire, and was escorted to his quarters in the Pavilion Marsan, one of the wings of the Tuileries. After presenting his obeisance to the Empress his hostess the King went to visit the Tzar in the Élysée, who returned the visit next morning. Later in the day Napoleon and his guests drove to Longchamps to witness on that field a review of 60,000 French soldiers. It was not the first review that William had seen there, nor was it to be the last. In 1814 he had witnessed the combined hosts of Prussia, Austria, and Russia march past the saluting-point; at which a Russian, an Austrian, and a Prussian monarch sat on horseback. Russian and Prussian monarchs were now again at the same saluting-point; the grandson of Francis was to come later—for the moment he was being crowned King of Hungary on the Krönungsberg of Pesth. Four years later William was to look again on an armed pageant on the Long-champs sward, when his host of 1867 was to be his prisoner and the troops he was to review the conquerors of France.

Bismarck made himself visible to the Parisians in his Landwehr cuirassier uniform crowned by the spiked helmet; and it is recorded that the Parisians 'were getting reconciled to him on account of his martial bearing in the field.' Neither the Tzar nor the King was very popular in Paris. Cries of *Vive la Prusse !*' were few and far between; and the angry shouts of

'*Vive la Pologne!*' had been yelled at Alexander ever since he had stepped out of the Gare du Nord. But at all events nobody tried to shoot William, whereas Berezovski interfered with the Tzar's ability to boast of the same immunity. After *fête* on *fête*, on the 14th the King bade adieu to his host and hostess and was back in his own capital next day. His simplicity of manner was noted by the Parisians, just as the English in 1814 had marked that characteristic of his father. To a fussy official he quietly said : ' Pray make no bother on my account—regard me as one visitor more to Paris.' When he went away he simply thanked the Emperor very warmly for the cordial reception he had met with, and left 40,000 francs to be distributed among the servants who had attended on him.

Notwithstanding the courtesies which passed in Paris in the course of the Exhibition of 1867, there was no love lost between France and Prussia ; and no little jealousy was caused on the part of the German people by the famous ' Salzburg Interview ' which made some stir throughout a great part of the Continent. Accompanied by his consort, the Emperor Napoleon in the course of the latter half of August 1867 travelled through South Germany on his way to meet their Austrian Majesties at Salzburg. The ostensible reason for this journey on the part of the French Imperial couple was simply the desire to offer their personal condolences to Francis Joseph on the tragic end of his brother Maximilian of Mexico, who had fallen a victim to that French propensity to interference with the concerns of others which now roused the ill-feeling of Germany. That State did not believe that Napoleon's visit to Salzburg was so simple as was avowed ; and he himself had considerable reason to recognise this incredulity in the course of his courageous passage through South Germany. Official courtesy, it is true, was frigidly observed for the most part ; but at Augsburg some hospitable cheers were instantly drowned in angry hisses and yells. The press of Germany raised its voice unanimously in no ambiguous tone against the tortuous and time-seeking foreigner whom it believed to be plotting against the unification of the Fatherland.

CHAPTER XIII

THE OUTBREAK OF THE FRANCO-GERMAN WAR

THINGS were going wrong in France. Dear bread in the rigorous winter of 1868 and a consequent scarcity of work served the turn of an implacable Opposition. Seditious cries had been heard in the streets: the 'Marseillaise' had been sung with the result of arrests and imprisonments. The Finance Minister had to put forth a huge loan of twenty-eight millions sterling in order to bring into system the resources of the State. The Government had asked that the army, with the reserve, should be increased to a strength of 750,000 men ; and that the Garde Mobile, which was expected to afford some 300,000 men in the course of a few years, should be instituted as a second reserve. M. Thiers contended that the army was strong enough ; that there would always be time to organise the Garde Mobile in rear of the 500,000 regular troops when war should threaten ; and that M. Rouher had exaggerated the military resources of the great European Powers. MM. Rouher and Baroche, and above all Marshal Niel, supported the Government measure. Its necessity was manifested by the persistence with which the Opposition described France as being at the mercy of Germany ; yet it was denounced by the enemies of the Government as an additional burden wantonly cast upon a suffering people.

How unpopular had become the Government towards the close of 1868 was manifested curiously. The Day of the Dead in November was turned by the Parisians to a political account. The grave was casually discovered of Baudin, a leader of the Reds in the *Coup d'État*, who had been shot on a barricade in that bloody time. For seventeen years Baudin had lain in his forgotten grave, when it was suddenly recollected that he had fallen in resisting the myrmidons of Napoleon, and that he perished in the defence of what was then the law and the Constitution. The opportunity of gratifying dislike of the Emperor was promptly seized. It was proposed to erect a monument to the memory of this enemy of tyranny. The suggestion was eagerly caught at, but probably it would have soon faded out, and Baudin's name would have fallen back into the oblivion from which it was temporarily exhumed, had not the Emperor and his advisers resolved to treat this petty matter as a case of sedition and to prosecute those who had subscribed to the monument as well as the newspapers which had published the subscriptions. Such incidents, though comparatively trivial in themselves, served to indicate the spirit of the nation. If anything was made clear, it was that the Napoleonic dynasty was not taking firm root in France. The masses were the reverse of conciliatory to the Imperial Government. In every vacancy in the Legislative Chamber where there was a chance of independent success the Imperialist candidate was defeated and a candidate hostile to the dynasty was elected. The plebiscite of May, 1870 was little else than a gigantic fraud, notwithstanding the boasted figures.

In August, 1869 Marshal Niel died suddenly, and was unfortunately succeeded by Lebœuf as War Minister. Marshal Niel had been the soul of the military reorganisation which was in progress when he was lost to France. He left his task far from complete, and his successor was not the man to carry out the undertaking. It is true that when Marshal Niel died the Garde Mobile was little more than a project. But he had pushed forward the manufacture of the chassepots that were to carry farther than the Prussian needle-guns, and it was under his superintendence that the first experiments with the mitrailleuses were conducted. Niel was an engineer officer of the highest capacity, who had served with distinction in Africa, the Crimea, and in Italy ; he was popular with the people and enjoyed the entire confidence of the Emperor. In the course of this year the life of Louis Napoleon hung in the balance for weeks. The Opposition journals bitterly assailed the sick man. Not content with the exaggeration of every unfavourable rumour and *canard*, the more venomous journals called into their service medical writers of the baser sort, to inform their readers how soon the unfortunate Emperor would probably die. The brutality of the articles on the sufferer that appeared in the 'Rappel' and the 'Réveil' would not have been tolerated in England for a day. It was announced that the Emperor read the medical articles in which he was sent to an almost immediate death, and which informed his subjects how the vital functions would soon fail to repair the waste of force caused by his ailment. He was a brave man—brave to stoicism ; and he endured with calmness the perusal of the gutter literature. Rochefort, who was supposed to be a gentleman, allowed himself to speak of the Emperor as 'the lodger of the Tuileries'—as it happened it was in St. Cloud where the Emperor lay ill.

The session of 1869 was closed in November with a speech by the Emperor when he declared himself responsible for order, which had the ominous aspect of being seriously menaced. On Jan. 2, 1870 the Emperor called on M. Émile Ollivier to accept the Premiership, and in the same day the list of the Ollivier Ministry appeared in the ' Moniteur.' When the Emperor confided the Government of France to the responsible Ministry of which M. Émile Ollivier was the head, he retired from the active direction of public affairs and restricted himself entirely to the position of a Constitutional Sovereign. With the appointment of the Ollivier Administration the *rôle* of the Emperor as active ruler ended ; yet he must be held to have been in a measure responsible for the policy of the Cabinet which six months later led to the ruin of his dynasty and to the most disastrous war of modern times. There is no space here for detailing the scandal connected with the name of Prince Pierre Bonaparte—Louis Napoleon was constantly unfortunate in regard to his relatives. May 8 was the day appointed for the nation to vote on the new Constitution, and on the transmission of the sovereign power from father to son in the Imperial family. A heated and turbulent discussion arose in the Corps Législatif, in the course of which M. Pelletan shouted that the Empire had given France eighteen years not of repose, order, and security, but ' of shame and of crime.' The result of the plebiscite—the

last one of the career of Napoleon—although it showed
7,257,379 'Ayes' and but 1,530,000 'Noes,' indicated a
settled hostility in Paris and most of the other large
cities of the Empire. The circumstance that the army
recorded nearly 50,000 votes against the Sovereign was
a serious matter ; and not less serious was the fact that
during the agitation of the plebiscite a plot to assassin-
ate the Emperor was discovered. On the nights of
May 9 and 10 serious riots occurred and barricades
were thrown up.

The last ceremonial function of the reign of Louis
Napoleon was held on May 21, when the result of the
plebiscite was formally conveyed to the Emperor in the
Salle des États of the Louvre. Never had the Empire
worn an aspect seemingly more splendid and prosperous
than when Napoleon advanced surrounded by his family
amidst the acclamations of the assembled Chambers and
took his seat on the daïs while M. Schneider, President of
the Corps Législatif, addressed the Head of the Nation.
' In supporting the Empire by more than seven millions
of suffrages,' said President Schneider, ' France says to
you, " Sire, the country is with you ; advance confidently in the path of progress, and establish liberty
based on respect for the laws and the Constitution.
France places the cause of liberty under the protection
of your dynasty." ' The Emperor thanked the nation
for having given him, for the fourth time, an overwhelming proof of its confidence. He closed his speech
with the words : 'Who can be opposed to the progressive march of a dynasty founded by a great people
in the midst of political disturbance and fortified by
liberty ?' Those were brave words ; but in three and a

half months from their utterance that dynasty was in the dust and the man who proudly spoke them was a prisoner of war in a foreign land.

There had been some sort of an intrigue in Paris in the summer of 1869 for the promotion of the candidature for the vacant throne of Spain of Prince Frederic, a younger son of the old Prince of Hohenzollern-Sigmaringen, the house of which King William of Prussia was the nominal head. It was said that the Empress Eugénie favoured the project and that Prince Frederic might marry a relative of hers. Perhaps such credentials hardly recommended him to the Spaniards and no offer of the Throne of Spain was made to Frederic. In the autumn of that year it was that Marshal Prim's project of inviting the candidature of Frederic's eldest brother Prince Leopold was first mooted. In the summer of 1870 Prince Leopold signified his readiness to accept the Spanish Crown if the choice of the Cortes should fall upon him. The tidings of this contingent acceptance reached Paris from Madrid on July 3. It was stated that a deputation had been despatched to Germany to offer Prince Leopold the Spanish Crown. A *communiqué* in the 'Constitutionnel' announced that the proffer had actually been accepted, and astonishment was expressed at the spectacle of the sceptre of Charles V. being placed in the hands of a 'German Prince.' So far as regarded blood it was a fact that Leopold had closer affinity with the Imperial dynasty of France than with the royal family of Prussia ; for his paternal grandmother was Princess Antoinette Murat, while his mother was a daughter of the Grand Duchess Stephanie of Baden, sister of Hortense

Beauharnais the mother of Napoleon III. His wife
was a sister of the King of Portugal. Dynastically,
therefore, Prince Leopold actually stood nearer to the
French than to the Prussian Throne ; but there was no
doubt that he held himself more a German than a
Frenchman. He regarded King William as the head
and patriarch of his race ; he was a colonel in the
Prussian army ; he lived much at the Court of Berlin ;
and his political sympathies were with the German
movement of the time.

The political horizon of Europe in the beginning of
July, 1870 was so delusively clear that an English statesman who certainly had strong claims to be considered
well informed affirmed publicly that it was without a
cloud. It is true that on the 4th the French *Chargé
d'Affaires* at Berlin went to the Foreign Office ' to communicate the painful impression which the acceptance of
the candidature of Prince Leopold had caused in Paris.'
The Prussian Under-Secretary in Bismarck's absence
declared ' that this affair had no existence for the
Prussian Government, which, therefore, was not in a
position to afford any information.' In truth, up to the
end of the first week in July Prussia, and with it the
whole of Germany, had full confidence in the continuance
of peace ; while in France M. Émile Ollivier, the Prime
Minister, had on June 30 declared that ' the peace of
Europe never rested on a more secure basis.' In the
Prussian army nothing was doing beyond the common
routine. The usual preparations were being made for
the autumn manœuvres. The draft of a new official
text-book for infantry exercise had just been submitted
to the King ; and a new instruction on outpost duty had

recently been issued. A partial issue of improved needle-guns had to be sent back into store when hostilities became imminent, and the old weapons re-issued for the sake of uniformity of pattern. A great number of officers both of the staff and of the line had received leave of absence during the interval between the regimental inspections and the autumn manœuvres; and many of those had gone to the camp of Châlons to witness the operations there. The ironclad squadron of the navy commanded by Prince Adalbert was away on cruise. The King was at Ems; Bismarck was still unwell at Varzin; Moltke was residing on his Silesian estate; and most of the other Ministers were abroad on tours of inspection or recreation. There is no doubt that in France the prospect of sudden and immediate war was equally remote; for in June the French War Minister had ordered a great number of horses to be sold, as in consequence of the persistent drought there were apprehensions of a failure of forage. And further, on the 30th of that month the Legislative Chamber had accepted the Bill for reducing the annual contingent of recruits from its usual figure of 100,000 to 90,000, on which occasion Émile Ollivier made the declaration as to the peaceable state of Europe already mentioned.

On July 4, however, Baron Werther the Ambassador to France of the North German Confederation, had obtained leave of absence and was about to pay his respects to King William at Ems; and the Duc de Gramont, the French Minister for Foreign Affairs, begged the Baron to describe to his Prussian Majesty the excitement which was agitating the French nation in regard to the Prusso-Spanish matter, and to entreat the

King to induce Prince Leopold to withdraw his candidature on pain of a 'catastrophe.' 'Do you mean by "catastrophe" a threat of war?' demanded the astonished Ambassador. '*Oui*,' replied M. Ollivier, '*oui, il y a menace de guerre.*' Baron Werther promised to make the desired communication to the King and departed for Ems on the following day. On July 5 M. Cochery, a Deputy of the Left Centre, made an interpellation to the Foreign Minister with regard to the Spanish Throne succession ; 'put up' intentionally, it was understood, in order to afford the Minister an opportunity of making a sensational and truculent reply. In the course of the 5th there were two Ministerial councils at neither of which did the peaceful sentiments of the Cabinet undergo any change. But after the evening conference the Empress was said to have had a long conversation with her husband, the result of which, as rendered next day by the Duc de Gramont in the Corps Législatif, was tantamount to a challenge to Germany. He declared that he was not privy to the negotiations between Marshal Prim and the Hohenzollern Prince ; he announced emphatically that it was not the duty of France to meddle with the internal affairs of the Spanish nation in the exercise of its own sovereignty. 'But,' continued he significantly, 'we do not believe that respect for the rights of a neighbouring people imposes on us the obligation of enduring that a foreign Power, by placing one of its own Princes on the Throne of Charles V., should disturb to our detriment the existing balance of power in Europe and endanger the interests and honour of France. We have a confident hope that such a circumstance will not occur, reckoning as we do on the prudence of the

German and the amity of the Spanish peoples. Should this, however, turn out contrary to our expectations, we shall in reliance on your support and that of the nation know how to do our duty without hesitation or weakness.'

This declaration was received with rapturous applause by the great majority of the House. Some members insisted that the Budget which just then was being debated must necessarily be fundamentally remodelled in view of the imminence of warlike preparations ; but as a matter of fact those were already in full train. Immense activity was known to exist at the French War Ministry ; and large quantities of stores and warlike material were being transported by rail by night and with the utmost secrecy through Paris from the south and west towards the east. The *pourparlers* were becoming ominously formal, and the Prussian *Chargé d'Affaires* at Paris was on July 9 instructed once more to signify to the Duc de Gramont that, 'the question of the succession to the Spanish Throne was one which concerned Spain and the candidate alone, and with which Prussia and Germany had absolutely no concern.' Seeing that it was impossible to fix a quarrel on the German diplomatist, Gramont determined on the attempt to involve the King personally. From his cure at Wildbad Benedetti was curtly ordered by telegraph to hasten to Ems, where he arrived on the 9th. The instructions awaiting him there from Paris were to the effect 'that he should endeavour to persuade the King to issue *an order* to the Prince of Hohenzollern to abandon the candidature.' Benedetti was received most cordially by the Prussian monarch. When he ventured to make the demand just mentioned his Majesty replied, that in his quality of King of Prussia he knew absolutely nothing of this candidature; that as head of the Hohenzollern family it was true that he was aware of it; but that he had no right to order Prince Hohenzollern, who was of full age, either to accept or to refuse the Spanish Crown, which he therefore declined doing. The Ambassador went on to appeal to the King's wisdom by pronouncing a word that would ' restore peace to Europe '; to which enigmatic remark his Majesty replied that the disquiet of Europe arose not because of any act of the Prussian Government but in consequence of the declaration made by the Imperial Government to the Legislative Chamber on July 6.

Baron Werther returned to Paris on the 11th, and after his departure Benedetti had a second interview with the King, with the same result as before: his Majesty adding that he had no idea where the Hohenzollern Prince was at that time. Hearing, however, of the complications that had arisen, the Prince immediately determined to abandon the candidature and thus, so far as he was concerned, remove every pretext for dissatisfaction between France and Germany. He informed the Spanish Ministry of his decision and begged his father to announce it widely; so that when Baron Werther reached Paris on the evening of the 11th the Spanish Minister Olozaga had already received the intelligence from his Government. Werther and Olozaga went together to the French Foreign Office on the 12th, for the purpose of handing over officially to the Duc de Gramont the telegrams announcing the renunciation of Prince Hohenzollern. M. Émile Ollivier also appeared and took part in the conversation. Up to midday of the

12th the Prime Minister seemed to consider the affair
as having been definitely arranged by the Prince's renunciation; and he told several Deputies in the Salles des
Pas Perdus of the Palais Bourbon that there was no
longer any object of contention in existence. The Duc
de Gramont, however, used very different language, and,
to the great astonishment of Baron Werther, declared
that the renunciation was merely a *subordinate incident*,
as France would not have in any case permitted the
Prince to ascend the Spanish Throne. The main point
still remained to be settled, namely the asserted slight
offered to France by the King of Prussia having permitted the Hohenzollern Prince to accept the candidature without having first come to an understanding with
France. Gramont suggested as a satisfactory means of
atoning for this slight 'that King William should
address an autograph letter to the Emperor Napoleon,
stating that in granting that permission he never had
thought of injuring the interests or affecting the dignity
of France, and that he cordially accepted the renunciation of the Prince.' Such was the sense of this letter,
of which there are many discrepant versions. A *naïf*
confession was incidentally made by the two French
statesmen—that for the sake of the Ministry they absolutely needed a compromise in order to allay the popular
excitement. Baron Werther, who must have been
greatly amused by this droll frankness, remarked quietly
that such a measure had been rendered very difficult
because of the terms used by the Duc de Gramont in
the Chamber on the 6th inst. The Prussian diplomatist
did not think it his duty to lay this insolent demand for
a letter of apology before his master by telegraph,

as the Duc de Gramont had required him to do; he did, however, communicate with Bismarck, who replied characteristically 'that he could not take any notice of this language unless the French Government thought proper to address it through its Ambassador at Berlin.'

Gramont was unappeasable, and his obdurate insolence recoiled on himself. On the evening of the 12th he telegraphed to Benedetti at Ems that he (Benedetti) should exact from the King not only a public approval of Prince Leopold's withdrawal, but also an engagement that his Majesty would never again allow the Prince to be a candidate for the Throne of Spain. On the morning of the 13th the King saw Benedetti hurrying to meet him on the Ems promenade; he handed the Ambassador a newspaper containing the statement that the Prince had withdrawn from his candidature; and he added that he had not yet received direct tidings from Sigmaringen, but would assuredly do so in the course of the day. Benedetti stated that he, too, had received from Paris news of the renunciation, whereupon the King remarked that he considered the affair now definitely settled. Quite unexpectedly Benedetti brought forward a fresh demand—that the King should give a positive assurance that he would never give his consent to the Prince's candidature should it ever again be mooted. The King positively refused to undertake any such engagement, and he remained steadfast in his refusal to the demand which Benedetti repeated with constantly increasing importunity; whereupon they parted. At noon the King received a letter from Prince Leopold's father in which was confirmed the news of the Prince's renunciation already conveyed by telegraph.

Prince Radziwill was at once sent by the King to Benedetti with this intelligence; and with the statement b
the King that he now sanctioned the withdrawal of Prince
Leopold 'in the same sense and to the same extent' as
he had approved his acceptance of the Spanish Crown,
adding the remark that he now looked upon the affair as
finally settled. The French Ambassador, urged on by
repeated telegrams from Paris, still insisted on an
audience; but he was several times in the course of the
afternoon informed by Prince Radziwill that his Majesty
had nothing to add to what he had already said. 'I
have just met the King at the railway station,' was
Benedetti's final telegram to Paris of the 14th; 'he
simply said he had nothing more to tell me, and that any
further negotiations would be conducted by his Government.' Benedetti expressed a wish to take leave of the
King, who took the opportunity of courteously recognising the Ambassador. From Ems Benedetti left for
Paris; King William went to visit the Empress at
Coblentz, and from the moment of the parting of the
King and the Ambassador war between France and
Germany was in effect inevitable.

On the evening of July 13 Roon and Moltke dined
with Bismarck in Berlin. During dinner came a telegram
which King William had ordered his secretary to despatch
from Ems. It gave an account of the demand made by
Benedetti that the King should bind himself for the future
to forbid a Hohenzollern from accepting the Crown of
Spain, and stating also that his Majesty had peremptorily
refused to make any such promise. In the concluding
sentence of the telegram the King suggested to his
Minister that the latter should communicate its contents

to the press, and inform the representatives of Prussia at foreign Courts of the new demands made by France and of their rejection. There was no instruction to publish the exact words of the telegram. Bismarck took a pencil and composed a summary of it, which he described in terse and vigorous terms. He then ordered this somewhat truculent summary to be inserted at once in an extra edition of the 'Nord Allgemeine Zeitung.' Before sending from the room this forceful edition of the Ems telegram, he read it to his two guests, whereupon Moltke exclaimed : ' *Vorher war's chamade, jetzt ist's Fanfare*!' The three great men well understood the effect which the promulgation of the telegram would have on public opinion.

During the night it was wired to the foreign representatives of Prussia, with instructions that they should communicate its terms to the Governments to which they were respectively accredited. On the morning of the 14th, while the French Ministers in Paris were congratulating themselves on their triumph over Bismarck in the immediate future, the German Ambassador presented himself to announce that he had received orders to demand his passports and to quit France. They also presently received a telegram from the French *Chargé d'Affaires* at Berlin, containing the tidings of the communication which had been promulgated there and which had appeared the night before in the German official newspaper, as also its effect on public opinion. Immediate war could not now be averted ; but it is fair to recognise that Bismarck resorted to arms only in order that he might anticipate an attack which he was aware to be in course of preparation against Germany. The recently-

published Memoirs of the late General Lebrun conclusively prove that a coalition of the French Emperor and
his allies against Germany had actually been formed.
That General was deep in the confidence of Napoleon.
In June, 1870 he was sent to Vienna to settle a plan of
campaign against Germany in which France, Italy, and
Austria were to join. The political preliminaries had
been agreed upon. In case of success Italy was to have
Rome ; Austria was to have restored to her the Silesia
which Frederick the Great had rent from her ; and
France was to receive Belgium and the left bank of the
Rhine. The treaty was actually drawn up—all it wanted
was the signature of the three Powers ; but it was not
signed when war broke out in July. This was not
the fault of the Emperor Napoleon. His cousin Prince
Jerome (Plon-Plon) has told us that the chief cause of
the hesitation was the intense feeling existing in the
Clerical Party in France against handing over Rome to
the Italians. But the difficulty as regarded Rome was,
after all, not the principal reason why the treaty was not
ratified. The Emperor Napoleon had calculated—he
was no strategist—that by rapidity of concentration he
might gain some advantage over Germany and perhaps
even win an important battle. If so, he would offer
peace to the King of Prussia on terms of alliance against
England, assistance for the conquest of Belgium and the
cession to France of the left bank of the Rhine ; Prussia
in return to receive a perfectly free hand in Germany.
The governing idea of the Emperor was the formation
of a strong alliance against England. This is proved
in actual documents ; and the diary of the Emperor
Frederick II. shows conclusively that Napoleon III. did

not abandon it even after Sedan. One might commiserate his downfall even if he had been an unscrupulous man ; but to be plotting coolly against the nation in the bosom of which he had found cordial sympathy, friendship, and a free asylum, was a baseness from which the most cynical of men might recoil.

The King of Prussia journeyed to Berlin on July 15. At Brandenburg he was met by the Crown Prince, Bismarck, Moltke, and Roon ; and he immediately gave orders forthwith to mobilise the whole army of the North German Confederation. His reception in Berlin was most enthusiastic. After some rest the King worked out with Bismarck, Moltke, and Roon all the necessary dispositions, which were completed early on the morning of the 16th, so thorough was the state of Prussian preparedness ; nor was the readiness for war in the South German States far behind. On the 16th Bismarck explained to the Federal Council the sequence of circumstances of which the climax had been reached by the manifest determination of France to force on Germany either humiliation or war ; and on the 19th during a sitting of the Reichstag he entered with the announcement that he had just received from the French *Chargé d'Affaires* the formal declaration of war ; 'the first and only communication received from the French Government on the subject which had engrossed the attention of the world during the previous fortnight.'

The powers of the Emperor Napoleon, both mental and physical, had been deteriorating during the later troublous years of his reign. He had lost his grip as well of men as of things ; and his domestic and social influences warped him to his hurt. During the swift and sudden events that led up to the actual outbreak of the Franco-German War, Napoleon was more than ordinarily enfeebled by his sufferings from the cruel disorder which at intervals he had endured for years. The advocates of personal government were constantly endeavouring to draw him back to the Constitution of 1852. The Clericals were for war, and for the disintegration of the powerful Protestant State beyond the Rhine. At home the populace yelled for war on the pretext that France had to avenge Waterloo. The effect of the wild war-cries of Paris was the gradual but natural estrangement from France on the part of the Powers. As the negotiations ran their swift course, the foreign Governments became convinced that France not only thirsted for war but was wantonly inciting it. Public feeling had become almost beyond the control of the Government. But the Government, under pressure of events, was fast losing the control of itself. Gramont wrote to Benedetti that further delay in the King's answer would not be endured, adding : 'We must begin ; we only wish for your despatch to call out the 300,000 men. If the King will not counsel the Hohenzollern Prince to renounce— well, it is war at once, and in a few days we shall be on the Rhine.'

It turned out that it was the Emperor Napoleon him-self who, at ten P.M. of the 12th, ordered Benedetti to insist on an engagement on the part of the Prussian King that Prince Leopold should not re-enter the lists as candidate for the Spanish Throne. 'So long,' said his Majesty, 'as we have not an official communication from Ems, we have not received a reply to our just demands ; so long as we have not received such a reply, we shall continue our armaments.' A communication from Lord Lyons inclined the Ministry to peace; but the war-party would not yield. With the one hand that party was precipitating the war; with the other it was putting off the adoption of the only means of waging it with success. Meantime there were hesitation and indecision in the French Cabinet. At a meeting of the Cabinet on the afternoon of the 14th, after a protracted discussion it was resolved that the reserves should be called out. The Emperor was ailing, and he remained a silent listener until the Duc de Gramont suggested that the question might be solved by an European Congress. That was the Emperor's favourite expedient; but this time it was to fail him. Another council met the same evening. When the Ministers had parted at six o'clock peace appeared assured; at ten it was war. The sudden change was attributed to the communication to the French Government of Bismarck's interview with Lord Augustus Loftus in which the Prussian Chancellor formulated the demands he had determined to make, and to the news of the movements of German troops towards the Rhine.

In the Cabinet of the night of the 14th Napoleon was the only person who had scruples and difficulties. He repeatedly asked of his Ministers, 'What guarantees they could offer him?' Of course, it was guarantees of success that he required—a successful war would have given him intense satisfaction, but he did not believe in the prospect of it. The dilemma presented itself—internal revolution with the fall of the dynasty; or war for the success of which he fain would have guarantees. He might have found some spurious comfort in Lebœuf the War Minister. That valiant impostor declared in the council that the French army was perfectly prepared for war. Asked specifically what he meant by that, he replied boldly and confidently, ' I mean that the army is perfectly supplied in every respect ; and that it will not require the purchase of a single gaiter-button for a year to come—*elle est archiprête.*' The war-party was certainly in force that night. It was in the ascendant in the Palace and among the friends of the dynasty. It had the sympathies of the Empress, who indeed was the chief instigator of the war because she expected that it would secure the Throne to her son. She also approved the war because she believed that the honour of France demanded it ; but no unbiassed person can conceive that her share in its responsibilities was traceable to other than patriotic motives.

On July 15 M. Émile Ollivier demanded a credit of 500 million francs to carry on the war, announcing at the same time that the reserves of the army had been called out. On the 19th the declaration of war was presented at Berlin by M. Le Sourd, the same *Chargé d'Affaires* who had made the first verbal inquiry with regard to the candidateship of Prince Hohenzollern.

Lebœuf's boast of the efficiency of the French army was falsified within a fortnight after it had been uttered. The French army was anything but prepared for war, and the very mobilisation showed how defective were the arrangements made by the War Ministry. The main fortresses on the eastern frontier were not put into a partial state of defence until it was almost too late—some, indeed, were not restored at all. It was not until the beginning of August that the corps on the frontier could draw their rations out of the magazines, previous to which time the soldiers had to live on an allowance of a franc per day. Neither in Metz nor in Thionville were there any supplies. Horses had to be bought at any price at the last moment. There was an immense quantity of maps, but they were all maps of Germany. General Douay, appointed to command the 7th Corps, on July 27 was still doing duty at Paris as aide-de-camp of the Emperor; while on the same day the Minister of War was ordering him to report from Belfort where his divisions were and how far their organisation had progressed. General Michel reached Belfort on July 21 ; and reporting his arrival to Paris stated that he could find neither his brigade nor the general of his division nor could he ascertain where his two regiments were.

In the last week of July there were on the eastern frontier of France and somewhat in rear eight Army Corps, as follows : the 7th Corps at Belfort and Colmar and the 1st Corps at Strasburg, on the right wing. The 5th Corps at Bitche and the 2nd at St. Avold, in the centre. The 4th Corps at Thionville, on the left wing. As reserve to the 5th and 2nd Corps the Imperial Guard and the 3rd Corps at Metz, behind the centre. As general reserve for the whole army the 6th Corps, at Châlons, Soissons, and Paris. Those troops if complete in their full war establishment should have represented a total of 337,000 combatants; but the reserves not having joined promptly and later only in deficient numbers, the infantry battalions were considerably below their proper strength. The Emperor had reckoned on a field army 300,000 strong at the beginning of August, but probably there were not above 220,000 combatants in the first line, with some 50,000 reserves and 1,000 guns including mitrailleuses. The Germans entered France 384,000 strong with double that number of reserves.

On July 28 the Emperor, accompanied by the Prince Imperial, departed to join the army in the field. In a retired part of the park of St. Cloud a level passage had been cut and a small platform provided, enabling the Imperial family to join the railway without passing through Paris. Presently the Emperor, along with the Empress and their son, issued from the private apartments and walked towards the park entrance, shaking hands with and addressing kind words to those whom he met on his way. Napoleon wore the dress of a General of Division ; the Prince Imperial that of a Sub-Lieutenant. While the Generals were entering the carriages the Emperor remarked that the suite and entourage formed a *corps d'armée* of themselves. The train was ready, and after one last embrace to husband and son the Empress descended to the platform. The signal was given and the whistle sounded ; and as the train moved the Empress called out to her son, ' Do your duty, Louis ! ' All present uncovered, and the train moved forward amid shouts of ' *Vive l'Empereur !* ' Napoleon's health was very seriously impaired before and during the war of 1870 ; possibly he had the presentiment that he was looking for the last time on the beautiful château which had been his favourite home.

On his arrival at Metz the Emperor was painfully disappointed by the state of things he found in the army. He could not but recognise that it was still unable to take the field, and lamentations came pouring in from all quarters as to the innumerable and serious deficiencies of the military administration which, as it seemed, no amount of exertion could remedy. Napoleon must have had the sad realisation that France, notwithstanding the repeated assurances of the official authorities and the confidence of the nation, was totally unprepared to carry on a great war. Yet the proclamation which he issued when at Metz he assumed the Command-in-Chief of 'the Army of the Rhine' contained expressions of proud hope, intermingled, however, with others which betrayed apprehensions; and it carefully refrained from representing the enemy as likely to be easily vanquished, as the so-called public opinion of France was freely assuming.

But the army had to be doing something for its credit's sake; and the Emperor determined on making an advance against Saarbrücken, a small Prussian town on the river Saar, about two miles inside the frontier line between France and Germany. Saarbrücken was an open town totally destitute of defences; it had been occupied since the declaration of war by a battalion of the 40th Hohenzollern regiment and three squadrons of the 7th Uhlans. The force detailed to attack this little place with its insignificant Prussian garrison consisted of three French Army Corps or about 80,000 men. The 5th Corps (Failly) was on the right; the 2nd (Frossard) in the centre; and on the left the 3rd (Bazaine). The direct attack on Saarbrücken was to be executed by Frossard's Corps, which for some days previous had been in bivouac on the Spicheren plateau about four miles south-west of Saarbrücken. About ten A.M. of Aug. 2 Frossard began the advance. Bataille's division of the 2nd Corps formed the first line. On the right of the high-road Bastoul's brigade descended the Spicheren heights, crossed the intervening valley, and moved on the ridges covering Saarbrücken ; on the left Pouget's brigade moved forward towards the drill-ground. Three squadrons of chasseurs scoured the ground to the front. In rear of Frossard's right wing followed Micheler's brigade of Laveaucoupet's division; in rear of the left Valaze's brigade belonging to Vergé's division. The remainder of the Corps followed in reserve.

Meanwhile the two Prussian companies in front of Saarbrücken moved out at once into the line of outposts. The post of the Winterberg which was most immediately threatened, was promptly strengthened. The company in St. Johann doubled out to the ' Rothe Haus ' post. The Löwenburg was occupied and part of a company went to St. Arnual. A skirmishing division and two guns brought up from Raschpfühl under Lieutenant Meyer received with a brisk fire the enemy debouching from the Stiftswald. General Micheler on his side also brought up a battery ; but Meyer maintained his position in spite of the French skirmishers. The Prussian garrison had thus been successful in maintaining timely opposition to the French at all points. But it was impossible for a force so scanty to resist for any length of time the enveloping attack of a whole Army Corps. A steady and deliberate retreat with frequent brisk rallies and occasional conflicts with the French skirmishers at the point of the bayonet was carried out with entire absence of hurry. The Saar was crossed and the gallant little garrison of Saarbrücken retired upon Raschpfühl.

It was on this day, Aug. 2, 1870, that the Prince

Imperial, then a boy of fourteen, in the words of his father 'received his baptism of fire.' I was watching from the drill-ground above Saarbrücken the oncoming swarm-attack of Bataille's tirailleurs, firing as they hurried across the plain. The tirailleurs had passed the Galgenberg, a low ridge on the bosom of the valley about midway between the Spicheren hill and where I stood. Presently the Galgenberg was crowned by two horsemen followed by a great staff. The telescope told me that without a doubt the senior of the two foremost riders was the Emperor Napoleon, and that the younger, shorter and slighter—mere lad he seemed—was the Prince Imperial, whom we knew to be with his father in the field. The exertion of the day told cruelly on the Emperor. An eye-witness wrote : ' After Saarbrücken Lebrun and Lebœuf had to lift him off his horse. The Prince was by his side all the time and looked very distressed, for his father had scarcely spoken to him during the engagement. But after they got into the carriage the Emperor put his arm round his son's neck and kissed him on the cheeks, while two large tears rolled down his own. I noticed that the Emperor had hardly strength to walk from his horse to the carriage.' On Aug. 4 appeared the following despatch in the ' Journal Officiel' : ' To-day, Aug. 2, at eleven A.M. the French troops had a severe engagement with the Prussians. Our army, assuming the offensive, crossed the frontier and invaded the territory of Prussia. In spite of the strength of the enemy's position a few of our battalions sufficed to carry the heights which command Saarbrücken, and our artillery soon drove the enemy from the town. The *élan* of our soldiers was so great that our losses have been slight.

The engagement, which began at eleven, was over at one. The Emperor was with the Prince Imperial, who has received upon the first battle-field of the campaign the baptism of fire. His presence of mind and coolness in danger were worthy of the name he bears.'

The Emperor addressed to the Empress the following private despatch : ' Louis has received his baptism of fire. His coolness was admirable ; he was not in the least degree excited. . . . We were in the front, and the balls and bullets fell at our feet. Louis has kept a ball that fell near him. Some of the soldiers wept on seeing how calm he remained. We had only one officer and ten men killed.—NAPOLEON.'

It is rare that a ' severe engagement ' occurs in which only one officer and ten men are killed. As a matter of fact, according to the official record the French loss in the Saarbrücken skirmish amounted to six officers and eighty men. The Prussian casualties were four officers and seventy-nine men.

CHAPTER XIV

FROM SAARBRÜCKEN TO SEDAN

THAT four companies of Prussian infantry and three squadrons of Prussian Uhlans should have made a deliberate and orderly retreat before a French Army Corps scarcely wore the aspect of a great triumph for the Army Corps, but nevertheless the petty affair at Saarbrücken was regarded in Paris as an important success. Napoleon knew better ; he was not a great commander, but he was quite aware that the loss of 'one officer and ten men killed' could scarcely be said to constitute a 'severe engagement.' After Saarbrücken on Aug. 2 the 2nd, 3rd, and 4th French Army Corps remained inactive on the left bank of the Saar until the 4th, when the defeat of General Abel Douay's division at Weissenburg on that day became known. The Emperor then gave orders to concentrate the army and to recall it towards Metz ; and he gave to Marshal Bazaine the command of the three Corps of the Saar. The 2nd Corps, however, remained on the Spicheren plateau until the 6th, from which position on that day it was driven with heavy loss by bodies of Prussian troops of about equal strength. On the same day Marshal MacMahon, while holding the strong position of Wörth on the eastern foot-hills of the northern Vosges with the 1st Corps and a division of the 7th, was assailed in greatly superior strength by the army of the Prussian Crown Prince; and after a long, bloody, and desperate battle was utterly defeated and his army shattered into headlong rout. The 5th Corps, which had been ordered to join MacMahon's force, could not reach the Marshal in time for the battle, but de Failly joined the retreat from the Bitche vicinity and the two Corps hurried in disorder across the Vosges towards Luneville. The defeats of Spicheren, Wörth, and all the early ruin, presage true of the wretched end, came bickering and crumbling about the ears of the unhappy Emperor. Bazaine in the real stress of things had got the handling of those three Corps 'of the Saar,' one of which, the 2nd, had already been badly mauled on the 6th in the Spicheren battle. Insubordination and confusion hampered him at every turn. All he could do was to work out there in the front, conducting the retreat, covering the ragged edges, trying to keep the men in heart. At length, in a paroxysm of worry, the Emperor came out from Metz to consult with Bazaine, the man to whom he turned when he found Lebœuf and the others to be like the crackling of thorns under a pot. The rendezvous was Faulquemont, a little dunghill village to the south-east of Metz. Bazaine's advice had a ring of soldierhood in it, but the Emperor, quivering with nervousness because of the Paris mob, would accept no suggestion that involved the uncoverment of Paris even in appearance. So Bazaine was bidden to take up a line of battle nearer Metz and 'give up this new hope of being allowed to make an effective diversion.'

The blackness of the cloud overhanging the Empire grew denser, and the plot began that was to ruin Bazaine.

Pietri telegraphed an urgent 'confidential' from the Empress that it should be insisted on that the Emperor must surrender the Command-in-Chief to Bazaine. The message thus continued : 'If misfortune should still pursue the army, Bazaine then would be the subject of obloquy and so take the onus of the responsibility off the Emperor's shoulders.' Bazaine did not know of the plot, but he distrusted his own capacity for the high duty of the Command-in-Chief. There were two officers in the army who were his seniors. So when he got the 'letter of service' to take the command, he betook himself to the Imperial headquarters and urged that both MacMahon and Canrobert were older and better officers than himself. MacMahon had other work re-served for him ; Canrobert was equal to his Crimean antecedent of shirking reponsibility. 'You are the right man,' said the Emperor to Bazaine, 'and it is an order I give you to take the duties.' The Emperor must have felt a thrill of compassion for the man on whose shoulders was laid the cross which he had let fall. In the letters which the Emperor wrote to Bazaine, both after the capitulation of Metz and while Bazaine lay under the sentence of death pronounced by the Trianon court-martial two years later, there are expressions which have a note of genuine tenderness. ' I find,' wrote Napoleon from his Wilhelmshöhe captivity, 'one real consolation in the depths of misfortune into which I am plunged, in knowing that you have always been staunch to me.' He could say no less to the man before whom loomed the fate of being stripped of everything dearest to the soldier—of reputation, of decorations cut from out the hostile ranks, because he had held himself bound to the allegiance to which his soldier-oath had pledged him.

A Commander-in-Chief in name, a buffer and a scapegoat in reality, Bazaine had toiled hard amidst many discouragements to get the army out of Metz and forward on the march of retreat towards Verdun. At that army's rear the masterful Prussians had struck hard on the 14th and so brought about the battle of Borny as the French call it, or Colombey as the Germans name it, on the eastern face of Metz. No great organiser, Bazaine was in his element the moment that the war-music began to make the air throb. He turned fiercely and skilfully at bay, and although the fight won for the Prussians the delay for which they had made it, Bazaine charged them a considerable effusion of blood for the advantage which he had no alternative but to concede. Bazaine was a man to whom fortune was never stingy in the matter of wounds. In the Borny fight a shell-fragment struck him on the left shoulder; but it had been almost spent and gave him only a severe contusion. The fight over and the troops now again beginning to move through Metz westward towards Verdun, Bazaine bethought himself of his master's anxiety to know the situation. That master was the white elephant of Bazaine and the army; but in the countries where white elephants are, they live objects of sanctity. The Imperial headquarters were for the night in the Château of Longueville, a residence on the left bank of the Moselle valley nestled comfortably under the guns of Fort St. Quentin. Thither in the dead of night, struggling his way through the retreating army jammed in the narrow streets of Metz, Bazaine betook himself, carrying his bruised shoulder from the battle-field. Of what followed it seems best to let Bazaine tell in his blunt but surely not ineffective way :—' I found his Majesty unwell and in bed '—the malady that killed Napoleon a few years later had long previously been debilitating him— ' and I was immediately admitted into his bedroom. The Emperor greeted me with his wonted kind affability. I told him what had passed, about the battle, &c., and I gave vent also to my anxieties in regard to the next few days. I mentioned that I was suffering physically, and adding my fear that I could not endure the pain the contusion caused me when on horseback, I begged that he would relieve me from the command. His Majesty, touching my shoulder where the torn epaulette showed the spot on which I had been struck, answered me with that kind humour which charmed all who came within its influence : " This is nothing serious, dear Marshal; it is a matter of but a few days ; and the blow you have received to-day is but the token that it is you who are destined to break the spell of our ill-fortune." Those were the Emperor's very words. He gave no hint that he had any other thought than to remain with the army.'

' " I wait," ' continued Napoleon—seemingly still nourishing his illusions—' " I wait for answers from the Emperor of Austria and the King of Italy, who at the beginning of the war evinced a disposition to befriend us ; for Heaven's sake risk nothing by rashness and above everything avoid any fresh reverse. I am leaning on you," were Napoleon's final words.' As Bazaine passed through the outer room the officers of the Imperial entourage called out to him, ' You are going to fetch us out of this hole we have got into, are you not, Marshal ? '

'I am going to do my best, gentlemen,' answered Bazaine; '*tout mon possible;* none of us can do more, and there are none of us who would do less!' And so the sorely troubled man went out into the darkness and consoled his bruised shoulder with a few short hours' sleep.

This was on the night between Aug. 14 and 15. What happened next morning was told me in Zululand by the Prince Imperial. He was asleep in the bedroom next to his father's. A crash awoke the lad, and he was still bewildered when the Emperor rushed into the room : 'Get up and dress ; quick, Louis—quick! The German shells are falling through the roof!' It was so ; a Prussian battery had galloped up on the opposite bank of the Moselle to within range and the gunners had opened fire on the Château of Longueville. As the Prince looked out of the window while he hastily dressed he saw a shell fall on the table in the garden at which some officers of the Guard were breakfasting ; and when the smoke of the explosion blew aside three of the officers were dead men. The carriages and baggage might follow—Gravelotte was the rendezvous given ; but meanwhile the business in hand was to get from under that shell-fire. There was a hurried cup of coffee for Louis and his father ; then they and the suite went quickly to horse and the abominable German shells were soon left behind. Near the village of Lessy the high-road to Gravelotte, cumbered with the impedimenta of a disorderly retreat, presented an absolute block. An interminable delay threatened to befall the Imperial party. But Prince Louis during the early days at Metz, while as yet the Germans were afar off, had done much

riding about the adjacent country. Quietly bidding
some soldiers to make a gap in the fence he called out,
'Follow me, father!' and led the way across country by
a vineyard track the trend of which he knew. So the
lad conducted his seniors down into the valley by Chatel,
then up on to the ridge which three days later was to be
littered with corpses, past the *auberge* of St. Hubert not
yet battered into dust and blood, down into the Mance
ravine not then a ghastly shamble, and so up the slope
between the poplar-trees to the village of Gravelotte,
lying in the angle where bifurcate the upper and the
lower roads from Metz to Verdun.

Thither, at least as yet, came no German shells, and
the hunted Napoleons could draw breath. The Emperor, after resting an hour, took to tramping to and fro
in front of the post-house which he had made his
quarters. It was his habit in trouble. I saw him later
doing just the same thing in the potato patch of the
weaver's garden on the Donchery road on the way from
Sedan, during the interval when Bismarck left him. As
Napoleon stalked up and down pondering uneasily, he
was unconsciously making history, and just as unconsciously he was moving in the heart of a scene waiting
to be made historical ere many hours had passed ; for
over against him was the old church of Gravelotte on
the edge of the graveyard of which the dead of the
impending battle were to be utilised for breastworks.
To the Emperor, about one of the afternoon, came
the harassed Bazaine. Like Martha, the Marshal was
'careful and troubled about many things.' He
tells : 'I complimented his Majesty on his *fête* day' (a
cheerful *fête* day truly!) 'by presenting him with a

little nosegay I had gathered in the garden of my last night's quarters.' The Emperor gave thanks for the courtesy; and then, his trouble recurring on him, he asked in a troubled voice, 'Must I quit the army?' Bazaine, in surprise, bewilderment, and embarrassment, begged of him at least to await events yet a little longer. So Napoleon turned to his people and said, 'We will remain, gentlemen, but do not have the baggage unpacked.' 'During this colloquy,' says Bazaine, 'the soldiers, melancholy and beaten out, continued to defile along the road in front of the post-house. Not a single cheer; not one " *Vive l'Empereur!*" came from the broken and straggling ranks at the sight of that Sovereign and his son so enthusiastically acclaimed but a few days before. The moral influence of the retreat had already so lowered the tone of the army!' Is it not a sombre etching, bitten in deeply by a few strong strokes?

Those two men, Emperor and Marshal, parted on the following morning, and for ever. Bazaine thus abruptly pulls down the curtain: 'On the morning of the 16th the Emperor sent a galloper to find me. I lost not a moment, but rode alone at full speed to the Imperial quarters. I found his Majesty in his carriage along with the Prince Imperial and Prince Napoleon. General de France's cavalry brigade was already on horseback to escort the Emperor. I had got no intimation in advance of those arrangements. I rode up to the carriage without dismounting. The Emperor seemed to be suffering, and he said to me but a few words: " I have decided to leave for Verdun and Châlons. Get you on for Verdun as best you can.

The gendarmes have left Briey because the Prussian scouts are in that village." '

Bazaine recorded no farewell, so abrupt was the parting. Napoleon whirled away out of bad into worse, until what relief the very worst could bring came to him after Sedan. The same afternoon Bazaine was in the heart of the fierce *mêlée* of Vionville, stemming with his own sword through the dust of the hand-to-hand struggle a whirlwind charge of the Brunswick Hussars.

Towards evening of the 16th the Emperor reached the camp of Châlons, having ridden from Verdun in a crowded third-class carriage. His arrival in the camp was unheralded by drum or trumpet, and he installed himself in his quarters with the knowledge only of his staff. Marshal MacMahon had just reached the camp with the 1st Corps, only partially reorganised after the rout from Wörth. The 12th Corps, then in process of formation in the camp, was originally intended to be given to General Trochu, but its command ultimately was bestowed on General Lebrun. Neither the 5th nor the 7th Corps had as yet reached the camp. Disorder reigned supreme in the camp, which seemed to be given over to pillage. Instead of smart and peremptory generals there were commanders in dirty uniforms who seemed afraid of showing themselves to their men. Instead of the fine regiments of other days there was a mass of beings without discipline, cohesion, or mark of rank—the swarms of dirty, unarmed soldiers known as *isolés*. Outside the tents and huts, squatting or lying around the bivouac fires, without arms and their uniforms in shreds, were the *isolés* of MacMahon, the fugitives from Reichshoffen, the remnants of regiments overwhelmed and dispersed by defeat; soldiers of the line without rifles or ammunition-pouches, Zouaves in drawers, Turcos without turbans, dragoons without helmets, cuirassiers without cuirasses, hussars without sabre-tasches. The Emperor's pavilion had been looted by the ruffian ' Moblots '; his baggage plundered and his very shirts put up to auction.

The confusion was heightened by incursion after incursion of drunk and reckless Mobiles from Paris. Each contingent was more insolent and unmanageable than the one which had preceded it. Masses of undisciplined blackguards surrounded the quarters of the Emperor, heaping on him foul and brutal insults which nevertheless the officers did not care to resent. A council of war was held on the morning of the 17th, which was attended by Marshal MacMahon, Prince Napoleon, and several other generals including Trochu. It was resolved that the Emperor, having resigned the Command-in-Chief of the army, should return to Paris and there resume with vigour the reins of Government. General Trochu was appointed by the Emperor to the position of Governor of Paris, and also to the chief command of all the troops available for the defence of the capital, inclusive of the insubordinate levies of Mobiles who had been sent to Châlons but who were forthwith to be sent back to Paris. Trochu was to precede the Emperor and prepare everything at Paris for his Majesty's reception there. It was further decided on that MacMahon's army, as soon as concentrated in the Châlons camp, should march on Paris and accept a battle there if necessary for the defence of the capital. In Paris, however, the decisions of the Emperor were put aside without scruple. The

Empress-Regent and the Ministers professed that the Emperor's return to the Tuileries, having regard to the excitement existing in the city, would involve serious danger to the Emperor's life and to the dynasty; and they conveyed to him the most serious warnings against the project he had favoured. The retreat of MacMahon's army to Paris was also strongly opposed on the ground that such a step would gravely wound the national vanity.

The Emperor consequently abandoned the project of returning to Paris and resuming the direction of affairs; he determined to remain with MacMahon's army in the capacity of a private individual of distinction. Virtually, indeed, he abdicated at this time, in the height of a crisis when France was more than ever in need of the determined and energetic leadership of one man. To fill up the measure of France's disasters, not only did Palikao's Ministry arrogate to itself the right of interfering with military operations; but even the Privy Council and the Presidents of both Chambers did the same under the ægis of the Empress-Regent, instead of leaving the direction of military operations to professional soldiers.

It is impossible to describe in the space at command the details of the battles of Vionville-Mars la Tour and St. Privat-Gravelotte, the former fought on Aug. 16, the latter on the 18th. The hero of the first-named battle was the Prussian General Alvensleben II., commanding the 3rd Prussian Army Corps. With this single corps, a force of about 30,000 men inclusive of two cavalry divisions, Alvensleben for five long hours withstood the repeated attacks of the whole French Army of the Rhine. Bredow's cavalry charge from

Vionville up to the edge of the Roman road was an exploit that will live for ever in the history of war. Later in the day Prince Frederick Charles assumed the command ; the Germans were reinforced and fierce fighting continued until darkness set in. That the Germans, notwithstanding their inferiority in numbers achieved a great strategical victory cannot be questioned The slaughter was immense. The losses were about equal ; each side suffered to the amount of 17,000 men.

The battle of St. Privat-Gravelotte was a yet more stupendous struggle than the contest of Vionville-Mars la Tour. The French army with a strength of about 140,000 men occupied the long commanding ridge in front of Metz, from the village of St. Privat on the right to St. Ruffin on the left, a length of about seven miles. On the part of the French the whole disposition for the battle was purely defensive, and could not well have been otherwise. On the German right was the 1st Army commanded by General Steinmetz, consisting of the 7th and 8th Army Corps. The 2nd Army, commanded by Prince Frederick Charles, occupied the German centre and left, confronting the French centre and right. The 12th (Saxon) Army Corps was detailed to make a wide turning movement and strike in flank the French extreme right at St. Privat, at the same time that the Guard Corps should attack the hostile position in front. The operation was ultimately successful, but with appalling bloodshed. As nightfall approached the whole French front was driven back with the exception of the extreme left, which maintained its position until early on the following morning. During the night between the 18th and 19th the whole

French army was withdrawn to the vicinity of Metz, where it was concentrated under the protection of Forts Queuleu and Plappeville. The German losses on the 18th reached a total of over 20,000; the French losses were about 12,000.

The French Army of the Rhine was invested in and about Metz from the 19th and all direct communication between that fortress and the outside world was cut off: but Bazaine's latest despatches represented his military position in the most favourable light. He expressed the hope, after having devoted a few days to the re-equipment of his army, of being able to reach Châlons by St. Menehould. Should this route be found blocked, he announced his intention of marching by Sedan and Mézières. By the Regency in Paris it was insisted on that MacMahon should make an offensive advance in the direction of Verdun, with the object of co-operating with Bazaine and effecting a junction with him. The army of Châlons numbered about 140,000 men, but its condition was far from satisfactory. MacMahon could not dare to adventure a pitched battle in the Châlons position with troops most of which had suffered in their *morale*. On the other hand, he hesitated to carry out his plan of retreating on Paris. As a compromise he determined to march to Rheims, there to await events. On the morning of the 21st the march on Rheims began. After much hesitation MacMahon determined on sacrificing his military convictions in favour of a movement having for its object the relief of the Army of the Rhine. There came to him on the 22nd a telegram from the Minister of War to the Emperor, which must have greatly influenced

MacMahon's decision. Palikao wrote: 'If you do not march to Bazaine's assistance, the worst is to be feared here in Paris. It would be at once concluded in case of such a misfortune, that the capital could not defend itself.' MacMahon telegraphed that he would commence his march towards Metz on the 23rd. In diverging to Rheims he had lost two precious days; but at length on the 23rd the army of Châlons marched from Rheims to the Suippe. The shortcoming of supplies for his army compelled the Marshal to move further to the northward in order to avail himself of the resources of the railway, with the result of the loss of another day. The position on the 25th was from Rethel on the left to Vouziers on the right. Defection and insubordination were seriously manifested, especially after the distribution of rations had become so irregular and scanty that the soldiers resorted to requisitions on their own account. Bands of stragglers followed the army and wandered over the country, a terror to the peaceable inhabitants and a dangerous symptom of growing indiscipline. Great mobs of soldiers pillaged a railway train in the Rheims station and did not spare even the Emperor's private property.

After the battle of the 18th the 3rd and 4th German armies advanced on the 21st towards the Meuse, marching on a broad front. The Prussian King's headquarters were on the 25th at Bar le Duc, whither came a telegram from London conveying the intelligence that MacMahon was assuredly moving to the relief of Bazaine by a wide turning movement to the north, beyond the right flank of the German armies. The tidings were confirmed; the next day those armies, with extraordinary alacrity and deftness changed front to the right and moved northward with strenuous swiftness to thwart MacMahon's enterprise.

On the 27th the Marshal's headquarters were at La Chesne. The German cavalry were pressing on his flank all along the space between the Aisne and the Meuse—too well he knew that the German infantry were swiftly following the German horse. He had the clear consciousness that he was marching towards 'that disaster which he wished to avoid.' He therefore took the wise resolution to abandon an impossible undertaking and to retreat on Mézières ; and he promptly telegraphed to Paris his determination, giving his sound and cogent reasons. The Ministry were obstinate in their ignorant and headstrong folly. To the Emperor came the blunt message : ' If you leave Bazaine in the lurch there will be a revolution in Paris, and you and the army will be attacked by the united force of the enemy.' The message to the Marshal came in the shape of a peremptory order from Palikao : ' I require you to march to the relief of Marshal Bazaine by utilising the thirty hours' start you have over the Crown Prince of Prussia ; the dynasty is lost and all of us with it, unless you obey the demands of the inhabitants of Paris.' The Emperor besought the Marshal not to march on sure ruin, pointing out that since the despatches of a Minister were not orders he was free to act on his own judgment. But MacMahon was what is known as a ' duty soldier,' and he held himself bound to obey the requisition laid upon him. The rearward march, already in progress, was countermanded ; the troops had to retrace their steps along roads sodden with deluges of rain ; and weary, foodless, and disheartened they did not reach their destination until

late on the 28th—some, indeed, not until the following
morning.

All MacMahon's energies were now concentrated on
reaching the right bank of the Meuse by the bridges
of Mouzon, Villers, and Remilly, and this he actually
accomplished by the evening of the 30th. His personal
exertions fought hard with the inertia into which his army
had fallen. He failed, however, to conquer Failly's
lassitude; that feat remained for the Germans. At
noon of the 30th Failly's corps was taking things easy
in a valley near Beaumont, when a Prussian division
'announced its proximity by its cannon-fire.' The
French sprang to arms and fought with great impetuosity. In all the fierce war there were few struggles
more fierce than this 'Battle of Beaumont.' Over-
powered by numbers de Failly's corps, contesting every
step, was at length compelled, shattered and dispersed,
to fly in rout across the Mouzon bridge, its flight
covered by the heroic devotion of a regiment of Béville's
cuirassiers. The French loss in the battle of Beaumont
was 1,800 killed and wounded besides 3,000 prisoners;
the Germans had won their victory at the cost of 3,500
killed and wounded.

On the late afternoon of the 30th the Emperor and
the Marshal were on the heights of Mouzon with the
12th Corps. News came that the 5th Corps was retiring
on Mouzon. The Marshal then said to the Emperor
that all the army would soon have crossed to the right
bank of the Meuse. He himself would not leave
Mouzon until the operation was completed, but he suggested to the Emperor that since all was going well he
should repair to Carignan, where the 1st Corps must

have already arrived, and where the headquarters would be established. So little idea had the Emperor of the dangerous plight of the army or of the magnitude of the defeat of Beaumont, that he sent to the Empress the following telegram, the last he despatched : 'An engagement took place to-day, but not of any great moment.' Scarcely an hour later General Ducrot brought him very alarming tidings. The 5th Corps had been driven back in disorder and the enemy in great force were close at hand. At Ducrot's pressing solicitation the Emperor consented to go to Sedan by railway, and he and his staff arrived at the station of that town at about midnight. The Sedan station was half a mile from the town and the Emperor had to tramp through the mud to the Torcy Gate, where he was delayed some time by civilian sentries before he was allowed to enter the town. Finally, long after midnight, he found his way to the sub-prefecture, weary, ill, and depressed. MacMahon urged Napoleon to re-embark in the train and proceed to Mézières ; the latter, however, refused to quit Sedan. The same night General Vinoy with the advance of his corps reached Mézières. His movement was delayed for some hours, because a train destined for Avesnes carrying the Prince Imperial, 'his baggage, his escort and his suite,' blocked the way of Vinoy and his division to Mézières.

MacMahon had been present throughout the fighting of the 30th, always in the front, as his manner was. The defeat of the day and the attitude of the enemy made it necessary to abandon finally a movement in the direction of Metz. He might accept a battle in the strong position of Mouzon ; yes, but he recognised that

if he fought and was beaten the only resource was a
retreat across the Belgian frontier and resultant disarma-
ment. He remained long in doubt. 'I do not know
what I shall do,' he said after sundown to Ducrot's aide-
de-camp; 'in any case the Emperor should be sent at
once to Sedan.' Sitting later by a bivouac fire, he
called to him General Lebrun commanding the 12th
Corps and bade him retreat with his command on Sedan.
'We have had a bad time,' said the Marshal, 'but the
situation is not hopeless. The German army before us
cannot exceed 70,000 or 80,000 men. If they attack us,
so much the better; no doubt we shall be able to throw
them into the Meuse.' Then the anxious sleepless man
rode away, issuing to his forces as he passed the order
to concentrate on Sedan. To Palikao he sent the
laconic telegram, 'Marshal MacMahon informs the
Minister that he is compelled to retreat on Sedan.' No
further word—the Marshal's temper had reached the end
of its tether.

By the morning of the 31st three of MacMahon's
corps had reached the vicinity of Sedan after a straggling
and chaotic night march; the 1st Corps did not arrive
until the afternoon, having been charged with the duty
of covering the retreat. MacMahon, had he but realised
the situation, had brought his army into a veritable trap,
the only hope of extrication from which was by a march
towards Mézières in the early morning of the 31st along
the narrow wooded space between the Belgian frontier
and the head of the great bend of the Meuse below
Sedan. But throughout the 31st the unfortunate commander still pondered and hesitated. About midday he
expressed his resolve to march on Mézières, and stated

his belief that he could crush any opposition in that
direction ; yet at four P.M. he informed Ducrot that he
had 'no intention' of going to Mézières at all.   To Felix
Douay commanding the 7th Corps, who evinced anxiety
about the key-point of the defensive position, MacMahon
expressed himself : ' But I do not wish to shut myself
up in lines ; I desire to be free to manœuvre.'   ' M. le
Maréchal,' was Douay's grim answer, ' to-morrow the
enemy will not leave you time to manœuvre.'   Mac-
Mahon spent hours watching gloomily from the citadel
the ominous concentric advance of the enemy.   Everything seemed to go against him.   In the Sedan railway
station there was a provision train containing 800,000
rations ; some hostile shells fell close by and the station-
master in a flurry despatched the train to Mézières.   It
carried a company of engineers to blow up the bridge at
Vilette ; the engineers were duly dropped, but the train
carried away with it the explosives and implements.

The   situation   was   curiously   bewildering.   Mac-
Mahon's army took up positions as for a defensive
battle, the 1st and 12th Corps on the heights behind the
Givonne valley and facing eastward, the 7th Corps
fronting to the north-west from Illy to Floing, the
cavalry and the shattered 5th Corps in reserve in the
' old camp.'   But no orders for the morrow were issued,
and the night passed without any expression of a decision
on the part of the Commander-in-Chief.   ' The truth is,'
said MacMahon before the Parliamentary Commission of
1872, ' that I did not think of fighting a battle on the
ground we occupied . . . and I did not yet know on
which side I ought to effect my retreat.'   While he yet
vacillated the enemy forced his hand.

It has been said that when the Emperor reached Sedan at midnight of the 30th, it was suggested to him that he should forthwith continue his journey by rail to Mézières, where he would find the 13th Corps with which he might return to Paris. But Napoleon refused this proposal, since his departure on the eve of a great battle might tend to dispirit the troops. He declared himself firmly resolved to share the dangers and destiny of the army, whatever they might be. On the 31st he issued the following proclamation to the army, which, however, was but partially circulated :

'Soldiers! As the commencement of the war was not fortunate, I wished to hand over the chief commands of the armies to such of the Marshals as public opinion might designate. Hitherto success has not crowned your efforts ; nevertheless I understand that Marshal Bazaine's army has re-established itself under the walls of Metz, and that that of Marshal MacMahon has suffered but comparatively little yesterday. There is, therefore, no ground for despondency. We have prevented the enemy from advancing on the capital and the whole of France is rising in arms to hurl back the invader. Under these difficult circumstances, seeing that the Empress takes my place so worthily at Paris, I have preferred the position of a soldier to that of a Sovereign. No sacrifice shall be too great for me in order to save our country. It still, thank God, possesses brave men ; and if cowards should be found military law and public opinion will render justice on them.

'Soldiers! prove yourselves worthy of your ancient renown. God will not desert France if each of us only does his duty!'

Those were the last words addressed by the Emperor Napoleon to the French army; their uncertain, contradictory, and dispirited tone was not calculated to raise the self-confidence of the army, or to inflame the fighting spirit of the soldiers.

General Wimpffen, who was the senior General of the French army on active service, had been summoned from Algeria to Paris by the Minister of War in order to supersede de Failly in the command of the 5th Corps, and he reached the capital on Aug. 28. Wimpffen was a man of great self-confidence. Palikao told him that 'MacMahon fell in too easily with the suggestions of the Emperor; that his Majesty was in a false position and caused the greatest embarrassment.' 'Send me to the army,' replied Wimpffen. 'I shall impart the requisite boldness and decision.' With a letter in his pocket authorising him to succeed MacMahon should any accident befall the Marshal, he reached Sedan on the night of the 30th, to find the troops in utter disorganisation. As evidence of the disorder he found on the march three regiments belonging to as many corps, some cavalry and several hundred men of the 1st Corps who were under the command of a non-combatant officer. A similar confusion everywhere prevailed, and hungry and weary soldiers fell asleep as they dropped on the sodden ground. Wimpffen led them during the night to Sedan. Presenting himself to the Marshal on the morning of the 31st he was received by MacMahon very coldly, and by the Emperor with tears in his eyes and in great grief at the precarious position of the army; but neither of the two told him how things actually stood nor informed him regarding the plans for the future.

The orders for his assumption of command not having been issued, he informally intimated to General de Failly that he had come to succeed him in the command of the 5th Corps, to which he presented himself as its new Commander and bivouacked for the night on the ground in its midst. Wimpffen's later course of action will presently be detailed. In his subsequent report to the War Minister he wrote very tersely: 'I came, I saw, and I was beaten.'

CHAPTER XV

THE CATASTROPHE OF SEDAN

THROUGH the dense mist of the early morning of Sept. 1 the Bavarians advanced to the attack of Bazeilles. The wakeful Lebrun aroused his soldiers from their bivouacs and sent a message to MacMahon that his troops were already in action, a message which the Marshal received about five A.M. He mounted his ready-saddled horse, rode out to Bazeilles, saw that the defence there was being stoutly maintained, and then bent leftward on to the high ground overlooking the village of La Moncelle. As he sat on his horse there about half-past six, trying to penetrate the haze which enwrapped the valley, the fragment of a shell struck him on the thigh. He dismounted, fainted for a few moments, and then, rallying his strength, found the wound severe. He nominated Ducrot as his successor in the chief command, and was then carried in an ambulance to the sub-prefecture in the town. On the way the Emperor riding out to the field of battle, met the wounded Marshal and spoke to him some words of earnest sympathy. Later in the disastrous day they had a long interview, the Emperor seated by the Marshal's pallet. After the capitulation of the army of Châlons King William gave permission that the wounded

Marshal should be removed from the noise and squalor of Sedan to the Château of Pouru-aux-Bois in the Ardennes to the eastward of the town. On his recovery MacMahon shared the captivity of his army in Germany and returned to Paris in time to conduct the extermination of the Commune.

About eight o'clock, in virtue of the Marshal's nomination Ducrot was exercising command and ordering a retreat on Mézières, which, if it had been promptly and resolutely carried out, might have temporarily saved at least a portion of the French army. The Emperor, who had ridden from near Bazeilles to the height of La Moncelle and had inspected the positions there under a very heavy fire, returned from thence to Balan. Here he remarked with great surprise the sudden retrograde movement of the troops which he had seen shortly before perfectly steady and occupying strong positions. He sent a message to Ducrot desiring to know what was meant by this retirement, adding that he had no intention of interfering with the General's dispositions in the chief command. Ducrot sent the reply : ' The enemy is only amusing us at Bazeilles ; the real battle will be fought about Illy. I am therefore withdrawing the troops in good order, with the object of concentrating the army for the march towards Mézières.' The Emperor, whether satisfied or not with this explanation, remained faithful to his principle of non-interference, and allowed General Ducrot to carry out his own project. But presently General Wimpffen produced his commission from Palikao ; and Ducrot, although for the moment indignant at his sudden supersession, was probably not very sorry to be relieved from a situation so complicated.

Wimpffen countermanded the movement in the Mézières direction in favour of a hopeless attempt to break out to the eastward towards Carignan. Ducrot accepted the commands of the new Commander-in-Chief, and in accordance with the orders of the latter the 12th and 1st Corps reoccupied their original positions on the eastward front between nine and ten A.M. Shortly afterwards Wimpffen casually met the Emperor at Balan. His Majesty was by no means pleased at the sudden unexpected change in the Command-in-Chief, of which he had previously no intimation. He attempted to move Wimpffen from his purpose, but in vain. 'Your Majesty may be quite at ease,' said Wimpffen; 'within two hours I shall have driven your enemies into the Meuse.'

While the new Commander-in-Chief of the French Army was thus abandoning himself to illusions, the German troops were soon to surround the hapless bodies which were becoming more and more disorganised as the minutes passed. The Emperor had been under heavy fire soon after quitting the fortress in the early morning, but the heaviest fire was in the vicinity of Balan. He left his escort and most of his aides-de-camp with a battalion of chasseurs screened by a wall, and went forward followed by four of his officers. Two of those, General de Courson and Captain de Trecesson, fell wounded close beside their master; a third officer, Captain Hendecourt, was killed while carrying a message from the Emperor to General Ducrot. At ten o'clock the Emperor dismounted, and slowly, silently, and unmoved, walked to and fro under a hail of fire. Shells burst close to him and covered him with dirt and smoke. But he remained unhurt, and after having maintained his situation for several hours near the south-eastern angle of the defensive position, he rode towards the heights of Givonne. Arrived near the old entrenched camp he found it impossible to advance farther, because of the roads crowded with wounded and fugitives. Despairing of the possibility of gaining the heights of Illy, he decided to enter the town in order to confer with the wounded Marshal. On his way to Sedan the Emperor was compelled to force his way through bodies of fugitive troops who were thronging towards the fortress in straggling crowds. Shells were falling thus early in the streets of the town ; just as the Emperor entered Sedan a shell exploded within a few yards of him, killing two horses. By this time he was much exhausted, and he was racked with the pain of the ailment which constantly tortured him. He reached the sub-prefecture, had a conversation with the Marshal, and would have remounted and ridden out again ; but found the block in the streets so dense that he had to relinquish his purpose and remain in the sub-prefecture.

When the Emperor returned into Sedan is not to be precisely ascertained ; nor, except inferentially, at what hour he first directed the white flag to be hoisted. No person avowed himself executant of that order, but the flag did not long fly ; it was indignantly cut down, according to common belief by General Faure, MacMahon's Chief-of-Staff, who did not give himself the trouble to communicate with Napoleon either before or after taking this considerable liberty. Soon after two o'clock Wimpffen communicated to the Emperor his determination to force his way out, and appealed to his

Majesty in writing to 'place himself in the midst of his troops, who could be relied on to force a passage through the German lines.' Wimpffen waited an hour in vain for an answer; then, with the utmost difficulty he got together some 5,000 men whom in the first instance he led towards the heights of Givonne; but his attack was beaten off after half an hour's sharp fighting, and the last resistance of the French on this part of the field of battle was thus completely broken.

How anxious was the Emperor that a capitulation should be speedily effected; how obstinate was Wimpffen that there should be no capitulation, but resistance to the bitter end, is shown in the testimony of Lebrun and Ducrot. 'Why does this useless struggle still go on?' demanded Napoleon of Lebrun, who a little before three P.M. entered his apartment in the sub-prefecture; 'an hour and more ago I bade the white flag to be displayed as a request for an armistice.' Lebrun explained that to sue for an armistice a letter had to be signed by the Commander-in-Chief and despatched by an officer with a trumpeter and a flag of truce. Having duly procured the proper accessories Lebrun went forth to where Wimpffen was gathering troops for an attack on the Germans in Balan. As Lebrun approached, the angry Wimpffen shouted: 'No capitulation! Drop that rag! I mean to fight on!' and forthwith he set out towards Balan carrying Lebrun with him into the fight.

Ducrot had been fighting hard about Illy and the upper part of the Bois de Garennes; but recognising that his efforts afforded no hope of success, he determined to pass through Sedan and join in an attempt to cut a way with Wimpffen towards Carignan and Montmédy. He had not even a corporal's escort, but he sent word to Wimpffen by the latter's orderly that he would enter Sedan and attempt to collect some troops in support of Wimpffen's efforts. What Ducrot saw in Sedan may be told nearly in his own words. The state of the interior of Sedan he characterised as indescribable. The streets, the open places, the gates, were blocked up by waggons, guns, and the impedimenta and débris of a routed army. Bands of soldiers without arms, without packs, were rushing about, throwing themselves into the churches, or breaking into private houses. Many unfortunates were trampled under foot. The few soldiers still preserving a remnant of energy were spending it in abuse and curses. ' We have been betrayed!' they cried. ' We have been sold by traitors and cowards!' There was really nothing to be done with such men, and Ducrot repaired to the Emperor in the sub-prefecture. Ducrot writes as follows :

' Napoleon no longer preserved that cold and impenetrable countenance so familiar to the world. The silence which reigned in the presence of the Sovereign rendered the noise more startling. The air was on fire. Shells fell on roofs and struck masses of masonry which crashed down upon the pavements. " I do not understand," said the bewildered Emperor, "why the enemy continues his fire. I have ordered the white flag to be hoisted. I hope to obtain an interview with the King of Prussia and may succeed in obtaining advantageous terms for the army."' While the Emperor and General Ducrot were conversing the cannonade increased in violence from minute to minute. Women were wounded and children

were destroyed.   The sub-prefecture was struck ; shells
exploded every minute in garden and courtyard.   ' It is
absolutely necessary to stop the firing !' exclaimed the
Emperor.   ' Here, write this !' he commanded General
Ducrot : " The flag of truce having been displayed,
negotiations are about to be opened with the enemy.
Firing must cease all along the line."'   Then said the
Emperor, ' Now   sign   it !'   ' Oh   no,   Sire,'   replied
General Ducrot, ' I cannot sign ; General Wimpffen is
General-in-Chief.'   ' Yes,' replied the Emperor, ' but
I don't know where General Wimpffen is to be found.
Some one must sign.'   ' Let his Chief-of-Staff sign,'
suggested   General   Ducrot,   ' or   General   Douay.'
' Yes,' replied the Emperor, ' let the Chief-of-Staff sign
the order !'

The subsequent history of this order cannot be
traced, nor, indeed, whether it ever got signed at all.
Wimpffen had ridden back from the front on the double
errand of procuring reinforcements and of trying to
prevail on the Emperor to join him in his forlorn-hope
attempt to break out. ' About four o'clock,' wrote
Wimpffen, ' I reached the gate of Sedan.   There at
last came to me M. Pierron of the Imperial Staff, who
handed me a letter from his Majesty, telling me also
that the white flag was flying from the citadel of Sedan
and that I was charged with the task of negotiating with
the enemy. . . .   Not recognising the Emperor's
right to order the hoisting of the flag, I replied, " I will
not take cognisance of this letter ; I refuse to negotiate !"
. . . Having gathered in the town about 2,000 men, at
the head of this gallant handful I succeeded about five
o'clock in penetrating as far as the church of Balan ; but

the reinforcements I hoped for did not arrive and I then gave the order to retire on Sedan.'

On his return to the fortress Wimpffen forwarded his resignation to the Emperor, who then attempted in vain to persuade first Ducrot and then Douay to assume the command. Wimpffen was finally sent for ; and, in the presence of the Emperor, a violent altercation occurred between him and Ducrot, in the course of which blows were actually exchanged. Ducrot, who was the more excited, withdrew ; and in the words of the Emperor, 'General Wimpffen, after having twice obstinately refused to obey the Emperor's command to treat with the enemy, was brought to understand that having commanded during the battle, his duty obliged him not to desert his post in circumstances so critical.' Wimpffen would have been quite justified in persisting in not resigning. The situation had been a purely military one and he was Commander-in-Chief ; yet the Emperor, who had no military position whatsoever, had overridden Wimpffen's powers while as yet that officer was in supreme command.

From the hill-top of Marfée the Prussian monarch and his staff had been watching the course of the battle ever since the early morning. As the great ring of German soldiers was gradually closing in upon the environed French army, a last desperate effort was made to arrest the progress of the Teuton adversaries and to break their lines by a great charge of cavalry. General Margueritte was ordered to advance with his reserve cavalry division by echelons eastward of Floing, crush everything in his front, and then, wheeling to the right, roll up the enemy's line. The 2nd Reserve Cavalry division, consisting of the four cuirassier regiments commanded by General Bonnemain, was to follow up Margueritte's charge ; and several regiments of divisional cavalry commanded by General Salignac Fenelon were also brought forward to take part in this great cavalry attack.

Margueritte having ridden forward to reconnoitre the ground in his front was severely wounded and was carried to the rear.   Colonel Beaufremont was then the senior officer, and therefore assumed the command which Margueritte had perforce vacated. Gallifet's claim to have succeeded Margueritte in the command is wholly untenable ; he commanded in the charge merely his own regiment.   The whole of the French cavalry with Salignac Fenelon's lancers in the front swooped down upon the enemy like a hurricane and broke through the line of Prussian skirmishers, but were received by the deployed battalions with a point-blank fire so murderous that the French squadrons were actually mowed down.   The divisions of Margueritte and Bonnemain renewed their attacks thrice with the greatest gallantry and devotion ; but they were met with a fire so withering that heaps of killed and wounded men and horses were actually piled up in front of the Prussian lines.

As the afternoon drew on the French defeat was decisively apparent, yet, although the fierceness of the fighting waned, the now surrounded army remained heroically stubborn in its resistance to inevitable fate ; and so its final death-throe had to be artistically quickened up.   In the stern language of the German ' Official History ' ' a powerful artillery fire directed

against the enemy's last point of refuge appeared the
most suitable method of convincing him of the hope-
lessness of his situation and of inducing him to surrender.
With intent to hasten the capitulation and thus spare the
German army further sacrifices, the King ordered the
whole available artillery to concentrate its fire on Sedan.'
This command, so states the ' Staff History,' was issued
at four P.M., and was promptly acted on. Results of
the reinforced and concentrated shell fire were soon
manifested. Sedan seemed in flames. The French
return fire, gallantly maintained for a short time, was
presently crushed into silence. At this moment the
white flag was definitely displayed on the citadel
flagstaff, and the German fire at once ceased. As the
bruit of impending negotiations spread, hostilities ceased
everywhere save about Balan, where the contumacious
Wimpffen was still battling to no purpose. The white
flag being visible, the King directed two officers of his
Staff, Colonel Bronsart von Schellendorf and Captain
von Winterfeld, to proceed to Sedan under a flag of
truce and summon the French Commander-in-Chief to
surrender his army and the fortress. The Prussian
officers penetrated into the city and duly announced the
character of their mission ; but to Bronsart's surprise he
was ushered into the presence of the Emperor Napoleon,
of whose presence in Sedan the German headquarters
had not been aware. In reply to Bronsart's application
for a French officer of rank to be appointed to negotiate,
the Emperor simply informed him that the Commander-
in-Chief of the French Army was General Wimpffen.
This answer his Majesty desired Bronsart to take back
to the King ; and to intimate that he would soon send

out his aide-de-camp, General Count Reillé, with a letter from himself to the Prussian monarch.

Bronsart came back trotting hard up the hill to the Prussian headquarters. As he approached he spurred his horse into a gallop, and pointing backwards towards Sedan exclaimed in a loud voice : ' *Der Kaiser ist da* ' ; at which there was a loud outburst of cheering. It was about half an hour later, the time a quarter to seven, when the French officer, Count Reillé, rode up the hill at a walking pace, with a trooper in advance carrying a flag of truce and with an escort of Prussian cuirassiers. He dismounted, approached the King, and with a silent reverence handed to his Majesty the Emperor's letter. While the King, Bismarck, and Moltke conversed earnestly apart, the Crown Prince, with that gracious tact which was one of the most charming traits of his noble character, entered into affable conversation with poor forlorn Reillé, standing out there among the stubbles. Bismarck gave instructions to Count Hatzfeldt of the Foreign Office to draft the King's answer to the letter of the French Emperor. Sitting on a chair, the King used as his writing-desk the seat of another chair held up by Major von Alten, while he indited his reply to Napoleon. The following is the Emperor's letter to the King :

' Sire, my Brother,—Not having been able to die in the midst of my troops, there is nothing left me but to render my sword into the hands of your Majesty. I am your Majesty's good brother,

' NAPOLEON.'

King William's reply was as follows :

' My Brother,—While regretting the circumstances in which we meet, I accept your Majesty's sword, and request that you will appoint one of your officers furnished with the necessary powers to treat for the capitulation of the army which has fought so valiantly under your command. I, for my part, have appointed General von Moltke to this duty.

' Your loving brother,

' WILHELM.'

Reillé rode back into Sedan with the King's reply to the Emperor's letter, and as he rode down the Marfée hill the astounding purport of his visit ran from lip to lip through the exulting army, which now hoped that after this colossal success the days of ceaseless marching and fighting would now promptly end. Soon after seven P.M. his Prussian Majesty and his suite started on the journey back to Vendresse, where were the Royal headquarters. Bismarck and Moltke rode into Donchery there to take part in the conference for settling the terms of the capitulation, and the Marfée hill-top was deserted.

After supping in the Donchery hotel on a tough beefsteak and a bottle of Donchery champagne, Bismarck about midnight joined Moltke, whom the King had designated to treat for the capitulation of the French army. That was a strange conference which was held in the still watches of the night in a salon of a house on the outskirts of the little town. Wimpffen verified his powers, and presented to Moltke the French Generals Faure and Castelnau. Moltke introduced Count Bismarck and General Blumenthal to the French Commander-in-Chief. On one side of the table sat Moltke in the centre with

Bismarck on his left and Blumenthal on his right. On the opposite side was Wimpffen by himself; behind him, somewhat in shadow, stood Faure, Castelnau (who specially represented the Emperor), and a few other French officers. Moltke sat silent and impassive; and after an embarrassing pause Wimpffen asked what were the conditions which the Prussian King was prepared to accord. 'They are very simple,' replied Moltke: 'the whole French army to surrender with arms and belongings; the officers to retain their arms but to be prisoners of war along with their men.' Wimpffen scouted those terms, and demanded for his army that it should be permitted to withdraw with arms, equipment, and colours, on condition of not serving while the war lasted. Moltke adhered inexorably to the conditions which he had specified, and was adamant to the pleading of the Frenchman. Losing temper the latter exclaimed, 'I cannot accept the terms you impose; I will appeal to the honour and heroism of my army, and will cut my way out or stand on the defence at Sedan.'

Moltke's reply was crushing. 'A sortie and the defensive,' he quietly remarked, 'are equally impossible. The mass of your infantry is demoralised; we took to-day more than twenty thousand unwounded prisoners, and your whole force is not now more than eighty thousand strong. You cannot pierce our lines, for I have surrounding you two hundred and forty thousand men with five hundred guns in position to fire on Sedan; you cannot maintain your defensive there because you have not provisions for forty-eight hours and your ammunition is exhausted. If you desire I will send one of your officers round our positions, who will satisfy

you as to the accuracy of my statements.' Wimpffen
declined this offer ; and when assured that there could
be no mitigation of the terms he exclaimed, ' Then it is
equally impossible for me to sign such a stipulation ; we
will renew the battle!' Moltke's quiet curt answer was :
' The armistice expires at four A.M. At that hour, to the
moment, I shall open fire.'

There was nothing more to be said. The French
officers sent for their horses. Meanwhile not a word
was spoken ; in the words of the reporter, ' *Ce silence
était glacial.*' It was broken by Bismarck, who urged
Wimpffen not to break off the conference in a moment of
pique. The French General represented that he alone
could not incur the responsibility of a decision ; that it
was necessary that he should consult his colleagues ; that
the final answer could not be made by four A.M. ; and
that a prolongation of the armistice was indispensable.
After a short colloquy in low tones between Bismarck
and Moltke, the latter gave his consent that the truce
should be extended to nine A.M. ; whereupon Wimpffen
quitted Donchery and rode back to Sedan. He went
straight to the bedside of the Emperor, who, having
been informed of the German conditions, said, ' I shall
start at five o'clock for the King's headquarters and
entreat him to grant more favourable conditions.'

Napoleon acted on his resolution. Expecting that
he would be allowed to return to Sedan, he bade no fare-
wells. As he passed through the Torcy gate before six
o'clock the Zouaves on duty there cried ' *Vive
l'Empereur !* ' ' the last adieu which fell upon his ears
from the voices of French soldiers.' The open carriage
in which, with two officers with him and three more on

horseback behind him, the Emperor sat in the undress uniform of a general officer and smoking a cigarette, travelled towards Donchery at a leisurely pace. At a hamlet about a mile from Donchery there was a halt of considerable length while General Reillé went on to Donchery, to intimate to Bismarck that the Emperor had left Sedan and was desirous of meeting him. Reillé had scarcely turned his horse away from Bismarck's quarters in the little square of Donchery, when the Chancellor, in cap and undress uniform, his long cuirassier boots stained and dusty, came out, swung himself on to his big bay horse, and rode away on Reillé's track. He crossed the bridge at a walk and kept that pace for a little distance on the road to Sedan, but presently broke into a sharp canter. About a mile short of Sedan, near the village of Frenois, he met an open carriage on the right hand of the principal seat of which there leant back a man of impassive features. Bismarck dismounted, letting his horse go, and drawing near on foot uncovered his head and bowed low. The man to whom he spoke—the man with the leaden-coloured face, the gaunt-eyed man with the dishevelled moustache and the weary stoop of the shoulders, was none other than Napoleon the Third and last.

The Emperor wore a dark-blue cloak with scarlet lining thrown back and disclosing the decorations on the breast of his coat. The cortège moved on a few hundred yards in the direction of Donchery, when the Emperor, who seemed to be suffering, desired of Bismarck that he should be allowed to remain in the adjacent wayside cottage until he should have an interview with the King. A few minutes after seven the

Emperor and Bismarck ascended to the upper floor of the cottage. They remained there until twenty minutes past seven. Bismarck, remarking that the room was not clean, ordered two chairs to be brought out to the front of the cottage: the two then sat down facing the road, the Emperor on the right, and an outdoor conversation began which lasted about three-quarters of an hour. As they sat, Napoleon occasionally smiled faintly and made a remark ; but clearly Bismarck was doing most of the talking. Soon after eight o'clock Bismarck quitted the Emperor for a time, going to his Donchery quarters for breakfast and to dress.

Madame Fournaise, the wife of the weaver whose cottage was occupied for a short time by the two most conspicuous men in Europe, has left—she died several years ago—some interesting recollections of this eventful morning. The Emperor, she said, alighted, and came up her narrow staircase. To reach the inner room he had to pass through her bedroom, where she had just risen. The furniture of the inner room consisted of two straw-bottomed chairs, a round table, and a press. Bismarck, 'in a rough dress,' presently joined the Emperor, and for a quarter of an hour, said Madame Fournaise, they talked in low tones, of which she, remaining in the outer room, occasionally caught a word. Then Bismarck came clattering out—' *Il avait une très mauvaise mine.*' She warned him of the breakneck stairs, but he ' sprang down them like a man of twenty,' mounted his horse and rode away towards Donchery. When she entered the room in which the Emperor remained, she found him seated at the little table with his face buried in his hands. ' Can I do anything for your Majesty?' she asked. 'Only to pull down the blinds,' was Napoleon's reply, without lifting his head. In about an hour Bismarck returned in full uniform ; he preceded the Emperor down the stairs, facing towards him as if to 'usher him with a certain honour.' On the threshold the Emperor gave Madame Fournaise four twenty-franc pieces—'he put them into my own hand' ; and he said plaintively, 'This probably is the last hospitality which I shall receive in France.' With a kindly word of farewell, 'which I shall never forget,' the Emperor quitted the poor house in which he had suffered so much unhappiness. The Emperor's gift of the four twenty-franc pieces, Madame Fournaise, poor though she was, would never part with. Three of the coins bore the visage of Louis Philippe ; the fourth was a Napoleon. When near her end she directed the three 'Louis Philippes' to be expended in defraying her funeral expenses ; the 'Napoleon' was interred with her as her last behest, in the grave of the woman who had given to the unfortunate Emperor 'the last hospitality he received in France.'

Napoleon remained alone in the upstairs room of the weaver's cottage for about half an hour after Bismarck had left him ; then, with a face of mortal pallor, he came out and betook himself to sauntering moodily by himself along the path in the potato garden on the right of the cottage, his white-gloved hands clasped behind his back and smoking cigarette after cigarette. His gait was curious. He limped slightly on one leg, and he waddled in a sideways fashion, the left shoulder forward, and his whole motion crab-like and doddering. Later, he came and sat down among his officers in front of the cottage, maintaining an almost unbroken silence while they spoke and gesticulated with great animation.

At a quarter-past nine there came from the Donchery vicinity at a trot a troop of Prussian cuirassiers, who promptly formed a cordon around the rear of the cottage. The lieutenant dismounted two troopers and without recognising the French group or making any semblance of salute, marched them up to behind the Emperor's chair, halted them, shouted the order ' Draw swords !' and then gave the men their orders in an undertone. Napoleon started abruptly, glanced backwards with a gesture of surprise, and the blood rushed into his face—the first evidence of emotion he had evinced.

At a quarter to ten Bismarck returned, now in full uniform. Moltke accompanied him ; but whereas Bismarck strode forward to where the Emperor was now standing, Moltke remained in the group gathered on the road. Half-way to Vendresse Moltke had met the King, who approved of the proposed terms of capitulation but intimated that he could not meet the Emperor until they should have been accepted by the French Commander-in-Chief.

After speaking with the Emperor for a few moments Bismarck ordered up the carriage, which Napoleon presently entered ; and the cortège, escorted by the cuirassier ' guard of honour,' moved off at a walk towards the Château Bellevue, which lies somewhat nearer to Sedan than does the weaver's cottage. The pretty residence looks out through its trees on the broad Meuse and the plain on which stands Sedan. The garden entrance on the first floor is reached by a broad flight of stone steps.

The Emperor was ushered into the drawing-room in the central block, where he remained alone after Bismarck left him. He seemed ill and broken as he slowly ascended the steps with drooping head and dragging limbs.

After the departure of the Emperor from Sedan Wimpffen had summoned to a council of war the general officers of the army of Châlons, who listened to the unfortunate chief as in a voice broken by sobs he recounted the terms insisted on by Moltke. Ultimately the council became unanimous in favour of acceptance of the conditions. But Wimpffen, nevertheless, procrastinated unaccountably hour after hour, notwithstanding that the hostile batteries were everywhere taking up menacing positions. At length an officer whom Moltke had sent with the ultimatum that at ten o'clock hostilities would certainly be renewed unless by that hour negotiations should have been resumed, bluntly informed General Wimpffen that he had instructions to give the order as he rode back that the German batteries would open fire promptly at the hour named. Under stress of this argument Wimpffen accompanied Captain von Zingler to the Château Bellevue, in the dining-room of which soon after eleven o'clock the capitulation was signed by Generals Moltke and Wimpffen. Then the latter had a brief interview with his Imperial master, whom he informed with great emotion that 'all was finished.' 'The Emperor,' in Wimpffen's own words, 'with tears in his eyes, approached me, pressed my hand, and embraced me. My sad and painful duty accomplished, I rode back to Sedan, *la mort dans l'âme.*'

Meanwhile the Prussian King with his son and their

respective staffs awaited on the hill above Frenois the tidings of the completion of the capitulation. Moltke carried the convention to his Majesty, who commanded the momentous document to be read aloud ; and then he himself added a few words of thanks and acknowledgment to the German Princes and to the army by whose valour and exertions results of so great magnitude had been achieved. Then the great cavalcade rode down to the Château Bellevue. As William alighted Napoleon came down the steps to meet him. The contrast between the two Sovereigns was strange and painful : the German, tall, upright, square-shouldered, with the flash of success from the keen blue eyes from under the helmet and the glow of triumph on the fresh cheek ; the Frenchman, with weary stoop of the shoulders, his eyes drooping, his lips quivering, bare-headed and dishevelled. As the two clasped hands silently Napoleon's handkerchief was at his eyes, and William's face became full of concern. Their interview in the drawing-room of the Château lasted for about twenty minutes. Then the Prussian King rode away to greet and congratulate his victorious soldiers. Napoleon remained in the Château Bellevue until the following morning.

Sir William Fraser mentions in his ' Napoleon III.' that he possesses the volume of ' Essais de Montaigne ' which the Emperor was reading when the Prussian King arrived at the Château Bellevue. The following passage was deeply scored by Napoleon—the previous passage is on the immortality of the soul :

' Deux choses rendoient cette opinion plausible : l'une, que sans l'immortalité des âmes il n'y auroit plus de quoy

asservir les vaines espérances de la gloire, qui est une
considération de merveilleux crédit au monde l'aultre,
que c'est une très utile impression, come dict Platon, que
les vices, quand ils se desroberont de la veue et cognois-
sance de l'humaine justice, demeurent toujours en butte
à la divine, qui les poursuivra ; voire aprèz la mort des
coupables.'

Sir William has fallen into some errors in regard
to the Sedan period. Napoleon did not sleep in the
Château Bellevue on the night after the battle, but in the
bedroom in the sub-prefecture which he had occupied on
the two previous nights. Wimpffen found him there in
the early morning of the 2nd on his return from the
Donchery conference. It was on the night of that day
that he slept in the Château Bellevue ; and it was on that
night, and not on the night of the 1st, that he selected
from a bookcase in his bedroom Lord Lytton's novel
'The Last of the Barons,' and read it in bed for several
hours. The book lay face downwards on the commode
at the bed-head, presumably where the Emperor had left
off reading ; and it remained there untouched for hours
after Napoleon had crossed the frontier and reached
Bouillon. Not three but four gold pieces were over the
chimney-piece in the inner room of the weaver's cottage ;
three were 'Louis' and only the fourth was a 'Napoleon.'
'What about the four twenty-francs pieces ?' asked of
Madame Fournaise a pilgrim to Sedan—'No doubt you
have sold them over and over again ?' 'Oh, my God,
no !' she exclaimed. 'Never—never ! Did he not give
them to me with his own hand ? See ! the original four
are in that locked case with the glass top on the mantel
yonder. Over and over again I could have had 500

francs for the four pieces ; but no money would tempt me to sell them ! '

On the afternoon of the 2nd Napoleon was again visible ; he had come out into the little park of the Château to superintend the reorganisation of his train, which had come out from Sedan in the course of the morning. He looked very wan and weary, but still maintained his impassive aspect. The Imperial equipage in its magnificence, the numerous glittering and massive *fourgons*, the splendid teams of draught animals and the squadron of led horses, presented an extraordinary contrast to the plain simplicity of the King of Prussia's campaigning outfit. In gold and scarlet the coachmen and outriders of Napoleon glittered profusely. He of Prussia had his postillions in plain blue cloth, with oilcloth covers on their hats to keep the rain and dust off the nap. Zola, in his vivid but often grotesquely erroneous ' Débâcle,' has fallen into strange blundering in regard to the Imperial equipage. He thus refers to it : ' The Imperial baggage-train had been left behind in Sedan, where it rested in hiding behind the Sous-Préfet's lilac bushes. It puzzled the authorities to rid themselves of what was to them a *bête noire* by getting it out of the city unseen by the famishing multitude, on which its flaunting splendour would have produced the effect of a red rag to a mad bull. There came at length an unusually dark night, when horses, carriages, and baggage-waggons, with their silver stewpans, plate, linen, and baskets of fine wines, trooped out of Sedan in deepest mystery, and shaped their course for Belgium without beat of drum, over the least-frequented roads, like a thief stealing away in the night.'

The Imperial train, as has been said, was massed in the park of the Château Bellevue on the afternoon of Sept. 2. By the evening of Sept. 3 the capitulated French army was disarmed and enclosed under guard on the peninsula of Iges. There remained then in Sedan only its normal or less than normal population, far too crushed to attempt any irregularity. A German governor had been installed, German troops were in garrison, and Sedan would not have dared to remonstrate if the Imperial train had perambulated the city in face of the population all day long.

On the morning of Sept. 3 the Emperor and his suite and cortège left the Château Bellevue in a heavy downpour of rain, driving through Donchery and by Floing and Illy and across the battlefield of the 1st, and past the frontier to Bouillon in Belgium, *en route* for Wilhelmshöhe in Cassel. At Verviers on the morning of the 5th Napoleon learned from a newspaper sold to him by a newsboy on the railway platform that he was no longer a Sovereign. Accompanied by General Boyer, an aide-de-camp of King William, he reached Wilhelmshöhe the same afternoon.

CHAPTER XVI

THE ENDING OF THE CAREER

THE Prussian King during his interview with Napoleon in the Château Bellevue on Sept. 2 gave permission to the latter to despatch to the Empress in Paris a telegram in cypher. It was very brief. 'The army of Châlons has surrendered *en masse*,' so it ran; 'and I am a prisoner of war.' This was the earliest authentic message which reached Paris. The Palace of Wilhelmshöhe, which was to be Napoleon's luxurious place of detention for several months after his ruin on the field of Sédan, had belonged to King Jerome, the uncle of the Emperor, who when quite an infant had visited it with his mother Queen Hortense. It had now become the property of the Grand Duke of Hesse. In the picture gallery of the Palace Napoleon recognised the portrait of Hortense, painted when in full glow of her youth and beauty.

The first public act of the Emperor during his captivity was to write the following letter to General Wimpffen in reference to his official report on the battle of Sedan. It was as follows :

'General,—I have read your official report on the battle of Sedan. It contains two assertions which I contradict. If I did not accede to your appeal to cut our way out towards Carignan, it was because it was impracticable, as experience proved to you ; and because the attempt, as I foresaw, would only sacrifice the lives of many soldiers. I consented to hoist the white flag only when in the opinion of all the commanders of Army Corps further resistance had become impossible. I cannot, therefore, have impeded your means of action. Believe, General, in my sentiments.

'NAPOLEON.'

In a letter written by the Emperor to the Commission of Enquiry on the conduct of the war issued in May, 1872 he dealt as follows with questions relating to Sedan. 'The honour of the army,' he wrote, 'having been saved by the bravery which had been shown, I then exercised my sovereign right and gave orders to hoist a flag of truce. I claim the entire responsibility of that act.' No doubt, in acting as he did on the afternoon of Sedan Napoleon was actuated by humane motives ; but it is more than questionable whether, when he ordered the display of the white flag, he had any 'sovereign right' which gave him that power. His attribution to himself of 'sovereign right' on that fateful afternoon was incompatible with his statement to Bronsart that the French army was under the command of General Wimpffen.

The monotony of the life at Wilhelmshöhe was broken but once, when the Empress in the end of October came to make a short visit to her suffering husband. Her own experiences had been tragic. On the afternoon of Sept. 4, the day of the Revolution and of the *déchéance*, she quitted the Tuileries in a *fiacre* accompanied by Madame Lebreton and was driven to the house in the Avenue de l'Impératrice of the American dentist, Dr. Evans, where she spent the night. On the morning of the 5th the Empress quitted Paris. After many delays Deauville was reached the same evening. Dr. Evans prevailed on Sir John Burgoyne to carry the Empress across the Channel in his yacht the *Gazelle*, and the little vessel, barely forty-five feet long, put out to sea in very heavy weather at six o'clock on the morning of the 7th. In its dog-hole of a cabin were crowded the Empress, Madame Lebreton, Dr. Evans, and Sir John Burgoyne, while a tempest raged for three-and-twenty hours. At daybreak on the 8th the wind fell and the yacht entered the harbour of Ryde. After having rested for a short time there the Empress proceeded to Hastings and arrived in the afternoon at the Marine Hotel in that town, where she remained a fortnight, and where she was joined by the Prince Imperial who had come from Belgium. At Hastings, a busy watering-place, the Empress found herself involved in a stir and bustle which annoyed and disturbed her. An English friend who had known the Emperor in other times was willing to let his mansion of Camden House at Chislehurst, and about Sept. 20 the Empress took up her residence with her son in that abode where in the years to come she was to endure so many sorrows.

From Wilhelmshöhe Napoleon addressed his last proclamation to the French people. It is too long for insertion, nor is it of great interest. Referring to the defence maintained so long and so bravely by the Government of National Defence, he wrote: 'I found the Empire, which the whole nation had just acclaimed for the third time, upset and deserted by those who were bound to defend it. Giving truce to my natural and just resentment, I exclaimed, " What matters the dynasty if the country can be saved ? " And instead of protesting against the violation of the law my prayers were given to the national defence, and I have admired the patriotic devotion which the sons of all classes and all parties have shown.' The Emperor adhered to the conviction that his favourite nostrum of universal suffrage would redress his misfortunes and restore the Empire. He was confident that the millions of Frenchmen who had voted in his favour in the plebiscite of May, 1870, were still the staunch suppporters of himself and of his dynasty. But that illusion vanished when the tidings reached him of the result of the Bordeaux elections during the armistice of February-March 1871. He uttered no complaint ; but he was overwhelmed with grief and struck to the heart ; for he truly loved the people from which the shattering blow proceeded and which he had believed to be true to him. He had grown old, grey, and worn when, his long dreary imprisonment ended, he landed at Dover on March 20, 1871, and was warmly greeted by a crowd of old adherents and of Britons with whom he had always been popular. The Empress and the Prince Imperial were there to receive him, and they threw themselves into his arms as he stepped ashore. He was visibly cheered by the warmth of his English welcome. On April 15 the Queen drove to Chislehurst and paid him and the Empress a visit of friendly cordiality. On Aug. 15, his birthday—in marked contrast to his sombre birthday of the preceding year—Chislehurst was alive with visitors from France and bright with floral offerings and tokens of the loyalty of officers of the Imperial Guard. In September the Emperor went to Torquay with his son, while the Empress paid her mother a visit in Spain. Demonstrations of sympathy and regard were manifested wherever he appeared in public, as, for instance, at a review of the Woolwich garrison, and when he watched the thanksgiving progress of the Prince of Wales to St. Paul's Cathedral on his recovery from his recent illness.

This cordial welcome to the land of his old-time exile soothed but failed to cure the melancholy of the life at Chislehurst. His long-standing deep-seated ailment, which, curiously enough, he shared with old Kaiser Wilhelm of Germany, had been exacerbated by the physical exertions of the campaign and in especial by the long hours in the saddle which he endured in agony on the day of Sedan. During the period of his residence at Chislehurst he was on horseback only three times, and on the last occasion the effect was so deleterious that he never again mounted a horse. He moved but seldom beyond the boundaries of the park surrounding Camden Place. In the summer of 1872 he made some stay in the Isle of Wight, but the benefit was merely temporary. An intimate writes : 'The Emperor would walk up and down the long corridor of Camden Place with his arm on the young Prince's shoulder, while he talked to the lad of men and things. After the midday breakfast, at which the little Court met for the first time in the day, he would sit in the morning-room in his arm-chair by the wood fire and talk cheerfully with the Empress or with any visitors who had come. It was but a small circle in which the Imperial couple moved, but it was

one of steadfast friends.   The Emperor talked willingly
and freely of the remote past, but he was only a listener
when contemporary politics were under discussion.   If
he interfered, it was to counsel moderation of speech
or to protest against reprisals.'

About the beginning of July, 1870 the Emperor at
the instance of Dr. Sée had been prevailed upon to call
a consultation of the leading surgeons of Paris.   A telegram was sent to London requesting that Mr. Prescott-
Hewett the eminent English specialist should come
to Paris and make an examination in consultation
with the French surgeons.   Mr. Prescott-Hewett, however, did not see the Emperor until after the commencement of the campaign, either at Metz or at Châlons ;
and although the Emperor was much more fit for an
operation than a campaign he took the field.   The
mischief was progressing gradually, and at the close
of 1872 the Emperor's surgical advisers agreed that
operative measures had become necessary.   The series
began on Jan. 2, 1873.   Two operations were performed
with a certain success, but the patient's condition was
not satisfactory, although the physicians were far from
regarding his case as hopeless.   After the second operation performed by Sir Henry Thompson, during which
he was under the influence of an anæsthetic, the trouble
seemed of a purely local character and the inflammation
promised soon to subside.   As the pain, however, continued extremely violent, it was considered advisable to
resort to a powerful narcotic, and the Emperor passed the
last night of his existence in a calmness which seemed to
permit strong hopes of his ultimate recovery.   Sir Henry
Thompson, Sir William Gull, Baron Corvisart and

Dr. Conneau were to hold a consultation on the following day (9th) at eleven A.M. ; and it was understood that a third, and probably final, operation was to follow the consultation. At 10.25 o'clock of that morning, however, Sir Henry Thompson found that the pulse, which until then had beat with great regularity—80 to 84—suddenly became weak. He immediately discerned that Napoleon III. had but a few minutes to live ; he apprised his colleagues—who agreed with his opinion—and the Empress was immediately informed of the sudden sinking. She was at once by her husband's bedside ; but he did not seem to recognise her—he was rapidly sinking, notwithstanding the small doses of brandy which produced a momentary reaction. The Empress promptly telegraphed to Woolwich for the Prince Imperial to come with all speed, and also sent for the Abbé Goddard, the parish priest of Chislehurst. He arrived in a few minutes, and administered the last sacrament to the dying man. The Empress, the Duc de Bassano, Vicomte Clary, M. Pietri and Madame Lebreton were kneeling by the bedside, and nothing could be heard but the prayers of the priest and the sobbing of those present. The religious ceremony ended, during which the Emperor seemed to evince some signs of consciousness, the Empress approached the bedside and embraced her husband. The dying Napoleon made signs that he wished to give his last kiss to his devoted wife, heaved two faint sighs, and expired at 10.45 A.M. The young Prince did not reach Chislehurst in time to see his father before his death : his despair at being too late was pitiable. The Empress conducted him to the bedside of his dead father ; he kissed the dead repeatedly, and placed on his breast (as the Empress and the Abbé Goddard had previously done) a small spray of box. The medical men present were agreed that the death they witnessed was the result either of a rapid failure of heart-action or from arrest of circulation by a blood-clot.

The Emperor Napoleon expired at a quarter-past eleven on Jan. 9, 1873, at the age of sixty-five. His last words, faintly addressed to his life-long and devoted adherent Dr. Conneau were, '*Étiez-vous à Sedan ?*'

The vicissitudes which Louis Napoleon experienced almost from the cradle to the grave were probably all but unexampled. He was a fugitive before he could speak articulately. In the interval between his twentieth and his fortieth year he was a prisoner in Strasburg, Lorient, Ham, and the Conciergerie. He was an outlaw for more than half of his life. There were incidents, at Strasburg and later at Boulogne, which brought upon him the mock and jeer of Europe. He carried a bâton as a special constable in Park Lane on Chartists' Day. Then, by a sudden turn of fortune, he became President of the French Republic. The *Coup d'État* made him Emperor of the French ; and thenceforth for some fifteen years he was perhaps the most-considered man of Europe. It was said of him that on being asked whether he should not find it difficult to rule the French nation he replied, 'Oh no! nothing is more easy. *Il leur faut une guerre tous les quatre ans.*' This policy held good in a modified degree. The Crimean War was for him a success, although not precisely a triumph ; the Italian campaign, in spite of its hard-fought victories, ended abruptly in approximation to a failure.

The Mexican expedition was an utter fiasco. Yet Napoleon might have gone on with his programme of a war every four years but for the circumstance that there happened to be in Europe in the middle 'Sixties an infinitely stronger, more masterful and more *rusé* man than the dreamy and decaying Napoleon. When he and Bismarck walked along the Biarritz beach in October, 1865, Bismarck expounding his political speculations as they strolled—' Is he mad ? ' the Emperor whispered to Prosper Mérimée on whose arm he leant. Napoleon had very soon to recognise that madness had no part in the character of Otto von Bismarck. The Prussian Premier was his superior in energy, in determination, and in *finesse* ; and he foiled the French Emperor at every turn. After Sadowa Napoleon could not but have felt assured that war between France and Prussia was inevitable sooner or later. Yet the French army was gradually deteriorating and its discipline and readiness for war were becoming more and more impaired. Looseness on the part of the higher officers occasioned carelessness and irregularities in the lower grades and in the rank and file. Yet the reduction of the contingent of the year 1870 by 10,000 conscripts was held to be justified by the Prime Minister, who said : ' The Government has no uneasiness whatsoever ; at no epoch was the peace of Europe more assured. Irritating questions there are none. We have developed liberty, in order to assure peace ; and the accord between the nation and the Sovereign has produced a French Sadowa —the plebiscite.' Those complacent expressions were uttered on July 2, 1870 ; before the month was ended France and Germany were at war with each other, and soldiers of both nations had already fallen on the frontier.

From his accession to the Throne up to the autumn of 1860 Napoleon ruled, in effect, an absolute monarch ; and he would have acted wisely if he had never communicated his resolution to liberalise the Parliamentary groundwork of the Empire. After he made this concession to a nation which was quite content to live under a régime of benevolent absolutism, he was always more or less involved in political troubles. 'Constitutional Reforms' were simply the vestibule to the arena of heated and venomous political conflicts ; and the Emperor was frequently compelled to express disappointment at the manner in which his acts were misinterpreted. The view of the wise and shrewd Prince Consort was that in giving Constitutional Government to France the Emperor was but turning from dreams of conquest to visions of nationalities rehabilitated by revolutions. While Napoleon remained physically capable, Constitutional Government was tempered in a measure by the supreme sway of the Sovereign ; but about 1862 the germs of the ailment which tortured him for the remainder of his life began to rack him. He was a most temperate man, but he allowed himself freedoms in a certain way. A list of his affairs, from La Belle Sabotière of Ham down to and beyond Margot Bellanger, need not be given here. During his frequent and lengthened visits to watering-places for the sake of his health, Constitutional Government had a good deal its own way ; and, as has been already said, when he confided the government of France to the responsible Ministry of which M. Émile Ollivier was the head, he finally retired from the direction of public affairs and resolutely restricted himself to the duties of a Constitutional Sovereign. With the appointment of the Ollivier Administration the *rôle* of the Emperor as active ruler ended.

Mr. Jerrold has well remarked that to Napoleon III. Paris owes a great debt. 'The slums,' he states, 'lying between the Palais Royal and the Tuileries and the unfinished Louvre ; the unkempt and unlighted Champs Élysées ; the waste place bordered by *guinguettes* about the Arch of Triumph—such were the plague-spots which Napoleon and Haussmann stamped out ; substituting for them wide boulevards and spacious streets, flower-decked squares, markets, baths, a system of drainage, an abundant water-supply, and paths and gardens in every quarter. A great highway from the Tuileries to the Place de la Bastille was hewn through one of the most tortuous and swarming quarters of the capital. The Louvre was joined to the Tuileries—alas, no longer extant ; and the Place du Carrousel was levelled and laid out. The great boulevards were extended to the Madeleine. The Champs Élysées were decked with shrubs and flower-beds. The Palais de l'Industrie was built. The Bois de Boulogne was made a paragon of landscape gardening, brightened by a broad expanse of ornamental water ; and the Tour du Lac became the fashionable ride and drive of Paris. The Malesherbes quarter of Paris, with the Parc Monceaux and that region of palaces round the Arch of Triumph and flanking the beautiful avenue now no longer named " de l'Impératrice," was laid out and its stately structures were built over the waste ground of the evil days of the Revolution of February. The Tour St. Jacques

springs now from the bosom of a garden. The Hôtel
Dieu is no longer a disgrace to the capital. Nor was it
only in Paris that the hand of the Imperial reformer
was visible. Every city in France became eager to
follow the example of Paris. In Marseilles, Lyons,
Rouen, Amiens, Bordeaux, Tours, considerable improvements were effected. In short, there is not a provincial
town in France which cannot show marked amelioration,
the result of the initiative of the Imperial Government.'

Sir William Fraser in his 'Napoleon III.' writes
with great truth that the Emperor made no imputation
of misconduct against the commanders of the army
which was defeated at Sedan, in marked contrast to the
accusations made by his great uncle after Waterloo. Even
in his letter to General Wimpffen contradicting briefly
two assertions of the latter, there is no trace of irritation.
He wrote a kindly letter to Bazaine while the 'Army of
the Rhine' was still maintaining itself in the Metz position, a letter which it may be worth while to quote :—

'My dear Marshal,—It is a real consolation to me
in my misfortunes to learn that you are near me. I
should be glad were I able by word of mouth to express
the sentiments which I feel for you and the heroic army
which under your orders has fought so many bloody
fights, and endured with constancy unheard-of privations.
Believe, my dear Marshal, in my sincere friendship.

'NAPOLEON.

'Cassel, Wilhelmshöhe, Oct. 13, 1870.'

Earl Cowper, reviewing the Memoirs of the Duc de
Persigny in the 'Nineteenth Century,' remarks that
Persigny lays great stress upon the evils of duality in
the Imperial Council, the existence of two opposite

parties, the difficulties which time-serving Ministers felt in choosing between the Emperor and the Empress, and the vacillating, uncertain policy which was the result. Persigny strongly urges that at all events the difficulties between the Sovereign and his Consort might be adjusted beforehand. This paper continues Lord Cowper, is valuable for the light it incidentally throws upon the scenes that must have occurred, the undignified contentions between man and wife which scandalised the Council and brought contempt on the Emperor, and the unmixed harm which was done by a brilliant and accomplished lady who, acting as Regent with a full sense of responsibility and surrounded by Ministers of her own choice, might have played a considerable part.

Sir William Fraser avers that there can be no doubt that the Emperor Napoleon while in exile fully intended to make a final effort to regain the Throne which he lost on Sept. 4, 1870. It was not merely to obtain relief from suffering that he underwent the painful operations which caused his death. Resolute to return to France, he knew that it was necessary that he should ride into Paris on horseback at the head of an army ; and this he could do only as a favourable result of the series of operations. In his own words : ' I cannot walk on foot at the head of troops ; it would have a still worse effect to enter Paris in a carriage ; it is necessary that I should ride ;' and it was with the object of doing so that he submitted to the operations under which he succumbed. Sir William adds on later information : ' Not only was the Emperor's return to Paris intended, but every detail had been arranged. A private yacht was to be available for landing the Emperor at some undetermined port on the northern corner of France, or perhaps in Belgium. Landing secretly, the arrangement was that the Emperor should proceed through France to the camp at Châlons, where forty or fifty thousand men should be assembled for the purpose of manœuvres ; declaring himself, he was to head this army and march at once on Paris.' Sir William adds that his information was from the proprietor of the yacht, the late James Ashbury, who repeated the circumstances to him (Sir W. Fraser) the evening before his death. He states further that he had information to the same effect from a person who was to have supplied for the enterprise a large sum of money ; and another informant, holding a very high official position in a distant country, corroborated the statement with the remark, 'I was to have played a somewhat conspicuous part in the drama.'

The father who lost his life in the hope of being able to return to France, and the gallant young son who fell slain by savages in an obscure corner of South Africa, now sleep together in the mausoleum at Farnborough, each in his sarcophagus.

The following is the will of Napoleon III. :

'APRIL 24, 1865.

'THIS IS MY WILL.

'I commend my son and my wife to the high constituted authorities of the State, to the people, and to the army. The Empress Eugénie possesses all the qualities requisite for conducting the Regency well, and my son displays a disposition and judgment which will render him worthy of his high destinies. Let him never forget the motto of the head of our family, " Everything for the French people." Let him fix in his mind the writings of the prisoner of St. Helena ; let him study the Emperor's deeds and correspondence ; finally, let him remember, when circumstances so permit, that the cause of the people is the cause of France.

' Power is a heavy burden, because one cannot always do all the good one could wish, and because your contemporaries seldom render you justice ; so that, in order to fulfil one's mission, one must have faith in, and consciousness of, one's duty. It is necessary to consider that from Heaven on high those whom you have loved regard and protect you ; it is the soul of my illustrious uncle that has always inspired and sustained me. The like will apply to my son, for he will always be worthy of his name.

' I leave to the Empress Eugénie all my private property. It is my desire that on the majority of my son she shall inhabit the Élysée and Biarritz.

' I trust that my memory will be dear to her, and that after my death she will forget the griefs I may have caused her.

' With regard to my son, let him keep as a talisman the seal I used to wear attached to my watch, and which belonged to my mother ; let him carefully preserve everything which comes to me from the Emperor my uncle, and let him be convinced that my heart and soul remain with him.

' I make no mention of my faithful servants—I am convinced that the Empress and my son will never abandon them.

'I shall die in the Catholic Apostolic and Roman religion, which my son will always honour by his piety.

'(Signed) NAPOLEON.

'Done, written, and signed with my hand at the Palace of the Tuileries, April 24, 1865.

'(Signed) NAPOLEON.'

This will was published in the English papers with the following explanatory letter from the solicitors of the Empress :—

'Sir,—Incorrect statements having repeatedly appeared in both English and foreign newspapers regarding the will of the late Emperor Napoleon, we think it right, as solicitors to the administratrix, to state that all such rumours as have hitherto been published are without authority and inaccurate. Unavoidable circumstances have occasioned some delay in the publication of the will, but letters of administration *cum testamento annexo* have now been applied for; and in order to avoid the possibility of further misrepresentations, we are authorised to transmit to you a copy of the will for publication.

'The estate has been sworn under 120,000*l.*, but it is right to state that this sum is subject to claims which will reduce the amount actually received by the administratrix to about one-half of the sum named.

'Your obedient servants,

'(Signed)   MARKBY, TARRY, AND STEWART.

'57 Coleman Street, E.C., April 29, 1873.'

Among the papers found in the Tuileries after the fall of the Second Empire, there was discovered a document which was a bank statement from the House of

Baring Brothers of London, with whom Napoleon III. had an account. According to this statement it appeared that the Emperor in 1866 possessed 150,000*l.* in Russian stocks ; 100,000*l.* Turks ; 132,000*l.* Peruvians new and old ; 50,000*l.* Canadians ; 50,000*l.* Brazilians ; 50,000*l.* Egyptians ; 100,000*l.* Americans ; 25,000*l.* Mississippis ; Diamonds, 200,000*l.* ; and other items amounting to 75,000*l.* ; in all, 882,000*l.*

This ' statement,' no doubt, may be spurious ; yet it does not appear that anyone should have been interested in regarding it as such. Assuming it to be genuine, with his Civil List on a great scale unimpaired Napoleon could have had no motive in dissipating this huge total of assets. Between nearly a million sterling, and the modest 60,000*l.* specified by the solicitors of the Empress as the estate of the deceased Emperor after the liquidation of the claims upon it, there is a great gulf fixed.

The foreboding and pathetic will of the poor young Prince Imperial, written on the night before his departure for Africa there to meet his sad and premature death, is as follows :

' THIS IS MY TESTAMENT.

' 1. I die in the Catholic Apostolic and Roman religion, in which I was born.

' 2. I desire that my body may be laid near that of my father until the time when both may be transferred to the spot where the founder of our House reposes among the French people, whom we, like him, dearly loved.

' 3. My latest thought will be for my country, for which I should wish to die.

' 4. I hope that my mother, when I shall be no more,

will maintain for me that affectionate remembrance which I shall cherish for her to the last moment of my life.

' 5. Let my private friends, my servants, and the partisans of the cause which I represent, be assured that my gratitude to them will cease only with my life.

' 6. I shall die with a sentiment of profound gratitude towards the Queen of England, the entire Royal Family, and the country in which during eight years I have received such cordial hospitality. I constitute my mother my universal legatee, subject to the payment of the following legacies :

' I bequeath 20,000 francs to my cousin, Prince I. N. Murat. I bequeath 100,000 francs to M. F. Pietri, in recognition of his good services. I bequeath 100,000 francs to M. le Baron Corvisart, in recognition of his devotion. I bequeath 100,000 francs to Mdlle. de Lar- minat, who has always shown herself so much attached to my mother. I bequeath 100,000 francs to M. A. Filon, my tutor ; 100,000 francs to M. L. N. Conneau, 100,000 francs to M. N. Espinasse, 100,000 francs to Capt. A. Bigot—three of my oldest friends. I desire that my dear mother should constitute an annuity of 10,000 francs for Prince Lucien Buonaparte ; an annuity of 50,000 francs for M. Bachon, my former equerry, and of 2,500 francs each to Madame Thierry and to Uhlman. I desire that all my other servants shall never be deprived of their salaries. I desire to leave to Prince N. Charles Buona- parte, to the Duke of Bassano, and to M. Rouher, three of the most beautiful souvenirs that my testamentary executors may select. I desire also to leave to General Simmonds, to M. Strode, and to Mgr. Goddard three souvenirs which my testamentary executors may select from the valuables which belong to me. I bequeath to M. Pietri my pin surmounted by a stone (cat's-eye); to M. Corvisart my pin with the rose pearl; to Mdlle. Larminat a medallion containing the portraits of my father and mother; to Madame le Breton my watch in enamel mounted with my monogram in diamonds; to MM. Conneau, Espinasse, Bizot, I. N. Murat, A. Henri, P. de Bourgogne, S. Corvisart my arms and uniforms, except those I may last have worn, which I leave to my mother. I leave to M. d'Entroujues a pin surmounted with a fine pearl, round in shape, which was given me by the Empress. I beg my mother to be good enough to distribute to the persons who during my life have shown attachment to me the trinkets or less valuable objects which may recall me to their recollection. I bequeath to the Comtesse Clary my pin surmounted by a beautiful fine pearl, and to the Duke of Huescar, my cousin, my Spanish swords.

'NAPOLEON.

'All written by my own hand.

'I need not recommend my mother to defend the memory of my great-uncle and father. I beg her to remember that so long as a Buonaparte lives, the Imperial cause will be represented. The duties of our House towards the country will not be extinct with my life. When I die, the work of Napoleon III. will fall to the eldest son of Prince Napoleon (Prince Victor), and I hope my beloved mother, in supporting him with all her power, will give to us who shall be no more this last and crowning proof of affection.

'NAPOLEON.

'At Chislehurst : Feb. 26, 1879.'

The following letter, addressed to the newspapers of the day by the private secretary of the Emperor Napoleon in reply to some of the calumnies published against his Majesty, may be read with interest :—

'Wilhelmshöhe, Sept. 15, 1870.

'Sir,—Since the occurrence of the recent sad events in France, the Emperor Napoleon has been the object of the most violent attacks and of calumnies of all kinds, which he will doubtless only treat with contempt ; but if it is right in him to remain silent under such circumstances, it is impossible that those persons who are attached to him should permit the daily publication of these reports in French and other foreign newspapers to pass without contradiction. Among the most odious of them it is necessary to point out one in an English journal which has not hesitated to rank among the causes of the war an embarrassment of the Civil List, and the necessity resulting therefrom of borrowing yearly fifty millions from the Budget of the Minister of War—loans all traces of which were made to disappear by merging them in the expenses of a great war. So absurd an imputation convicts the writer either of an ignorance the most profound as to the laws which in France regulate the finances of the State, or of extraordinary bad faith. Malversations are hardly possible in France, for the auditing of the Civil List involves a strict examination, under the supervision of the Legislative Body and the Court of Accounts.

'Another journal asserts that it is known to all the world that the Emperor Napoleon has invested in Amsterdam a sum of ten millions in Dutch railway shares. I positively contradict the assertion ; and, what is more, I affirm that the Emperor Napoleon has not a centime invested in foreign funds.

'A German journal has represented the state of the Emperor in quite another light, for it alleges that so destitute was he of resources that the Prussian staff at Sedan had to advance him 2,000 thalers. This story, like the rest, is totally unfounded.

'I have limited myself to pointing to these assertions, so entirely contrary to the truth, not in the hope of putting an end to attacks upon a Sovereign who, under the misfortunes which have befallen him, ought to be safe from attack, but in order that all may know how very slender their foundations are, and to how small an amount of faith they are entitled.

'I trust, sir, that you will give this letter insertion in your journal, and in thanking you by anticipation I beg you to receive the assurance, &c.

'G. PIETRI,
'*Private Secretary to the Emperor Napoleon.*'

THE END

LIST OF AUTHORITIES

The following are some of the authorities consulted for the 'Life of Napoleon III.' :—

Memoirs of Queen Hortense. Compiled by Lascelles Wraxall and Robert Wehran. 2 vols.

Louis Napoleon, Emperor of the French. By James Augustus St. John. 1 vol.

Life of Napoleon III. By Blanchard Jerrold. 4 vols.

The Works of Napoleon III. Author unnamed. Published at the office of the Illustrated London Library, 227 Strand. 2 vols.

Napoléon III : avant l'Empire. Par H. Thirria. 1 vol.

Napoléon III : l'Empire. Par H. Thirria. 1 vol.

Napoleon III. Par A. de la Guéronnière. 1 vol.

Napoleon III. By Sir William Fraser. 1 vol.

Prisoner of Ham. By F. T. Briffault. 1 vol.

History of Ten Years, 1830–40. By Louis Blanc. 2 vols.

Memoirs of Madame Rémusat. 2 vols.

Memoirs of an Ex-Minister. By Lord Malmesbury. 2 vols.

History of the Coup d'État. By Maupas and Vandam. 2 vols.

Life of the Prince Consort. By Theodore Martin. 5 vols.

Memoirs of Christian von Stockmar. 2 vols.

Diary of Queen Victoria.

Réorganisation Militaire. Par Général Changarnier. 1 vol.

War of the Crimea. By Sir Edward Hamley. 1 vol.

The Crimean War. By Alexander Kinglake. 9 vols.

M. Thiers: Cinquante Années d'Histoire Contemporaine. Par C. de Mazade. 1 vol.

Life of Field Marshal Sir John Burgoyne. 2 vols.

Mémoires sur Napoléon III. Par Comte H. de Viel-Castel. 3 vols.

Victor Emmanuel. By Edward Dicey. 1 vol.

Italy under Victor Emmanuel. By Count Charles Arrivabene. 2 vols.

Memoirs of Count John Arrivabene. 1 vol.

Cobden. By John Morley. (Commercial Treaty with France.) 1 vol.

Cavour : Vie. Par C. de Mazade. 1 vol.

Englishman in Paris. By Vandam. 2 vols.

Rapports Militaires écrits de Berlin, 1866–70. Par Baron Stoffel. 1 vol.

La Journée de Sedan. Par Général Ducrot. 1 vol.

Guerres de 1870 *: Bazeilles—Sedan.* Par Général Le Brun. 1 vol.

Sedan. Par Général de Wimpffen. 1 vol.

Franco-German War. By Moltke. 1 vol.

German Official History of Franco-German War. Translated by Clarke and Wright. 4 vols.

Bismarck. By Charles Lowe. 2 vols.

Trochu. L'Armée Française en 1867. Une Page d'Histoire Contemp. La Politique et le Siège de Paris. 3 vols.

Rise and Fall of the Mexican Empire. By Count Keratry. 1 vol.

Épisodes de la Guerre de 1870, *et le Blocus de Metz.* Par l'ex-Maréchal Bazaine. 1 vol.

My Mistress the Empress Eugénie. By Madame Carette. 1 vol.

The Eve of an Empire's Fall. By Madame Carette. 1 vol.

Life in the Tuileries under the Second Empire. By Anna Bicknell. 1 vol.

Démocratie et Liberté. Le 19 Janvier—Compte Rendu aux Electeurs. Par Emile Ollivier. 2 vols.

Papiers Secrets du Second Empire. Arranged by La Chapelle. 1 vol.

Journal of a Staff Officer in Paris. Par Comte d'Hérisson. 1 vol.

Memoirs of Benedetti. 1 vol.

Life of the Prince Imperial. By E. Barlee. 1 vol.

Le Dernier des Napoléon. 1 vol.